BERLIN: THE DISPOSSESSED CITY

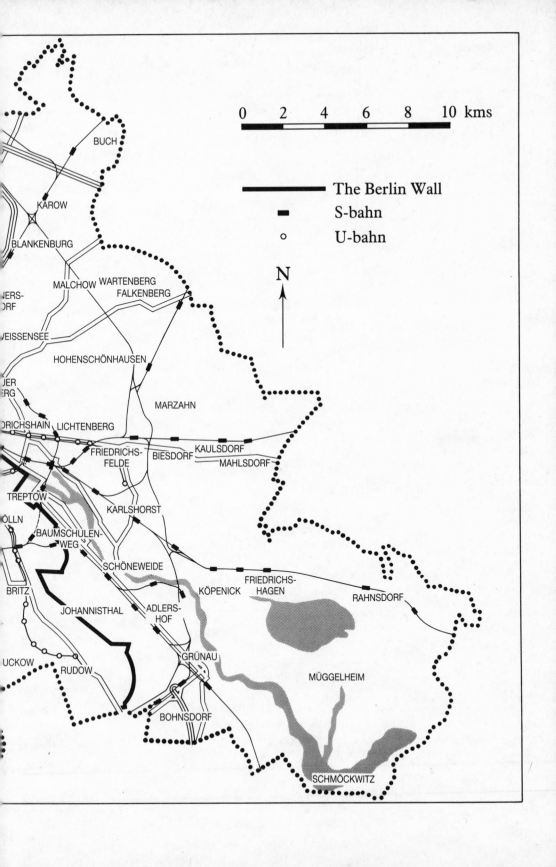

BERLIN
THE DISPOSSESSED CITY

MICHAEL SIMMONS

HAMISH HAMILTON · LONDON

HAMISH HAMILTON LTD

Published by the Penguin Group
27 Wrights Lane, London W8 5TZ, England
Viking Penguin Inc., 40 West 23rd Street, New York, New York 10010, U.S.A.
Penguin Books Australia Ltd, Ringwood, Victoria, Australia
Penguin Books Canada Ltd, 2801 John Street, Markham, Ontario, Canada L3R 1B4
Penguin Books (N.Z.) Ltd, 182–190 Wairau Road, Auckland 10, New Zealand

Penguin Books Ltd, Registered Offices: Harmondsworth, Middlesex, England

First published in Great Britain 1988 by
Hamish Hamilton Ltd

British Library Cataloguing in Publication Data
Simmons, Michael
Berlin: the dispossessed city.
1. Berlin (Germany)—Description—
Guide-books
I. Title
914.3'15504878   DD859
ISBN 0–241–12284–8

Typeset in 11/13pt Plantin by
Butler & Tanner Ltd
Printed and Bound in Great Britain by
Butler & Tanner Ltd, Frome, Somerset

Contents

For Angela

Introduction

Poetry comes to the prosaic, politicised city of Berlin in the spring. That is the time when old people in the queues at the dismal Friedrichstrasse crossing points carry great bunches of fresh flowers. They bring portable consumer goods and delicacies to eat and drink, of course, but—almost invariably—flowers as well. Very possibly, they were picked from a garden only a few hundred yards away, a spot which for the recipient must remain politically beyond reach for the time being.

Since 1961, the city has been formally divided. The Brandenburg Gate is no longer a gate, merely a symbol of eye-catching proportions that appears on postage stamps and postcards obtainable on both sides. Each 'half' of the city now thinks of itself simply as 'Berlin' and produces street maps which unrealistically choose to disregard what lies just beyond the Wall. But the whole of it, strictly speaking, remains an entity occupied by the four powers—several thousand troops from the Soviet Union, the United States, Britain and France. These troops will remain for as long as one side sees the other, however implausibly, as a 'threat' to its own security. The 'two Berlins', meanwhile, play an endless waiting game, growing further and further apart, run by totally different sorts of bureaucrats and officials who behave according to different sets of rules, abide by different values and priorities and teach their children different 'facts' of life.

There is no agreed 'Berlin' nowadays, just as there is no Germany, only a Federal Republic and a GDR. A West German colleague, pleading the case in early 1987 for a fresh appraisal of his country's history, declared that in West Germany there was no real 'establishment', no capital city combining political and cultural elites, but that there remained a deep preoccupation among 'the thinking classes' with what happened in the twelve years from 1933 to 1945. He could have written the same of East Germany. A country which cannot get itself into proper focus, however hard it tries to adjust the binoculars, is bound to have a bizarre relationship with its former capital. When the 'freedom' of that capital has to be dependent on military occupation, the city becomes a paradox.

But Berlin is also home to slightly over three million people—about two-thirds of the 1939 total—who, by virtue of force of habit, inheritance, residence permits, tax concessions, objection to military service, or a barely formulated wish to pursue an 'alternative' way of life, have chosen this city. Every one of them, whether he or she likes it or not, is playing a part in the political waiting game. The handful of Americans who wanted to demolish the shattered city in late 1945 and start again somewhere else did not have their way, so these three millions are here, pushed right up against the geo-political realities of the late twentieth century, and not somewhere else.

How the inhabitants of Berlin see their political future remains, for the time being, something they are not allowed to pursue. They can elect bodies and individuals to run their day-to-day affairs, but they cannot devise a corporate long-term future and see to its implementation. Any move in such a direction can only be made with the unconditional acquiescence, unlikely in the short term, of four like-minded occupiers. Berliners on both sides—as the activities associated with the 1987 anniversary of the city showed—can evince great pride at being Berliners; though this pride, one has to add, had to be buttressed by top-level visits from Moscow and from Washington.

Every so often in putting this book together, I came back to the question: who, at grassroots, are the Berliners? The most straightforward answer is what it has always been, that they are those who inhabit the city. But that doesn't mean they were born there, or that both parents were born there.

The impression I have gained is that Berlin is, as it has always been, a city dominated by incomers—by individuals or groups of individuals who arrived, from the Huguenots onwards, as refugees, who were drawn by some element of its cosmopolitan magnetism, or who have been drafted in, not always willingly, to meet the multifarious needs of a politically motivated government. The poet Heinrich Heine lived there in the early 1820s and decided that it was 'not a city at all, but a place where people come together'. Thirty years later, George Eliot—who thought the city ugly, but immensely likeable—was worried that there were so many 'puppets in uniform' to be seen, and said her legs were 'in constant danger from officers' swords'. Berlin, according to Christopher Isherwood, writing of the winter (1932–33) before Hitler took power, was 'cold and cruel and dead'. Its warmth, he suggested, was 'an illusion'. Both Heine and Eliot might hear echoes of their thoughts if they visited the place today. Isherwood, who was unimpressed, except by the durability of his old landlady, when he went back in 1952, would ask perhaps why he could not hear the echoes of his.

The men who have had a decisive say in the city's history—Rosa Luxemburg, the only woman who might join their group, was cut off in her prime—have often had little affinity with the city itself; and they have frequently made important decisions relating to it and to Germany as a whole when they were elsewhere. Bismarck, Wilhelm II, Goebbels, Hitler and Adenauer to name but a few, made it quite plain, at one time or another, that they did not particularly like Berlin, even expressly disliked it. What successive Soviet leaders have felt for their western outpost has been consistently unclear. Soviet Army officers stationed in or near the city have orders not to fraternise too enthusiastically with the Berliners (and certainly few Berliners would understand them if they did) and, of course, they have endorsed the Wall. They could not have done that if they coveted what lies beyond it.

The nineteenth-century novelist, Theodor Fontane, spent a great deal of his life in the city and devoted much of his writing to his ways of seeing it. In 1884 he described in a letter some of the ambivalence he felt about the place. 'Ach Berlin,' he wrote, 'how far you are from being a real capital of the German Reich. It is the machinations of politics that have turned you into one overnight, not your own efforts. ... The great city makes us energetic, nimble and smart, but it also makes us shallow. The great city has no time for thought and, what is much worse, it has no time for happiness. What it initiates a hundred thousand times over is only the desperate search for happiness, and this is the same thing as unhappiness. ...' Several times, feeling myself sitting in the roller coaster of Berlin's history as I wrote this book, I came back to that sigh: 'Ach Berlin. ...'

But Fontane, like the other nineteenth-century observers, put his finger on something essential about the city. It did not evolve as a capital. It was made into one—and was made into one as a result of war. Nor did it arrive at its present state of dispossession except as a result of war. Because it brought together a lot of people

ix

in a conurbation at various moments in its past, and especially in the last century, it has achieved many of the things one expects of a big city. But it does not really have greatness. That quality comes from the quickness in the atmosphere, the excitement one may feel perhaps in that moment when one steps through a hotel door onto the street. In both Berlins today, there is noise and bustle and even a certain expectancy in the air, but not quite that excitement.

The *Berliner Luft*, the air, is something different. It has led to a climate that is not only meteorologically different because the city lies more than a hundred feet above sea level. It has created an ambience, counterpointed by the history that speaks from almost every street corner, but which induces in almost every visitor the feeling that 'anything goes'. There is a certain kick in the air which somehow, willy nilly, urges the visitor on in what Fontane qualified as the search for happiness. There is no shortage of entertainment, at any time of day, in West Berlin. In East Berlin, the same applies but one has to know how and where to find it.

It is a city that wants to be friends, and shows itself, always self-consciously, in bright colours. Nothing, except the making of the city maps, is done by halves there. Nor does it seem quite to know when to stop.

Berlin has a distinct personality. To almost every visitor, it extends a hand of warm welcome, while keeping the other hand behind its back. It is a place of great conviviality, but where it can be difficult—even for Berliners—to relax in the company of someone who hesitates when the conversation turns to what his or her father did when Hitler was calling the tune. (But then Berlin is also a place where people argue most vociferously that there is more to the Germans and their history than just the twelve years of Nazism. . . . They did not by any means, as other Germans did, vote for Nazism with any enthusiasm.)

This book is not, precisely speaking, a history book. I am a journalist, not an historian. But it is written, with great warmth for both parts of the city, in an endeavour to guide the reader along some of the routes by which it has reached its present unusual situation. Often these routes have followed the course of German history. But much German history 'happened' outside Germany—in Paris, for instance, or in the Crimea, even in the now unlikely city of Tehran. I have restricted my canvas wherever possible to Berlin.

Acknowledgements

Acknowledgements are something a working journalist usually keeps to himself. In this case, that is not possible. Anyone who spends more than a little time dipping into any of the books listed in the bibliography will know very quickly to what extent I am indebted to their authors, living or dead. So will anyone—and especially the members of my family—who has borne with me when I have broached the subject of Berlin in conversation over the last few years, know how much I owe to them.

Margit Hosseini, at the West German Embassy, provided Berlin humour, encouragement when it was needed, and researched so successfully that the book couldn't have been done without her. Sarah Adie, typist and secretary extraordinary at the *Guardian*, managed to remain good-natured while typing the manuscript, and Christa Wichmann, at the Wiener Library, London, did the same when I taxed her with esoteric questions. The following, I hope, know how grateful I am to them: Neal Ascherson, Wolfram Bielenstein, Patrick Bunyan, Margrit Clegg, Doug Clelland, diplomats at both German embassies in London, the Goethe Institute and its librarians, Hilary Gray, Joerg Henschel, Ingeborg Hohndorf, Ilse Kaden, Paul Mason, Rainer Oschmann, Alexander Reissner, Geoffrey Rider, Hans-Jürgen Roeber, Mary-Ann Spatola, Kurt Strauss, Dan van der Vat, Bill Webb and Udo Wetzlaugk.

I am especially grateful to Rowohlt Verlag, Hamburg, for permission to use popular verses from Peter Rühmkorf's anthology, *Über das Volkvermögen*, at the start of each chapter. The translations in each case are basically my own.

But the biggest acknowledgement has to be to Berlin itself. Everyone who has by choice spent any time there will know what I mean by that.

Berlin[1]

Berlin, du deutsche deutsche Frau
Ich bin dein Hochzeitsfreier
Ach, deine Hände sind so rauh
von Kälte und von Feuer.

Ach, deine Hüften sind so schmal
wie deine schmalen Straßen
Ach, deine Küsse sind so schal,
ich kann dich nimmer lassen.

Ich kann nicht weg mehr von dir gehn
Im Westen steht die Mauer
Im Osten meine Freunde stehn,
der Nordwind ist ein rauher.

Berlin, du blonde blonde Frau
Ich bin dein kühler Freier
dein Himmel ist so hunde-blau
darin hängt meine Leier.

Wolf Biermann

---

[1]Berlin, you oh so German lass
I court you with desire
But oh, your hands are rough, alas
from cold winds and from fire.

And oh, so narrow are your hips
just like your streets so narrow
And oh, so tepid are your lips
I know I'll never leave you.

I can no longer leave you now
The wall is to the west
And to the east I have my friends
the north wind is the harshest.

Berlin, the oh so blonde-haired lass
I court with cool desire
Your sky is such a lousy blue
And there I hang my lyre.

(translated by Steve Gooch)

ONE

1871-1918

Heil dir im Siegerkranz
Pellkartoffeln mit Heringsschwanz
Heil Kaiser dir
Friß in des Thrones Glanz
Die fette Weihnachtsgans
Uns bleibt der Heringsschwanz
In Packpapier[1]

Berlin started life as a settlement and trading post among the forests of central Europe at least eight centuries ago, but it only came of age as the German capital in 1871. For a long time after that, and within the memory of people still living, it was rather disparagingly regarded for its parvenu qualities. Its remoteness and provincialism were decried, especially when compared with cities like Munich, Frankfurt or Dresden.

It was under the auspices of Otto von Bismarck, though hardly as a result of any vision he had, that the city in the late nineteenth century started to grow, at uncontrollable speed. Following victory in the 1870 war against France, Wilhelm I became Kaiser, Bismarck his Imperial Chancellor, and Berlin, almost overnight, an imperial capital with European pretensions. Suddenly, there was dizzy talk that it might become a *Weltstadt*, a world city.

The rapid growth in the *Gründerjahre*— or 'foundation years'— of empire was exciting certainly, as was the economic boom which immediately followed the war. But the growth was disturbingly uneven and the boom was short-lived. And before the great Bismarck was in the end forced away from centre-stage—he went very reluctantly—there were already political straws in the wind

---

[1] Hail to thee in the Victor's laurels – potato bits with herring's tail. Hail to thee, oh Emperor, and, in the imperial splendour, enjoy the Christmas goose. We'll make do with the herring's tail, and wrapping paper for a plate.

highly visible to the discerning. The calamities and the trauma which were to come had their beginnings in this time.

On the ground, Bismarck's legacy can most clearly be traced in the wide thoroughfare of the Kurfürstendamm. It was his encouragement of the developers and speculators of the 1880s that caused it to expand most dramatically. Today, beneath the decorated façades that can still be seen on some of its four- and five-storey residences, it mixes a weary salaciousness with a sort of boulevard elegance as the adopted 'centre' of West Berlin. In German, the word *Stildurcheinander* (mixture of styles) conveys its architectural, social and cultural diversity, even if it does not convey the noise and energy that are apparent every minute of the day and for so much of the night.

In earlier times, the Kurfürstendamm provided a pleasant route by which to reach the hunting grounds at Grunewald, further west. Then the wealthy moved in, choosing to live in this area at a time when, in other parts of the city, appalling poverty, overcrowding and unemployment were giving cause for concern. On the eve of the First World War, there were literally dozens of millionaires living in or near the 'Damm, just a few minutes stroll from each other's doorstep. The millionaires have gone, but their trappings remain; the poor, as any stroll round the city will show, have yet to leave.

But it is in the old royal and government area around Unter den Linden that this more recent history of the city has to start, rather than the Kurfürstendamm. Unter den Linden, which now cuts into East Berlin from the Brandenburg Gate, is something very different. Its heritage and its most distinguished buildings (when Bismarck was around) were Prussian in flavour and, given the interest of the East German leadership in earlier history, it is not surprising that some of this Prussianness has been preserved.

The area came into its own as the hub of a greater Germany one fine day in June 1871. The new Kaiser, who had been proclaimed some months before in the Hall of Mirrors at Versailles, was the seventy-four-year-old Wilhelm I. On that day, he headed a glittering procession, lasting all of five hours, from the Brandenburg Gate, up the Linden, to the Palace. He had become Kaiser with a reluctance that was only dissipated by the insistent ambitions of Bismarck. But his *Reich*, his empire, had been born out of war, and the salute of the crowds along the Linden was to victory in that war.

The cavalcade entered Berlin at the Halle Gate to the south, passing through Belle-Allianz-Platz (now Mehring-Platz), not far from today's Checkpoint Charlie. All the way, there were flowers and flags, and at the Pariser Platz white-robed girls stood in attendance. One of them gave the old man a kiss. The Linden itself was a riot of colour, with more flags and flowers and great painted placards hanging between the lime trees, depicting either victorious moments in the war or allegorical representations of the *Länder* (provinces) which were now constitutionally joined as Greater Germany. Captured French weaponry was laid out along the route, and guns were fired in salute. In the Lustgarten (now part of the Marx-Engels-Platz) next to the great Cathedral, massed military bands struck up with Martin Luther's 'Now, thank we all our God', and choirs of children sang '*Deutschland über alles*'. A whole variety of processions would be passing this way in the decades to follow, sometimes to the same musical accompaniment.

The diplomatic corps and guests of honour of 1871, stationed on viewing stands which had been erected next to the Opera House and outside the University opposite, represented three of the four powers who were to meet a hundred years later to hammer out the 1971 Quadripartite Agreement on Berlin. The fourth, France, must have had some interesting reflections, as victor rather than vanquished, when it attended the latter engagement.

But Wilhelm's hesitation before the edifice of empire was to be a key factor in the politicisation of the city. At one critical point during the final deliberation at Versailles, Wilhelm had grown so irritated that he almost abdicated there and then. Letters to his wife spell out his unhappiness at what he feared would be the shape of things to come.

If, in the great celebrations that June, there was any thought that Berlin's era of provincial complacency was now at an end, about to be replaced by a grand epoch of imperial expectations, the Kaiser's first public gestures were in the opposite direction. He still looked towards the Prussian past. So far as he was concerned, the high point of the day was the unveiling of a statue outside the Palace to his father, King Friedrich Wilhelm III, a ruler who had done much to foster the stiff Prussian virtues of discipline and orderliness which have been hung round German necks ever since.

The war just ended, Wilhelm declared, was one of the most glorious, but also one of the most bloody of modern times: 'If the King to whom we erect this statue could see us now, he would be well satisfied with his people and his army.' The following evening, when 700 guests sat down to a gala dinner at the Palace, he hesitated again. His first toast was to 'my royal father, the Hero King'; but his second was to 'a now united Germany, its monarchs and princes, present and absent'. Small wonder it was the Prussians (as Bismarck himself later confirmed) who were the most unwilling in the new set-up to let go of their positions and their inheritance.

Wilhelm would have been deluding himself if he thought the crowds of 1871 were greeting him with feelings only of undiluted adulation. Many felt loyalty certainly. For them, the victory and the new Reich opened up vistas of opportunity in the army, the diplomatic service, and in government. Though some conservatives may have thought their positions threatened by their peers from other Länder, the 1870s were in fact to present great opportunities for expansion.

In that decade the city's new business class was also emerging. Its self-interest had been fuelled by the recent take-off of the city as one of Europe's biggest centres for manufacturing and commerce. (It remains one of the biggest to this day.) But there was a highly significant group of others who, however deferential they may have appeared to the glittering ranks parading before them, were gripped by a very different self-interest. They were from among the thousands, often destitute and illiterate, who were converging on the new capital, day after day, to find work, food, and a roof over their heads. In a slum area of Blumen-Strasse, only a mile to the east of Unter den Linden, there had very recently been ugly skirmishes, later to reach the scale of riots, as the authorities sought to disperse a group of squatters. And there was disease—smallpox, brought in by French prisoners, for instance—where the sufferers had little hope of treatment. For those who knew where to look, even in this hour of triumph, there were ominous clouds of confrontation on the Berlin horizon.

Then there was a second victory procession in 1871, one which was totally different in character from the first, and much more poignant. This was in September, and involved several thousand troops, including reservists who were worn out, dishevelled and hungry, when they arrived by train at the old Anhalter railway

4

station. They were met by scenes of near pandemonium. Women and children milled about, having waited months to greet them, carrying wreaths, garlands and bouquets of flowers, laughing and weeping by turns, pushing military guards and platform barriers to one side in their collective determination to meet the incoming troop train. Out of this chaos, a sort of discipline emerged: women took hold of their men's weapons, while the men who were not wounded or disabled lifted up and carried their children, and another march set off up to and along Unter den Linden. At the Palace, Wilhelm, bemused no doubt by what he saw, once again took the salute. He was already too old to be worried by distant clouds.

Even in 1871, Berlin was a heterogeneous collection of human beings. Between 1865 and 1875, its population rose from 658,000 by nearly fifty percent to 964,000. The qualified welcome of 1871 came from a community twice as big as that which had thrown up an angry mob in the riots of 1848. In 1871 alone, nearly 134,000 people came into the city, of whom nearly forty percent found work and stayed. The removal of the old surrounding wall, which the authorities had started to dismantle a few years earlier, was a sign of the expansion. There was ample scope for political activity.

Representatives and hangers-on from the other kingdoms and states which were now embraced by the empire swelled the city's ruling class. Some built palaces, or palatial residences, in the vicinity of Unter den Linden and Wilhelm-Strasse; others gravitated towards Charlottenburg—until then a separate district which was 'in the country'—while others installed themselves in large villas south and west of the Tiergarten. Each of the aristocratic families had its own staff, and in a very short time there was something recognisable as Berlin 'society'.

Many of their very sumptuous homes, as well as the haunts they used to frequent, can still be found in the genteel surrounds of Wannsee, the Grunewald, and other picturesque parts of the city. Berlin (that is West Berlin) still has its low-profile aristocratic set; but there are elites on both sides, and on both sides the 'exclusive' nature of certain residential districts persists.

New arrivals in the early empire were often escaping from

feudal conditions in the country. They came with almost no belongings or only the clothes they stood up in. Tens of thousands were homeless as well as unemployed, and some were reduced to sleeping in holes in the ground on the city outskirts. Others put together ramshackle shanty-like structures in the woods beyond the city boundaries, though some managed to find space in wretched accommodation that was provided. For those subsisting in such conditions, it was debilitating in more senses than one. Not only were they without the creature comforts of a home; they were also an hour or more's walk to and from places where work might be found. Local farmers' instincts saw to it that prices for basic foods were higher outside than inside the city.

Where Berlin today is conspicuously a city of old people—at least one in five Berliners is over sixty-five years old—and especially old ladies with little dogs, it was in the 1870s inhabited above all by the young. Well over a third of the population was less than twenty-two. A large number found employment in the works and factories, as well as the building sites, which mushroomed round the city. Women had to work because wages were low, and child labour was much used. Earlier efforts to devise a viable trade union structure had failed, but political battle lines were beginning to become clear, as were the issues of homelessness, destitution, overcrowding and disease.

Misery and wealth existed side by side, often in the same building. Wealthier tenants (or occasionally the owners) occupied the first or second floors of a five- or six-storey house, while the lower orders, paying lower but still unreasonable rents, were kept to the ground floor or the basement beneath, or out of sight on the floors higher up. There was little contact between the floors. The compactness of the city was such that grinding poverty and wretchedly unhealthy living conditions could easily be found within five or ten minutes walk of the royal palaces.

The *Mietskasernen* or rent barracks which became the city's characteristic tenement blocks date from this time. In street after street they were let out in the fashion just described, often four blocks or more deep, layer upon layer stretching back from the street frontage with minuscule courtyards and little if any daylight in between. Each room in these gaunt blocks was commonly occupied by half a dozen or more people at any one time. Families had their own 'tenants', and all lived, ate, slept, and attempted to carry on a trade or piece-work in impossible conditions. At one time, within a generation of the launching of the empire, almost a quarter of the city's population survived in such surroundings.

Some of these blocks still stand in both parts of the city—in Kreuzberg and in Prenzlauer Berg, for instance—but large numbers have been adapted and improved to more enlightened twentieth-century standards. Inner blocks have been demolished and replaced by communal courtyards or children's play areas. The sunlight now gets through.

Occasionally, however, one may be suddenly confronted by a building that has barely changed: hugely elaborate doorways in ornate but flaking stucco façades give way to the bleak and plain brick fronts of the blocks behind. Children play on the street pavements, where the light is. However pressed they are by 'the housing problem' in both East and West Berlin, the authorities acknowledge that it is a source of embarrassment that Berliners (even if they happen to be Turkish or other Third World immigrants) should continue to live in such surroundings.

It is tempting to think the Berliners' very particular sense of humour may date from this time and these conditions. In the 1870s, many in the city decided to emigrate, often heading for New York and points beyond. But the majority stayed, and against odds which often verged upon the overwhelming they survived. If they laughed at life with a grim, gritty and bitingly cynical humour, who can blame them? If the city started to flourish as an entertainment centre, and the harsh art of the expressionists soon started to emerge, rubbing shoulders with equally harsh cabaret performers, who can be surprised?

As the city began to sprawl, small and barely noticeable communities in and around the city found themselves overwhelmed in the headlong rush to create suburbs. Growth has been such that some have finished up as today's inner city areas. At that time land prices went through the roof, and many peasants and farmers who had been working the land even within the city limits became rich overnight, selling off fields to developers and speculators for great sums. Schöneberg, for instance, between the Tiergarten and Grunewald and straddling the old road to Potsdam, housed a few thousand people around a village church. In the space of twenty-odd years Schöneberg grew almost tenfold, to reach nearly 100,000 by the late 1890s. It was soon very much on the map. By the time Hitler was addressing mass rallies in its now demolished

Sportpalast in the late 1930s, Schöneberg's population had reached 300,000.

Then there are totally contrasting places like Reinickendorf, an enclave in West Berlin to the north of the old city centre, which still—just—has it old village streets and cemetery, but which in the 1870s grew to become an industrial centre. It was here, close to Tegel airport, that Berlin's iron and engineering industries grew, and some of the biggest and best-known names in German economic history established themselves; they were later to play also a significant role in political developments. A different sort of 'industry' in this area was devoted to prison building. One went up in Tegel, while two others (to become notorious in Nazi times) were constructed further south in Moabit, close to the Tiergarten. Franz Biberkopf, archetypal anti-hero of the Weimar period novel, *Berlin Alexanderplatz,* by Alfred Döblin, was a Tegel inmate. Other real-life heroes were to include members of the anti-Nazi resistance. One of these was the young Pastor Dietrich Bonhöffer. Tegel Prison is still the biggest in Berlin.

Prenzlauer Berg was another of the districts which took off in the 1870s, relieving the congestion of the area just north of the Alexanderplatz, around the still serviceable Hackescher fruit and vegetable market. Part of this historically pregnant district is known as the Scheunenviertel (once the base for the grain trade) and is still fascinating to wander round. It is cluttered with older buildings and dominated by the noise of passing overhead trains. Here, the early communists were active, and political demonstrations and meetings of all descriptions, clandestine as well as public, were held, despite the anti-socialist laws which were pushed through by Bismarck and his successors. In this area too, in Hitler's time, many Jews managed to survive—though thousands also perished—and the underground resistance was active.

Schönhauser Allee, which sweeps rather grandly over a distance of several miles down through the heart of the city, from Pankow in the north to where the Schönhauser Gate used to stand, still has several great houses which are almost oppressively elaborate in appearance. One senses here as one senses on the Kurfürstendamm, the very mixed nature of turn-of-the-century qualities of life. The fortunate ones kept up appearances just behind the ornament, while the less fortunate lived and worked out of sight.

Despite welfare provisions introduced in the last years of the exclusively Prussian government administration, the caring facilities provided for the majority were not enough to prevent the outbreaks of sickness which so commonly occur in conditions of overcrowding and poor housing. Smallpox, typhus, tuberculosis, cholera, bronchitis and other diseases associated with malnutrition all took their toll. In harsher winters, unnamed, unknown corpses which were found in the streets ceased to cause surprise. On occasions, the severity of treatable outbreaks was such that prison cells were requisitioned to provide makeshift accommodation for the suffering—on the grounds, presumably, that any institutional care was better than none.

For those who squatted outside the city walls, perhaps near the Cottbus, Frankfurt, or Landsberg Gates, there was little treatment at all. These too were places known to the authorities as ones where attempts to evict people or move them on invariably led to violent confrontations and bloodshed. Today's suburbs must have been built over an unknown number of forgotten and unmarked paupers' graves.

Where social conditions were conducive, crime and prostitution prospered. The highly developed city police force of this time has been made much of by today's East German historians. It was kept constantly busy, particularly in poorer and overcrowded districts. Here, there were alcoholism and begging, crimes of violence, robbery and theft, extortion and blackmail, bribery and corruption. They yielded much source material for chroniclers of city life, from Theodor Fontane the novelist, who died in 1898, and later to Bertolt Brecht, who was born in the same year.

As elsewhere in the industrialising world (in Victorian Britain for example) it was a fertile time for do-gooders. These were preachers and purveyors of goodwill, invariably well-meaning but not infrequently representing an upper class which had neither desire nor reason to seek social change for its own sake. They set out to make life more bearable for the less fortunate; it was philanthropy at arm's length.

Adolf Stöcker was not typical. He was a former prison warder and army chaplain, apparently without notable class bias. But using words which were heavily laced with anti-Semitism, he sought to wean the workers away from what he perceived as political intrigue to become God-fearing servants of the Kaiser. When Bismarck made his moves towards the end of the 1870s to ban the Social Democrats, Stöcker launched his own right-inclined Christian Socialist Workers' Party. His cajolings won the party no seats in the Reichstag, but they did draw the politically inclined closer together, often under another socialist umbrella altogether.

Stöcker and his like failed in the end, as other Bible-thumping persuaders failed, partly because of the naturally a-religious inclination of most working-class Berliners. Only one in four Protestant marriages of this time was solemnised in church and only every other child was christened. Ironically, it was in spite of this sort of scepticism that many parish churches were built in outlying parts of the city. Many of them stand to this day, Gothic incongruities in fired red brick or stone which are barely used, but imposing monuments to the time of their erection.

The *Gründerjahre*, as their name suggests, were a time of infrastructural growth. They were the years when the city's multi-faceted transport system, already a flourishing enterprise, was fully developed. More and more railways were planned and laid, above and below the ground; new roads were laid and old ones widened—though many still had open sewers—and canals and waterways were dug. Extraordinary railway stations were constructed in all parts of the city, several of which are now almost or completely out of service, great and ornate mausoleums of an imperial past, but frequently of quite unusual fascination to the railway enthusiast. One or two are today used in true Berlin fashion: coffee bars have been laid out across railway lines that go nowhere, cut in half by the Wall—or flea markets have sprung up in disused railway carriages (as at the Nollendorfplatz), even bazaars offering oriental goods that 'ordinary' shops do not sell.

Horses were employed in the *Gründerjahre* by the tens of thousand. They cluttered the streets, some hauling commercial vehicles, others carrying passengers or goods. Whenever evictions were ordered (usually early April and early October), they were called into service to pull the evicted and their piled-up belongings to uncertain destinations—faint premonitions of rituals which were to be gone through in the same streets in and after 1945.

Industries grew. August Borsig, self-taught, had his early engineering production line in a converted dance-hall in Chaus-see-Strasse, not far from the Oranienburg Gate. After not many years, he was producing locomotives by the hundred. The gate to his factory still stands, as does his last head office at No. 13 Chaussee-Strasse, with the family name immaculately picked out in the stonework above the third floor windows. It is an unlikely monument in East Berlin to nineteenth-century capitalism.

Werner Siemens, an artillery officer who took early retirement, started up a small workshop in Schöneberger Strasse, near the Anhalter station. Here he was able to produce rudimentary electrical goods. Later, he was to expand on a much larger site, to the north of the Charlottenburg Palace, where as a beneficent employer he eventually developed an entire town-within-the-city called Siemensstadt. The Siemens' former residence at Gärtner-Strasse, in Lichterfelde, West Berlin, is now a research institute.

Emil Rathenau was different. He had studied industrial processes and management in the US, and started the Deutsche Edison Company from works on the Hohenzollerndamm in what has now become a largely residential area. Later, expansion obliged him also to move—to new sites in Reinickendorf and Wedding, and then into the already heavily industrialised central district of Moabit. By then, the group had become the Allgemeine Elektrizitäts Gesellschaft (AEG), and a factory which was to be designed for it some years later by Peter Behrens for the manufacture of heavy turbines was completed shortly before the First World War. This building came to be seen as one of Germany's outstanding contributions to twentieth-century architecture. It stands at the corner of Hutten-Strasse and Berlichingen-Strasse, a mile or so north of the Tiergarten, a monument with a certain political flavour, erected as it was when Wilhelm II was proclaiming himself sole arbiter of good taste and design.

These were by no means the only heavy industrialists who moved into gear at this time. Ancillary industries and companies were formed which were to supply and draw supplies from the primary manufacturers. Hundreds of small-scale enterprises came, went and were replaced. Sometimes handfuls of men worked informally together in twilight sectors of the economy. Sometimes one-person enterprises emerged—selling shoelaces or newspapers perhaps, or carting goods across the city—idiosyncratic phenomena which have been characteristic of the Berlin economic landscape throughout its history. Even though the East German Government sought at an early stage to take them over in its part of the city in 1950, by the late 1970s they were once again gradually re-emerging and, in a short space of time, officially encouraged. Berlin would not be the same without them.

The first years of empire accelerated the demand for piece-work labourers, thousands of whom were women working at home for textile or clothing manufacturers. Bettina von Arnim, in an angry book on social conditions written in the early 1840s, half a century earlier, had found what she called 'a colony of the poor'—close to the old Hamburg Gate—and she described the subhuman conditions in which 2500 people were obliged to live, eat, sleep and carry out piece-work in 400 rooms. Fifty years later the scenes were little different.

Banks came into being, many around Behren-Strasse, between the Palace and the Wilhelmstrasse, with branches forming in the most promising districts. Many had names which are still familiar institutions on the German financial scene (such as the Deutsche Bank and the Disconto Bank), and five of their very substantial buildings can still be seen in Behren-Strasse. One, built in 1899 as a finance house for city industrialists—Nos 32 and 33—has today been converted politically as well as structurally, into the East German State Bank.

Against this backcloth the Reich's politicians, based in Berlin, danced their separate minuets with their various notions of democracy. The Reichstag as an institution was light-years away from representing the interests, let alone the aspirations, of most Berliners. Men in the iron foundries in and around Invaliden-Strasse, or in the machine tool or engineering workshops nearby, and their women, who were sometimes putting in up to sixteen hours a day 'in service', had little in common with the posse of aristocrats who clung unrealistically to 147 of the Reichstag's 357 seats. At national level, these aristocrats represented approximately one per cent of the population.

The Reichstag parliament took a long time to settle down geographically. Its first meeting took place in March 1871, in the White Hall of the City Palace, an occasion dominated by the Kaiser and his generals. Three weeks later, there was a formal reception for the deputies at the recently completed 'red' City Hall, which stands in today's East Berlin across Marx-Engels-Platz from where the Royal Palace used to be. Then, the deputies were seated in a hastily converted hall of the Prussian Assembly building (yet another former palace) at Dönhoff-Platz. But some of them complained, saying the hall was a wretched, jerry-built affair and they moved again, into redesigned premises provided by the Court porcelain manufacturer. This time, at the very first meeting, bits of ceiling plaster and glass collapsed on some deputies' heads and desks, and it was back again to the Dönhoff-Platz.

In 1872, an international contest was launched to find a new Reichstag building appropriate to the new imperial capital. Bismarck's intention was to give Berlin an architectural fillip which would rival developments elsewhere in Europe. Paris, he knew, already had its Louvre, while Brussels was at work on a great new Palace of Justice, and Vienna had started on its new Parliament. London already had a Foreign Office fit to direct an empire.

Prizes were now awarded in Berlin as a result of the contest— but no building work was done. The second prize went to Britain's Sir George Gilbert Scott, who suggested a St Pancras Station-like orgy of neo-gothic not unlike the building eventually erected on the Reichstag site. A second competition was held in 1882. This threw up a monumental design, part-gothic, part-baroque, by a Frankfurt architect called Paul Wallot. At a grand ceremony in June 1884, the foundation stone was laid by the eighty-seven-year-old Wilhelm I. He did not live to see the structure completed, but he did live to hear that only ten weeks after the stonelaying the workers of Berlin were marching in a demonstration along the banks of the Spree River, carrying a red flag and shouting for liberty, equality and fraternity—all at a time when a ruthlessly applied Anti-Socialist Law was supposedly preventing just such things from happening.

The Wallot building is more or less still there today. It stands melodramatically right up against the dividing Wall and within hailing distance of the Brandenburg Gate. It saw the last few days of bitter, often hand-to-hand fighting in April and May 1945 between Soviet soldiers who had everything to gain and Germans who had almost nothing left to lose. Today it is surrounded on three sides by empty spaces, drenched by the same peculiar silence on the western side of the Wall as that which characterises so much of Unter den Linden. The number 69 bus, which runs from the Kurfürstendamm, turns round here, and cars belonging to Reichstag administrators park nearby. Schoolchildren on edu-cational visits from West Berlin and sometimes other West

German schools swarm about the place, strange apparitions amongst such historic masonry. The bustling Königs-Platz, which formerly stood before the grand entrance, has been obliterated and statues of famous men, like the roadways and flower-beds amongst which they stood, have been removed or destroyed. The flag of West Germany flies now from the Reichstag roof, and in the clinical, late twentieth-century accommodation beneath, political committee meetings are held, warily noted by officials of the occupying powers. Most poignant of all, an elaborate exhibition is perpetually there for scrutiny, asking, and selectively seeking to answer, pointed questions about German history.

The Reichstag took more than ten years to build. In other words, it was—how symptomatically?—almost a full quarter of a century after the inauguration of the Reich before the parliament was in its own premises. Even then, it was found not to be complete, lacking the sort of office accommodation that deputies expected, and woefully short of meeting rooms. The dedication above the entrance, 'To the German People', was not to be inscribed until the chaotic year of 1916, at the insistence of some of the deputies, even though Wallot had incorporated it in his original design. It was ironic: 1916 was a time when the war was going badly and people were starving.

Wallot himself did not live to see the inscription made, dying in 1912; nor did Bismarck ever speak in the building. He had left the political scene some years before the commissioning ceremony was finally performed, by Wilhelm II, in December 1894. (And that, incidentally, was the only occasion the Kaiser went near it.)

Bismarck, before he was dropped as 'pilot' of the Empire by Wilhelm II, was the towering political personality of the Reich. After 1870, according to one of Germany's most individualistic twentieth-century thinkers, Golo Mann, he became 'a clever, selfish, hard-hearted, neurotic old man', who 'barely understood the great change over which he presided'. Certainly, one change he mooted got nowhere at all. This was that the Reichstag should perhaps be moved out of Berlin altogether, possibly to Potsdam. There were, thought Bismarck, too many Berliners among the deputies.

While Bismarck probably appreciated the Kaiser's early uncertainties—on more than one occasion Wilhelm I thanked God for the 'gift' of such a capable person—as chief architect of the new Reich he could not be expected to share them. But the 'iron'

Chancellor was prone to sulks and bouts of histrionic behaviour, even tears. At the same time, he would also spend long spells away from Berlin. The 1871 procession was a rare public appearance.

Bismarck had lingered for several weeks in Paris after the formalities of January 1871, apparently unperturbed by the éclat of the Commune. He returned to Berlin with thoughts that the new imperial capital—already superior, in his mind, to Vienna which he said was 'not a German city'—should become a great metropolis to rival Paris. That fact in itself was not extraordinary: before Bismarck, and repeatedly since, the style and the flair of Paris as a city have been evoked as worthy of emulation. Berlin's architects, in the early days of the evolving Forum Fredericianum (the area around the Palace) were heavily influenced by their French peers, and even employed French working partners on royally approved projects. The evidence is still visible in the several pre-1871 palaces and parks of today's city and at Potsdam next door.

It is a piquant thought that Baron Georges Eugène Haussmann, whose transformation of the French capital so impressed Bismarck, had in fact been drummed out of office in the same year that Prussia inflicted its defeat on the French army. His prime sin was that he had grossly overspent, and neither his dismissal nor the reasons for it can have been good omens for a team, however ill-defined, which had thoughts of changing the face of Berlin in its first imperial years. The fact that Haussmann's plans for Paris had been abruptly curtailed in such dramatic circumstances did nothing to restrain the Berliners' cluttered vision for the city to come.

One hundred years on, the Kurfürstendamm stands as a tangible realisation of one Bismarck dream, even if its present form is not as he envisaged. Inspired by the Champs Elysées, he had proposed that Berlin should have its own *grande allée* to connect the administrative centre with Grunewald in the south-west, then being cosseted as a favoured retreat for the aristocracy and the elites serving the new empire.

Grunewald today is a visually attractive and relatively peaceful area of trees and lakes (which were once swamps) with many large detached villas and occasional concrete bunkers left over from the Second World War. Some of the villas were damaged by the events of 1945 but have been restored; then they were still homes for the well-off in an extension of what Bismarck called his 'West End'. The approach to the city centre is via the majestic Königsallee, and this in turn leads into the Kurfürstendamm. One villa in Königsallee became in 1963 the residence of Prince Louis Ferdinand, nephew of Kaiser Wilhelm II and titular head of the Hohenzollern household.

A large proportion of the houses built after the widening of the Kurfürstendamm in 1881 were destroyed in 1944–45, but among the boutiques, souvenir shops, hotels, cinemas, restaurants and office blocks that have mushroomed in the last forty years, the original *Jugendstil* bursts through. It offers grand evidence of an old flavour—a flavour which only ceases to be anachronistic because it is part of one of the curious patterns that characterise the whole of Berlin.

Bismarck did not otherwise go out of his way to imbue the city's planners or builders with flair or imagination. The city when he died (far away, at his country estate, in 1898) was hardly more grand to look at as a direct result of his actions than when he had arrived, as a teenager with his mother, in the early 1830s. At bottom, he never quite came round to caring for Berlin.

He owned no home of his own in the city. At the southern end of today's Otto-Grotewohl-Strasse (then the street of government, Wilhelmstrasse) he occupied No. 76, a palace which had become the residence of the Prussian Foreign Minister, and his existence there was curiously haphazard. Books and belongings piled up on chairs or tables; rooms were without carpets; and hospitality consisted of food brought in from outside caterers. He would often work into the small hours, and receive important visitors in the late evening, sometimes at a convenient hotel.

Nothing remains today of where he lived: more than forty years after the Second World War, it is just another patch on the bleak bomb-site, the size of several football pitches. It extends for most of the length of this erstwhile Whitehall, from close to the Leipziger-Platz and the adjoining Potsdamer-Platz—both of which were once hives of popular activity—up to the Pariser-Platz. A hundred yards or so to the west, and roughly parallel, runs the 1961 Wall, and well into the 1980s there was almost nothing but weeds and young trees to hide intriguing bumps of rubble in between.

Great houses—many of them palaces—and their gardens, which reached to the Tiergarten beyond, have all gone. But it was from buildings which once stood, heavily guarded, on precisely this bomb-site, that the Reich, its politicians and its people—and the

Hitlerian 'reich' which followed—were controlled. At its southern extremity, the Wall now turns round the back of the East German House of Ministers building (a solid erection authorised by Hitler for Hermann Göring's air ministry in the 1930s). Only then, beyond the Wall at that point, Otto-Grotewohl-Strasse becomes Wilhelm-Strasse once again.

Bismarck did not get his wish, uttered two years before he died, that a statue of him should stand on the Kurfürstendamm. But an heroically conceived memorial, depicting him half a dozen times larger than life in cuirassier uniform, was made by the less than distinguished sculptor, Reinhold Begas. It was erected on the Königs-Platz with accompanying mythical-heroic figures three years after the Chancellor's death, outside the Reichstag building he never entered. A little later, this group was joined at either side by similarly heroic, but smaller, memorials to Field Marshal Helmuth von Moltke (a thinking military strategist) and Minister of War, Albrecht von Roon (administrator and disciplinarian of the Prussian School).

These three were the ones who had decided on war against France—over dinner on 13 July 1870. Today, they are still together, shrapnel-scarred and weather-worn, and with some of the lettering lost from their titles. Hitler was to remove the Bismarck statue in 1935, and the whole group was only re-assembled after 1945, at a graceful but much less prominent position in the Tiergarten, by the Grosser Stern. Not many passers-by stop to stand and stare at them now, and the Königs-Platz itself is an open green space, favoured for picnics or impromptu football matches by the city's Turkish community, or by evangelists who set up their marquees, or by the organisers of occasional rock music concerts.

Bismarck's farewell from the city, when it came, was a theatrical and sentimental affair. Ministers and generals performed, bands played, crowds cheered and waved—even though many were pleased to see the back of him. His posthumous progress through German history books has not been easy, but today he is remembered on all sides. When Thomas Mann tried to deliver a public reassessment of the man's achievement at Berlin University in the 1920s, the students howled him down. This, too, was ironical: Bismarck had been a wayward student himself in the same university less than a century before, almost overlapping during his stay with the marginally less wayward Karl Marx. However, in the mid-1980s, the East Germans felt able to publish a detailed evaluation of the man and his role in building 'the German nation' in a book which was discussed respectfully and at length in the West German press. Overall, he is remembered with a sort of qualified, uncertain pride—but not as a bloody dictator.

Probably the most momentous year in Berlin during the peculiar balancing act of the partnership between Bismarck and Wilhelm I was 1878. In that year, there were two assassination attempts on the Kaiser, both made in Unter den Linden, not far from the spot where Bismarck too had been fired at. In the first, a young apprentice called Max Hödel stood on a cart outside the Russian Embassy, firing shots which missed. In the second, on a Sunday afternoon three weeks later, a disoriented intellectual called Kurt Nobiling fired more accurately, but not fatally, from a second floor window of No. 18 Unter den Linden.

The Kaiser, though well past eighty, recovered, helped on perhaps by the knowledge that many in the city crowded round the palace for hours on end and positively wanted him to recover.

A few weeks after this event the city, as a *capital*, dressed itself up to act as host to Europe's 'great powers' for the Congress of Berlin. So far as Berliners were concerned, this meant around 1000 distinguished guests commuting, when they were not in conference discussing 'the Eastern Question' and territories nearer home, between palaces, embassies and sparkling new hotels (the Kaiserhof had recently opened), drinking champagne and feasting beneath the chandeliers, taking trips up the river or to Potsdam. Much of the business was conducted in French with Bismarck taking charge; the Crown Prince Friedrich had a small walk-on part. Disraeli, present as Lord Beaconsfield, was apparently much impressed with Berlin; it was, he wrote, 'a fine city' and its streets had 'an air of architectural splendour'.

But in the city's own political history, 1878 was also the year of Bismarck's *Sozialistengesetz,* or Anti-Socialist Law. Although no one had been able to prove any link between the known opposition parties—specifically the now emerging Social Democrats—and the assassination attempts, parties that represented the steadily growing conservative middle classes (blurring at the edges into the old aristocracy) were moved quickly from concern to

18

outrage when they heard that the incidents had occurred. The law, after some argument, was finally passed in a feverish Reichstag by 221 votes to 149, with Bismarck gaining support for the measure from the National Liberals. The more left-wing Progress Party and the Catholics' Centre Party were denounced, along with the SPD, as enemies of the Reich.

The first clause of the new law said it all: 'Associations which aim by social democratic, socialist or communist means to overthrow the existing state or social order, are banned. . . .' This ban was to remain in force until shortly before Bismarck's departure in 1890—a twelve-year period which saw increased powers granted to the city's police and the magistrates. They presided over an increasing flow of charges brought for sedition and anti-state activities. Meetings of socialists of varying hues continued to be held, but were regularly broken up by police raids, whether they were orderly and behind closed doors, or openly demonstrative, in public parks such as the Friedrichshain or Treptow. House searches and the harassment of individuals were beginning to become the norm.

Such activities occurred despite the appointment—also in 1878—of a relatively liberal Lord Mayor, Max von Forckenbeck. He held out against Bismarck and other conservatives to see through administrative measures for the city in the way its accounts were managed, in the loosely defined but burgeoning area of culture, and in the increasingly complex area of traffic control. He outlasted the Anti-Socialist Law and Bismarck by just two years, but his tenure was nevertheless a period in which social and political tensions in the city, exacerbated by the yawning gap between very rich and very poor, could only increase.

The Social Democratic Workers' Party, forerunner of the SPD, had been formed in 1869 after a stormy three-day meeting at Eisenach. An early leading light in the years preceding this meeting had been Ferdinand Lassalle, a somewhat unpredictable character of colourful wit, erudition and evident abilities. He had befriended Karl Marx in London—though Marx was less certain of him—and had addressed workers' meetings in the Oranienburg district of Berlin. He was young and impressionable, apparently willing to compromise on constitutional matters and to meet Bismarck for unsuccessful clandestine tête-à-têtes in the search for an amicable modus vivendi. But despite his brilliant efforts on behalf of the workers, and his ability to fuel Bismarck's nervousness, he was also a man of susceptibilities—being infatuated for much of his life with an aristocratic lady—and he was to die suddenly, aged only thirty-nine, in a duel fought in Switzerland.

The Eisenach meeting turned to August Bebel, a lathe operator still in his twenties, and to Wilhelm Liebknecht, a one-time theological philosopher in his forties, for leadership. Bebel, at this early stage, was not yet political to his finger-tips, preferring to educate and enlighten his fellow workers in a non-political atmosphere, while the more cerebral Liebknecht, another friend and follower of Marx, was for more direct political action. By the time of the war against France, both men were speaking and voting against war credits and were therefore tried for 'treasonable intentions' and imprisoned. They represented, said the leading right-wing polemicist of the time, Heinrich von Treitschke, 'a party of moral degeneration and political demoralisation'—but theirs was a group which was to resurface untidily and to lead from the front for a long time after Bismarck's departure.

In 1875, still three years before the banning law, reformists and radical Marxists had joined forces despite acknowledged splits in thinking among the nascent membership, at the historic meeting (in Gotha) to launch the Socialist Workers' Party. The commemorative scroll for this founding congress, a copy of which can be seen in the permanent exhibition in the Reichstag, shows Karl Marx and the late Lassalle, standing shoulder to shoulder but looking in opposite directions. Bebel and Liebknecht, who had by now both completed two-year prison terms for treason, are also depicted. They look (to the right) in the same direction as Lassalle. Marx, it soon became clear, had deep reservations about 'the Gotha programme'.

In that year, steps were taken to form the Central Association (Zentralverband) of German Industrialists. Confronted by a precarious political situation, this association sought to offer members a measure of self-protection. Its emergence led in turn to the ascendancy of a different breed of politician: men no longer from an aristocratic of 'landed' background, but with vested interests and—which inevitably led to splits—with minds of their own. The old Prussian conservative right to hold high office, and through it to exercise power, was broken in this period. The Prussian hold on the government bureaucracy, the military machine and the diplomatic service remained disproportionately strong, but it was not so formidable. The muscle-power, and the money, of big industry were from now on to play a critical role in the city's and the country's political evolution.

The city's property-less poor and the *Lumpenproletariat* somehow found the will and the energy to attend, more and more, discussion groups and evening classes which were organised on their behalf. Sometimes these were under the auspices of aspiring politicians who had been proscribed from participating more openly in public life. Sometimes they were a result of the sense of mission of well-meaning students from the universities of Berlin and, recently established, Charlottenburg. Speakers as well as listeners seemed to be looking for knowledge and enlightenment rather than wholesale change or an overthrow of the system. There was, however, at least one unequivocally class-struggle-oriented institution, the Workmen's Improvement School, which was founded (in 1891) by Wilhelm Liebknecht on the premises of an old brewery in Friedrichshain.

Instruction and argument would go on—if the police did not intervene—until the small hours. 'They come,' wrote a Berlin journalist in 1890, 'in their working clothes, covered in traces of hard work.... During the discourse, there is a soundless silence. Then there is an hour of well ordered debate. Those taking part are workers and only workers....' And out of such meetings came a creeping increase in the hard politicisation of the city's workforce. It was an inevitable by-product that the protest demonstration now started to become a feature of city life. There may not yet have been a discernible profile of working-class coherence—the impetus was still missing—but for many, politics was beginning at last to look like the art of the possible.

Liebknecht, drawing on the resources of both his own eclectic education and a peculiarly sardonic humour, persevered. In earlier years, picnics and arguments he had had on Hampstead Heath in London with Marx and Engels had sharpened his resolve and the nature of his commitment. They had also given him the political wherewithal to nurse and inspire the young Bebel. Liebknecht's Berlin home was at 160 Kant Strasse, not far from the Zoo station, now one of the city's busiest junctions.

Bebel was the son of a non-commissioned officer in the Prussian army. His character was in some ways colder than that of Lieb-knecht, but there was a shrewd side to him which was puritanically moralistic and demanding of high standards. The loyalty he commanded was such that when in 1872 he was committed to prison for his beliefs, the railway guards lined the station platform to salute as he went past. When he reached his cell, he devoted whatever time he could to reading Marx and John Stuart Mill. Until well into his sixties, from his home in Schöneberg, he was regularly declaring himself 'a mortal enemy' of the Kaiser and his system, and shortly before his death (in 1913) he forecast with uncanny accuracy the horrors that were to come in the trenches of 1914–1918 and the economic chaos that was to follow. East German historians speak of him today as 'to his death a loyal proletarian revolutionary'.

The depression which hit Berlin with a Stock Exchange crash in May 1873 had also hit the rest of Europe, but in Berlin—and elsewhere in Germany—it ran an unpredictable course. As prices and profits fell, so output and trade, like the organism of the city itself, continued to grow. The price of land, and consequently of rented accommodation, went on climbing, but organised rent protests were prohibited by law. Fortunes continued to be made—and lost. Scores of companies each year were going into liquidation, and the collapse of the Henry Bethel Strousberg's railways-construction-publishing conglomerate was the talk of the city for several years. After this collapse, Strousberg was obliged to leave a 'palace' which he had built for himself on the Wilhelm-strasse, one of the most imposing in central Berlin, for more modest accommodation. A short while thereafter his old palace was taken over and converted to become the British Embassy.

Commercial interests began to set new trends in architecture, domestic as well as industrial. Occasionally, as with the Behrens AEG factory which was to be erected in 1910, the structures were successfully iconoclastic; but more often they were of mediocre quality, handicapped by ill-trained or imitative architects and by incompetent builders.

To this day, as one looks at the fabric of the city, there is a hangover of unevenness from this period at almost every turn. In many neighbourhoods, buildings do not seem to complement one another, or they may be striking to the eye (for reasons negative or positive) simply because of their incompatibility. The 'spirit' of neighbourhood tends to exist only on a small scale: individual streets or blocks may have an ambience of their own, while the districts in which they are situated have proved intractable and formless. The 'spirit' of Berlin certainly does not lie in its architectural homogeneity, and the city barely figures in architects' books about cities. By the 1890s, Athens on the Spree, as idealists had perceived it, had become Chicago on the Spree, a reflection voiced originally by one of the city's more distinguished personalities, the businessman-traveller Emil Rathenau.

Feeling for the city's 'spirit' was of course very different at that time. Among those who cared in any creative sense, there was a tug-of-war between neo-traditionalists, recalling in their assorted designs what they liked most about the past, and wilful modernists, driven on by visions of progress, usefulness and technology. A backward-looking imperial Prussian demand for order was thus in conflict with *laissez-faire* disorder. An uncertain establishment was beginning to hear inchoate demands for radical change. At ground level, it meant the monumental was clashing with the functional, the frills of neo-Gothic with the clean lines of aspiring modernism, the wilfully aesthetic with the technically necessary.

The Kaisers' own contributions—and especially the quirkish extravagance to come from Wilhelm II—were usually retrievals from the past. Statues which he commissioned echoed his grandfather's time or even earlier: the *Marstall* (Royal Stables) between Marx-Engels-Platz and the Breite-Strasse is approximately Renaissance in style, but was only completed in 1901. The *Siegessäule* (Victory Column), was begun by Wilhelm I in 1864 to celebrate famous victories, and was dedicated at a grand ceremony on 2 September 1873. Later it was complemented by Wilhelm II's *Siegesallee,* an avenue of thirty-two statues of the historically great of Prussia and the Reich, unveiled to an incredulous and somewhat disdainful public also in 1901. Today the avenue is still there, cutting across the Tiergarten, but the statues have all gone.

In the face of such opposition, a designer like Peter Behrens was bound to be breaking new ground with his AEG turbine factory. So was Alfred Messel, teaching at the university, and then designing, for a prime site on the now totally changed Leipzigerstrasse, the Wertheim department store. Even Le Corbusier, a hallowed if controversial figure in the literature of architectural design, was later able to look back on his brief Berlin period (in 1910) with mixed feelings. It was one which gave him some of his best ideas in thinking up 'the city of the future', but which taught him that 'functionalist' architecture, as then practised in Germany, did not always produce things of satisfying beauty.

Wilhelm II's authorised contributions to the city were nearly always unambiguously portentous. In 1892, he declared: 'There is nothing in Berlin to captivate the foreign visitor, except a number of palaces, museums and the army.' It was a situation for which, in some measure, he felt personally responsible. Then, a few years later, he was to announce: 'Art which goes beyond the laws and the parameters which I lay down is no longer art. .... If art is to fulfil its proper role, it must affect people deeply—but it must be uplifting and not degrading.' Joseph Goebbels was to echo such sentiments forty or so years later. Perhaps the Kaiser was more honest when, on yet another occasion, he said succinctly enough: 'I never feel really happy in Berlin.'

Wilhelm I proclaimed the city's museums to be his pride and joy, and it is to his credit that he gave Wilhelm Bode, already a widely known figure of the art world, a brief to build and then fill the city's museums and galleries with whatever he found worthwhile. Bode, skilful at acquisition both of works of art and of money with which to buy them, had studied law in Berlin; from the early 1870s he played a central role in building up Berlin's art and museum collections. He went on playing that role until well after the end of empire, and many of the outstanding pieces and 'old masters' which can even now be seen in museums and galleries on both sides of the Wall are the result of his assiduous collecting. The Kaiser Friedrich Museum, opened on the Museum Island complex across the Linden from the Palace in 1904, has been given his name by the East German authorities.

The 1890s were a time in which the arts generally seemed to flourish—though often with political checks and balances. The French Impressionists, for instance, had finally become acceptable and sought after throughout Europe—but not in Berlin, where the traditional adjudicators of 'taste' had no taste. Max Liebermann, who was later to be seen as the notional 'leader' of the German impressionist group, had returned to Berlin (his birthplace in 1847) in 1884, gaining for himself the reputation of a painter of the workers and their environment. However, he was largely a solitary figure, immuring himself in a studio on the Pariser Platz.

Edvard Munch, the Norwegian artist, was another solitary figure. He provoked a storm of uninformed criticism when he accepted an invitation to hold an exhibition of his paintings in Berlin in 1892. This storm led to a breakaway group, which understandably called itself the Berliner Sezession, formed in 1899 with Liebermann as one of its founders and leaders. Käthe Kollwitz, revered ever since as a social-realist painter and accomplished draughtswoman ahead of her time, followed. She was balanced by Heinrich Zille, quirky but very telling in his satirical drawings and cartoons of approximately the same sort of social subjects, and perenially popular with a wider public. Both artists exposed aspects of Berlin society which its higher echelons preferred to ignore.

Concert halls and theatres became busy and more numerous in the 1890s. And, in spite of the Kaiser's diktats, discriminating audiences were finding a way of satisfying even minority tastes. Cosmopolitan Berlin was beginning, for instance, to cater for the social and entertainment needs of its homosexual population.

Such developments did not stop the establishment from making its own 'creative' thinking clear. The great Cathedral, across the Spree river from the City Palace, was an early casualty: in 1895, after half a century of debate, the building—its inside containing work by Schinkel—was pulled down, and eleven years later a new, spuriously Gothic, cathedral was consecrated. There were even plans at this time to alter radically the appearance of the Brandenburg Gate, converting it into a memorial to Wilhelm I. Drawings and models were made, but the work went no further than that.

While these things were happening, the Kaiser Wilhelm Gedächtnis Church was built, at one of the city's busiest points, where the Kurfürstendamm meets the popular shopping street of Tauentzien-Strasse. This was a heavily unimaginative creation, and again a spurious Gothic. It has become a sort of West Berlin trade mark, but has never been popular with Berliners, even though it is a carefully preserved war ruin. It is hardly a hallowed place: there are graffiti over many of its walls. The architect was Franz Schwechten, who was earlier responsible also for the new Anhalter railway station—of which just one craggy eye-catching corner of red and yellow brick now remains. In East Berlin, Schwechten is remembered for a brewery, which looks like a church and stands in the Schönhauserallee.

No account of Berlin at this period is complete without mention of the city's Jews. Ever since the *Gründerjahre* got under way, they had shown themselves to be active, and increasingly numerous, in many areas of city life. They were in government, at national and municipal level; they were also in banking, the law and the press. They owned several of the big new department stores; and they distinguished themselves in the arts. In 1871, the Jewish population was a little under 50,000 out of 826,000; by 1910, it was more than three times that out of a total of just over two million.

Anti-semitism had taken root early. A new political party, the Anti-Semitic League, was formed (though it made little effective headway); and Heinrich von Treitschke, the historian who has since become something of an albatross round German necks for his right-wing sentiments, was expatiating on his theme that '*die Juden sind unser Unglück*' ('the Jews are our misfortune'). It was a theme to be repeated with ominous regularity in the years to come.

Treitschke was intellectually opposed by a more tolerant fellow academic, Theodor Mommsen, but he found a qualified endorsement in the thinking of the philosopher, Friedrich Nietzsche, who wrote in 1885, 'I have not met one German who is well-disposed towards the Jews....' With the music of Wagner ringing in the seekers' ears, it was as if the imminently unstoppable though not yet hair-raising search for readily identifiable scapegoats had begun. Slogans devised at this time were to be heard with disturbing frequency over the next half-century, especially after Konstantin Frantz, an intellectual of the time, had allusively declared Berlin to be more like the capital of a Jewish Reich than a German one.... 'They control the whole city,' he wrote in 1879.

Small organised groups, committed to anti-Semitism, were formed at the university. Franz Mehring, a leading social democrat, said of this period that 'irrespective of political, religious and social beliefs', there arose among the 'cultured' groups of Berlin society 'a deep animosity against the Jewish character'.

Envy played its part in the growth of this animosity. When business was good for more or less everyone who was 'in business', the animosity against the city's Jews was not so pronounced, a trend confirmed by the mid-1890s when there was an identifiable resurgence in what today might be called business confidence. But every so often, when there was a need for scapegoats, the Jews were the ones who suffered.

The sense of order and discipline, by which the Prussians set so much store, was seriously eroded when Wilhelm I died in 1888.

His funeral in March was the obverse of the great procession of 1871. Bismarck could not appear: he was ill. The temperature was a biting 20 degrees below zero, and it was snowing. A pinched and starving stillness, rather than clamour and acclamation, was the hallmark of the day's crowds. Banners along the Linden this time declared that 'the faithful people of the grateful capital shed warm tears for his going home.'

The princes, potentates and generals whose position had been so secure during his reign, were there to see him go, and there were memorial services for him in London, Vienna and St Petersburg. But by then, Germany was about to prepare to leave the European mainstream.

On his death, Wilhelm was succeeded by his eldest son Friedrich, who had been operated on only a few weeks before for cancer of the throat. He had acted as regent ten years earlier after the assassination attempt against his father, and had earned himself a reputation as a distinguished soldier, a political Liberal who was frequently but not always openly at odds with Bismarck, and a thinking intellectual. But he was a dying man when he came to the throne and had to put his orders down on paper—one of them to sack his too outspoken Interior Minister, Robert von Puttkamer—and after only ninety-nine days he died. It was the emerging and gradually consolidating Social Democrats and other would-be progressives who were most disappointed that he did not achieve more and who were therefore also initially most disoriented by the noisy entrance of his son, Kaiser Wilhelm II.

Wilhelm hit Berlin like a bull in a china shop. He claimed he would lead the people to a splendid future, and proceeded to spend lavishly on his Palace, to dress his entire staff in new uniforms, to commission a royal yacht, a royal train, and so on. His élan may have been worthy of some praise, but his naturally self-righteous conservatism, and the distance of his extraordinary lifestyle from the majority, which soon became apparent, were not good omens. The urge to expand which grew out of such ostentation contained the seeds of its own destruction, a sort of pride before the fall.

By the turn of the century, Wilhelm II had started looking acquisitively out from Berlin to the wider world, even as the entrepreneurs in his government and in commerce did likewise. The world was also beginning to take an interest in the city—and not just the businessmen. Queen Victoria, for instance, came and was much impressed. Top-class hotels soon began to appear. The Kaiser himself and members of his court attended opening ceremonies at some and became regular patrons at others.

Industrial and trade fairs were the chosen way of expressing the expansionist mood. The biggest was held in the Treptow Park, laid out in the 1870s and 1880s, which stretches along the banks of the Spree in the south of the city. It took place in 1896, a year which brought nearly three quarters of a million visitors to the city. They came then to see all the marvels of modern science and technology, including the city's first electric tram. (Today, almost every official visitor and certainly every Soviet citizen who comes to Berlin makes his or her way to Treptow for markedly different reasons: a huge Soviet war memorial there dominates the park, with mass graves for 5000 Red Army soldiers who died in the fierce and final days of the Second World War. Red marble used in the construction of the memorial was taken from Hitler's former Chancellery in the Wilhelmstrasse.)

Like Bismarck, Wilhelm II did not particularly care for Berlin; and, like Bismarck, spent much of his time away from the city. He had announced that he expected homage as God's 'equal', and from elderly, nostalgic Prussians, from the obsequious and the misguided, he received it. He also postulated that Berliners, in the shape of his appointed forces of law and order, should be ready to shoot other Berliners if he demanded it. Presumably, in the light of such a postulation, he smelt something he did not like in the city air.

It was ten years into his reign when the redoubtable Rosa Luxemburg, then twenty-seven, arrived. With the characteristic agility of her highly unusual mind, she quickly recognised the necessity that she should fulfil a role: as a hard-hitting observer of the social scene and as a thinking revolutionary. She soon found herself dissatisfied by the city's motley collection of political activists. They tended to be people willing enough to make decisions relating to the human condition, but never quite capable of making decisions which were viable or which acknowledged the human element. With varying degrees of intensity, this gap between conception and execution was to plague the otherwise determined labour movement in Berlin—and Germany—up to the 1920s and beyond. (It was to hit the Communists in East Berlin, too, in 1953 when building workers and others suddenly found they could not accept government orders, and it was to hit the SPD administration in West Berlin in the late 1960s when it was overtaken by student riots.)

Rosa Luxemburg, being Polish and Jewish, saw Berlin initially with some detachment. 'It is the most repulsive place,' she wrote to a friend, 'cold, ugly, massive—a real barracks, and the charming Prussians with their arrogance as if each one of them had been made to swallow the very stick with which he had got his daily beating. . . .' Her happiest Berlin home was at 58 Cranach-Strasse, in the Friedenau district of Schöneberg, today a trim and settled residential area. She liked privacy and would walk each day in the Tiergarten, but was also susceptible to loneliness and to the city's moods. 'You have no idea what darkness there is in Berlin during the winter,' she wrote. 'How I long for sunshine.'

By the time Rosa arrived, the public demonstration, and the uncompromising tactics employed by the police to break it up, had become familiar features of city life. The poor unemployed with families, especially if they were living on top of one another in cramped conditions, could frequently only resort to the streets. Agitators of almost every colouring would come out in support, their favoured rallying points being in and around the Alexanderplatz.

Rosa quickly made it her business to be among the people on such occasions. She was on hand when an outbreak of food poisoning hit a hostel for the homeless in Fröbelstrasse (near today's Ernst Thälmann Park) and she accompanied some of the victims to the city hall. Here she was struck by what she called the *Kaltblutigkeit* (cold-bloodedness) of the officials, who appeared to be stiff and pompous in the face of misery and reports of death. Such insupportable wretchedness, Rosa wrote, tears away the mask of Berlin's respectability.

Karl Liebknecht was the son of the old Social Democrat. He was the same age as Rosa and surfaced in Berlin at about the same time. He, too, was a politician of the streets but he had a touch of the impetuous demagogue, which he carried on occasions into the Reichstag committee rooms. He had grown up during the time of the Anti-Socialist Law (and had been born while his father was in prison), studied law and politics at Leipzig and Berlin universities, and did a spell with the Kaiser's Pioneer Guards at Potsdam before committing himself to politics, and to Marxism specifically.

In popular memory, and at the Friedrichsfelde memorial cemetery for socialists, these two out of a dozen prominent figures get particular attention and are remembered together. It is not so assiduously recalled that they argued vehemently as frequently as they agreed.

Many in Berlin and abroad respected Liebknecht as a remarkable and courageous fighter. Others thought of him as a lesser person than his father (who died in Berlin in 1900), never quite doing things well, seemingly disorganised. Even so, his utterances and his published polemics were enough to earn him spells in prison, and it was from prison that he won a seat as an anti-militarist, always pro-Marxist, member of the SPD. His Berlin homes were An der Spandauer Brücke (then by the Marx-Engels-Platz S-bahn station, but now gone) and later, at Hortensia-Strasse, by the Botanic Gardens in the West Berlin district of Dahlem.

Two other emerging and important politicians of this time were Friedrich Ebert and Philipp Scheidemann. Ebert, born three weeks after the Reich itself, was a Heidelberg tailor's son, who trained as a saddler. He was a gradualist by nature who sought better living conditions and social improvements for the working class, only entering active politics after the dropping of the Anti-Socialist Law. In 1905 he became SPD secretary-general and his administrative abilities, helped by a natural authority and common sense, assisted in the creation of a streamlined party machine.

These paper qualifications, as well as his natural astuteness, made him the automatic candidate to follow Bebel, on his death, as party chairman in 1913. But in Berlin's most acute hours of need, which were to come in a very few years, these qualities were not apparent. It was as a decidedly unrevolutionary opponent of Liebknecht and of Marxism, fitting in with the then prevailing thinking of his party, that his later actions as the republic's first president were to be judged, as well as the decision that he should 'go along with' the Imperial Government of Prince Max von Baden.

Scheidemann, six years older than Ebert, came to Berlin from Kassel and worked as a journalist before entering the Reichstag in 1903. He wavered about the centre-right of the SPD spectrum, apparently endorsing the Kaiser's imperialist ventures in the

Middle East. Like Ebert, he was 'unrevolutionary' by nature, but he seemed to be coy about taking office while the Kaiser remained in power. Until the revolution, he was vociferously unsure of the SPD's capability of even governing—though he was the one, in the end, who was the first to proclaim the new republic. He was unsure of himself in the tumult of Berlin during the war: calling on the party, on the one hand, to keep and encourage the goodwill of 'the masses' while in the next breath dismissing these same 'masses' in most disparaging terms.

The years before the war sharpened differences between the rulers and the ruled. Wilhelm chose a succession of Imperial Chancellors—notably Prince Bernhard von Bülow—who were close to him in their political outlook. With them, he grew ever more preposterously expansionist, searching, as one of them was to put it, for Germany's 'place in the sun'. As the Army and Navy waxed strong in support of these aims, the agitation and uncertainties in the streets intensified. Bülow was finally to resign after a row at the Palace which followed a sabre-rattling interview that had been given by Wilhelm to the London *Daily Telegraph*. A suddenly fraught situation was only marginally eased with the appointment of Theobald von Bethmann-Hollweg to succeed him.

Since the authoritarian inclinations of the Kaiser were slightly diminished as a result of the interview, Bethmann tried, without much success, to effect a popular compromise by putting more liberal policies into practice. His own credentials were appropriate enough: he came neither from the aristocracy nor the landed gentry, but from the civil service (and from a banking family). He represented a break with tradition.

In the 1900s he sought as Home Affairs Minister to harness the workers' movement and to keep it, where it could be defined, 'within the existing social order'. But it was not long before he was clashing with the entrenched generals and with the steadily advancing Admiral von Tirpitz every time he queried the Kaiser's international ambitions. Popular politics, meanwhile, had moved into the streets and anti-war rallies were becoming unexceptional events. On one well-ordered occasion, more than 200,000 people gathered in such a cause in Treptow Park—in September 1911.

Elections were held in the following year and the SPD was able to achieve its best performance to date, winning 110 seats out of 390, from more than four million votes. It was now the largest party in the Reichstag, and had earned a huge endorsement from the people of the city. Three Berlin voters out of every four had given it their support. The way in which the majority had now voted was a pointer, if one was still needed, to the growing irrelevance of the Prussian way of doing things. Even so, the practitioners of this 'way', many of them cultivating moustaches imitative of the Kaiser's own, still had unquestionable control of the civil service. He and they went through the motions of uttering loud and jingoistic sounds of national fervour, but it was becoming increasingly clear that previously sure, or notionally sure, social and political foundations were being rocked as they had never been rocked before.

It was not long before the changes became visible. In May 1912 a session of the Reichstag had to be suspended because socialist deputies had launched an attack on the thinking of the Kaiser himself. Elsewhere in the city, representatives of a still disparate collection of trade unionists and co-operatives' representatives were coming together to air their grievances. They needed little spurring on: wages were being cut in a whole variety of jobs and unemployment was beginning to grow. While the generals and senior members of the foreign service regaled each other with talk of war, men and women of the Left talked more and more about revolution.

The news from Russia, since the revolution of 1905 in St Petersburg, was being brought first-hand by associates of Rosa Luxemburg. Russians were soon arriving to seek sanctuary in Berlin, and Lenin came at least a dozen times between 1895 and 1917. The first time, he was still in his twenties, with uncertain revolutionary aspirations but suffering severely from pneumonia, and he had left Russia to seek medical treatment. He stayed in a boarding house at No. 12 Flensburger Strasse, near the Belle Vue Palace north of the Tiergarten, and complained in a letter to his mother: 'I understand the Germans with the greatest difficulty or, worse still, I don't understand them at all....' By 1912 an 'illegal' visitor, he was staying round the corner at Klopstock-Strasse with a builder called Rauchfuss (near the Tiergarten S-bahn station), arguing intermittently with Rosa Luxemburg but, at this period, anticipating war between Austria and Russia as a precursor to revolution. This time he wrote: 'I have got so used to it here (in Berlin) that I almost feel at home and would be quite happy to stay a while longer. . . .'

By 1912, the city was still being treated to displays of the Kaiser's strutting arrogance. Sometimes he would stride out with his sons through the Mitte area, expecting and usually getting adulation, or he would ride magisterially down to the Brandenburg Gate for a turn in the Tiergarten beyond. In May 1913, when the Princess Viktoria Luise was married, Tsar Nicholas II and King George V of England, both relatives by marriage, were among the guests. A few weeks on in the same summer there were celebrations again, this time to mark the twenty-fifth anniversary of Wilhelm's accession.

The brightness in the Berlin air started to take on a certain brittleness. The arms 'race' between Germany and France intensified, as did the rivalry at sea between Germany and Britain. The motives of the Russian Tsar, although he had been a wedding guest, were seen as increasingly suspect. Which ever way one turned, there was talk of war.

The people's own chosen leaders, on the other hand, spoke in the streets of 'solidarity of the people' and continued to argue against war. For many of 'the people', however, such arguments can only have been perplexing: the city now had a throbbing life of its own and there was colour in the streets. The sexually amoral behaviour of the upper classes in the area of the Linden and Friedrichstrasse had begun to spread further west—and to other classes.

After five in the evening, one contemporary journalist reported, 'the country's preachers and precept-bearers will surely raise their eyebrows at the brazen girls to be seen strolling along the Kurfürstendamm or the adjoining Tauentzienstrasse, arm-in-arm, ogling at passers-by. No gravitas, clearly, in these streets.' He could have written these words today; in fact they were printed the day after the assassination in Sarajevo of the Archduke Ferdinand, on 29 June 1914.

The storm clouds were bound to break sooner or later. Towards the end of July, the city's Lord Mayor, Adolf Wermuth, came back hurriedly from holiday and was thrown into a state of some consternation by the agitation that met him on his return. He was urged, despite a known shortage of municipal funds, to get in extra stocks of food. A few days later, a senior army officer told crowds in Unter den Linden to be ready for war. On 31 July the

Kaiser himself spoke from the Palace balcony: 'We are being forced to defend ourselves; the sword is being pressed into our hands. I urge you to go to church, to kneel before God, and plead with Him to aid our courageous army.'

The following day war was declared on Russia. The Kaiser went again to his balcony: 'I no longer know parties; I only know Germans. . . .' He demanded of those who heard him that, regardless of party, class or religious faith, their differences should be buried and that, 'through thick and thin', the people should place their trust in him. He summoned Reichstag deputies to the Palace and repeated his message. The Great White Hall, where the Imperial Reichstag had first met more than forty years before, responded with cheers, and Bethmann-Hollweg declared unconvincingly that Germans were 'united to the last man'. The theatrically inclined Kaiser had pulled off his most histrionic act yet.

An unquantifiable number of Berliners, and very possibly a substantial majority, were delighted to oblige, their enthusiasm only minimally alloyed by the doubts of the few. 'Hero figures' emerged overnight, and once again there were kisses and flowers at the city's railway stations, as men in new uniforms—products of the city's own textile industry—headed for the fronts. Chalked slogans talked naïvely in terms of an 'excursion to Paris', said that 'every shot fired' would hit a Russian, and that every stab of the bayonet would get a Frenchman. At this moment, perhaps, Berlin's skills at graffiti were born.

These few days, weeks at the most, were the nearest Germans were ever to get in that pre-war era to a feeling of corporate national pride. It is arguable whether Hitler at his most exhortatory and euphoric was able to induce the same feeling; what is not arguable is that the feeling of August 1914 was something very rare indeed.

The exhilaration could not and did not last long. Within a matter of weeks several of the city's theatres, museums, even street markets, pubs and night bars were closed, and there were cuts in public transport and electricity supplies. The city's mood grew darker as meat and flour supplies were placed under official control; and bread, potatoes, lard, eggs and milk were put on ration. Then, suddenly, shops were being broken into by people who were hungry as well as poor, even for potatoes. The farmers, it seemed, began to lose faith in money. Prices, many negotiated informally in farmyards or possibly at the city's railway stations, began to climb.

Even the escapists who sought refuge in entertainment could not escape completely. The 'language of the enemy', which in earlier moments had given the city its touch of cosmopolitan raciness, was suddenly expunged. The Palais de Danse on Behrenstrasse, for instance, became the Tanzpalast; the Café Piccadilly on the Potsdamer Platz became the Fatherland Café, and so on. Then the decision was made that street lights had to be out by 1 a.m. The city's police authorities, under Colonel von Kessell, were given powers to carry out house searches and to make arrests in the name of 'order'.

News of 'setbacks' on the front and of the Imperial Army losing important initiatives began to percolate through, but only slowly. The Kaiser and his circle went on with their crazy routine—eating and drinking at the newly opened, elegant hotels. But the gap which existed between the waiters and the servants on the one side, and those whom they waited upon and served on the other, grew disconcertingly wider. 'The scene has fundamentally changed,' wrote Rosa Luxemburg, six months after the war had started. 'Gone is the ecstasy, and gone are the patriotic street demonstrations.... No more do trains filled with reservists pull out amid joyous cries from enthusiastic maidens. No longer do we see laughing faces smiling from train windows....' The people, she added, are going about their daily tasks with a 'disturbed' look about them.

By 1916, the disturbingly high number of the war's casualties could no longer be hidden. The gloom spread to many new corners of the city as rationing was extended still further. Wool and cotton were in short supply—needed at the front—so clothes were rationed. Coffee, tea and tobacco were hard to get, the black market spread wider, and substitutes were devised. All sorts of food and drink were created out of turnips, of which there were plenty. Women began to drive the horse-drawn buses of the city for the first time. Petrol had been requisitioned.

On 1 May 1916, at the Potsdamer-Platz, Karl Liebknecht addressed an anti-war rally of several thousand, exhorting them to remove the government and end the war. He had been released only shortly before, after an enforced year on the Russian front—burying the war dead—which he had served in addition to a spell in prison. He was now arrested again. At the same time, Rosa

Luxemburg was taken into 'protective custody'. Eight weeks later, on the day of Liebknecht's trial, an estimated 50,000 machine workers downed tools and converged upon the courthouse. The government did more for the revolution to come, in other words, by trying Liebknecht and again imprisoning him, than he could do himself. He did not achieve such crowds when he was free. A statue to him was erected in Potsdamer Platz after his death; twenty-five years after the Second World War, only the plinth remained.

With the abrupt removal of these two, the leadership of the embryo communists fell to two of Luxemburg's friends, Franz Mehring and Klara Zetkin. Mehring, a journalist and committed Marxist, was shattered when Luxemburg was murdered in the January after the war was over, and died himself not long afterwards. Zetkin survived long enough to work with Lenin and, in 1932, to roundly denounce Hitler from her place in the Reichstag.

Disenchantment grew cruelly as the war ground on. The Kaiser started increasingly to absent himself from the city, seemingly happier at the front among men in uniform. At home, the potato harvest failed, but there were always turnips. Substitutes were developed—and the word 'ersatz' became common currency—for traditional jams and soups, and for soap. The city's horses were commandeered for the war effort; though those that could not work were sometimes eaten. Casualties in the battle areas were now being counted in millions.

Out in the southern suburb of Lichterfelde, meanwhile, British prisoners-of-war were engaged in road building. They were 'a most unkempt lot', reported the English wife of a German aristocrat. Other British prisoners were held at Ruhleben racecourse, near Spandau. A sewage works has since been built on this site.

In the absence of leadership from the Kaiser, Bethmann Hollweg, the 'gentleman' who occupied the Chancellor's seat, sought to ward off intolerable pressures from Left and Right. The Left, if it believed its own street orators, had power in its grasp; the Right felt a victory of sorts might still be attainable. Even at this late stage its supporters were still being invited to contribute to the war effort—by paying a donation for the honour of hammering nails into a great wooden image of Field Marshal General Paul von Hindenburg which had been erected outside the Reichstag. Finally, Bethmann-Hollweg, confused and broken, departed,

and the Army under Hindenberg and General Erich von Ludendorff took over the running of the country.

At this point, the SPD splintered into disarray; Liebknecht and
Luxemburg led one group and announced the formation of the
Spartacus Alliance, precursors of the German Communist Party.
Another group called itself the Independent SPD but, while it
preached opposition to any prolongation of the war, it declined
also to enthuse for revolution. A third group, the less equivocal
Revolutionary Shop Stewards, kept closer to feelings on the shop
floor and sought to organise trade union thinking.

By early 1917, it was the shop stewards who seemed to have
won the hearts and minds of the sullen crowds in the street. They
intervened at a meeting of the Metal Workers' Union and were
able on 16 April to exhort around 300,000 to down tools and
march through the city. The bread ration had just been halved
and their demand was for food. The authorities responded with
threats of general conscription and the strike folded. But the case
for revolution had been heard—a committee to bring it nearer was
formed.

At this time, coincidentally, the sealed train bearing Lenin
and his supporters on their fateful journey to Petrograd passed
through Berlin. It stopped on the morning of 11 April at the
Potsdamer station—with police cordoning off the platforms in
case of trouble—before being transferred to the Stettiner station
and departure. Despite his hopes for revolution in Germany,
under Liebknecht, Lenin did not return to Berlin.

Hindenberg was seventy and of old Prussian Junker stock. He
had spent his life (from the age of eleven) in the Army and knew
more about victories than about defeat. From the front, he wrote
to General Wilhelm von Groener, in Berlin and responsible for
supplies, and urged that 'the workers' should be further 'enlightened'. The devious Groener chose for undisclosed reasons to
make his own use of the contents of this letter. Our worst enemies,
he announced to those Berliners who cared to hear, were not at
the front but 'in the midst of us'; they were the strike agitators.

This was enough to light the proverbial powder-keg, and
towards the end of January, further strike meetings were held.
The ultimately non-committal but always shrewd Ebert, as well
as the aggressive Liebknecht, were among the protagonists. Ebert
was heckled, Liebknecht was not, and by 27 January the city was
as close as it had ever been to civil war. Almost half a million

workers, it has been estimated, stopped work. Most milled about the city streets in directionless confusion. The more militant of them overturned buses and trams, while the less militant saw to it that what remained of the city's transport was paralysed.

Many of the workers were unarmed, and they were able to offer only token resistance when the police moved in to make arrests. A tactical retreat was ordered and the workers' own shock troops were organised to defend the bigger factories in the city. The ultimate aim, so far as the Revolutionary Shop Stewards were concerned, was to make these troops 'masters of the streets', to win over whoever was ambivalent, and to persuade as many of the dispirited military as they could to the justice of a people's take-over. Somehow or other, more arms were found: either by raiding army stores, by buying them from a variety of sources, or by swiftly appropriating them from soldiers who were home on leave. Not all of these men were willing to back the cause, but many were cajoled into doing so.

As such convulsions were seizing the city of Berlin, French and British troops, supported by Australians and Canadians, were over-running German positions and taking thousands of prisoners. Kaiser Wilhelm, the Supreme Warlord, communicated to his generals that he wished to sue for peace. First Quarter-master General von Ludendorff was one of a few willing to fight on, but the pressure grew for peace and for an abdication.

The Kaiser's authority in Berlin was falling day by day, and, so far as the majority was concerned, there was almost no adulation left for him. On 12 October Liebknecht was one of a group who were released from prison. Later that month, the Kaiser left his Palace to be driven down Unter den Linden and through the Brandenburg Gate for the last time. He was heading for Spa, in southern Belgium, his headquarters behind the front line and a place where, as Supreme Warlord, he would be in the more congenial company of his officers. The crowd which saw him on his way from Berlin was one of the thinnest he had ever had to contemplate.

TWO

1918-1933

Deutschland Deutschland über alles
Über alles in der Welt
Überall ist großer Dalles
Nur in Deutschland ist kein Geld[1]

Joseph Goebbels, the Rhinelander, wept when he heard that the Allies had bombed Dresden in early 1945: the Third Reich had only a few months left. A dozen or so years earlier, however, during the first weeks of the same Reich, he dismissed a telephone call to his home that the Reichstag was on fire as 'a bit of a wild fantasy'. Then, the news confirmed, he hurtled down the Charlottenburg-Chaussee, with his dinner guest—Hitler, of course—to see the worst. 'There is no doubt,' he told his diary, 'but that Communism has made a last attempt to cause disorder by means of fire and terror, in order to seize power during the general panic ... (but) not for a moment does the Führer lose his composure; wonderful to watch him giving orders....'

After an hour's sleep—by his own account—Goebbels was feverishly at work, banning 'Marxist' newspapers, approving measures to deal with the 'Red' parties—and inspecting damage. 'The hall,' he wrote, 'is a sad picture of devastation. Wreckage upon wreckage. The Communist Party will have to pay for it dearly ... the worst is over. We hope that the last breakdown is happily overcome....' It was as if he were already rubbing his hands in satisfaction at a job well done. Certainly no one was able with any authority to answer his charges against the communists. The probable guilt of Hermann Göring was only to emerge at a much later date.

It is difficult today not to be haunted by the Reichstag building.

[1] Germany, Germany, is the greatest, the greatest in the world. Everyone around is bankrupt, but only Germans have no cash.

Some architects have described it as overpoweringly monumental—and standing close to it and looking up, it does have the
grim power of a great cliff. It is neo-baroque, or it is a free play
with the ornate forms of the High Renaissance, depending on
one's point of view—and it is still less than a hundred years
old. Succinctly, it has embodied a century's triumphs, phoney
triumphs and tribulations. It also still carries some of the graffiti
scrawled by Red Army soldiers in May 1945.

Like the Brandenburg Gate, two hundred yards or so to the
south, the building has a peculiar arrogance. Having withstood
disdain from the Kaiser, disinterest from Bismarck, contempt
from the fire-raising Nazis, and assaults from Allied bombers and
Soviet occupiers, it now stands, like the 'colossal wreck' (but
refurbished) in Shelley's sonnet to Ozymandias, with 'lone and
level' stretches of grassland on three sides. But it is no longer at
the centre of anything. The nearest West Berlin building is several
minutes' walk away; the nearest one in East Berlin a stone's throw
across the Wall at its back.

Inside, the building is no longer the creation of its architect,
Paul Wallot. Rather, it is a space-age experience. Heavily dec-
orative and eminently combustible woodwork which he incorporated have long since gone. The inside has been gutted, and the
paintwork of the new offices, meeting rooms and corridors is in
varying shades of clinical white. There is air-conditioning, and
the 'modern' furnishings, some worryingly self-conscious in their
design, are of man-made materials that could only belong to the
late twentieth century.

Along one corridor, there is a display of rather faded photographs. They show how the Reichstag looked soon after it was
built, how it looked after the 1933 fire, after the Allied bombing,
after the last hand-to-hand fighting of April and May, 1945—and
finally, a distinct anti-climax, how it looked after reconstruction.
The latter process took more than ten years to get under way and
lasted three times longer than the war, from 1956 to 1971. It cost
scores of millions of marks. Fifteen years on again, and there has
been a proposal to reinstate, after all, the great central dome.
That, too, will be a very costly affair. The whys and wherefores
in the determining of such priorities—in a city where housing has
always been a central problem—are endlessly fascinating.

This dead-and-alive Reichstag receives streams of visitors—
tourists as well as working politicians and officials. The tourists

40

snap each other at the grand entrance, usually on the steps, unknowingly watched by the imperial eagle in the coat of arms just beneath the gable. Many spend time in the elaborate museum inside which seeks, in the most appropriate environment, to answer 'questions about German history'. Uniforms, documents, trinkets, and paraphernalia pertaining to the 'ideas, forces and decisions' are all there. It is mainly photographs which try, mutely, to convey the intermittent trauma.

When the First World War ended, Berlin, according to the painter George Grosz, looked like a stony grey corpse. 'The houses were cracked, paint and plaster had crumbled away, and in the dull, grimy eye-sockets of the windows you could see the caked traces of tears; the tears of people looking for familiar faces that were never to return. . . .' There were presentiments there of a certain continuity. Grosz, as his Weimar period pictures show, was a harsh and penetrating observer of the city, and he could be describing with these words one of his own later pictures, a Brecht backcloth, a setting for a Nazi demonstration, or any one of several corners in either Berlin today. The waiting in this city is not only for détente; it is also frequently for a coat of paint, and for sympathy with a huge but unquantifiable predicament. There were many faces, more than once, that were never to return. . . .

Early on Saturday afternoon, 9 November 1918, the Königsplatz which then stood before the main entrance reflected the chaotic uncertainty in which Berlin then found itself. There were reports of insurrection among sailors at Kiel, and the Kaiser had taken himself out of what he perceived as immediate harm's way to Supreme Headquarters near the front line in Belgium. Defeat, unthinkable until this moment, was now staring him in the face. It came together with the inevitability of abdication, and none of the officers around him tried to persuade him otherwise. Hours before, Prince Max von Baden, who had been in many senses 'his' Imperial Chancellor, had handed over office to Friedrich Ebert. He, in spite of all his proletarian pretensions, had also taken the title of Imperial Chancellor. Oddly, it had been a solemn but totally unconstitutional act, between two men who were both constitutionalists at heart.

In the city streets, it was a fertile time for rumour and counter-rumour. Large numbers of the city's population were battle-weary, but mostly ignorant of how badly the last stage of the endless war was going. They were bewildered and hungry, and moved about dizzily with no clear notion of what would happen next. Meetings in the preceding few days had achieved nothing that could be clearly grasped; and now one of the crowds, impatient as well as apprehensive, converged upon the Reichstag. It consisted of people who were too tired for any exultation; many were armed.

In a restaurant for deputies on the second floor (now incorporated into the museum) Philipp Scheidemann was trying to snatch some lunch. Soldiers and sailors were standing, and sometimes, lying about. They had removed their badges of rank and had, in many cases, brought their women with them. They had effectively taken the building over. Ebert was also there, but Scheidemann was prevailed upon—somewhat against his will— to address the crowds below. He spoke of 'the accursed war' which was ending, of Germany's 'downfall', of the 'workers' government' currently being formed by 'our friend, Ebert', and of the miracles which had occurred. 'Stand united and loyal,' he shouted from his upstairs window, 'and be conscious of your duty.... Nothing must be done to dishonour the workers' movement. The old and the rotten have broken down. Long live the new! Long live the German Republic!...'

And that, apparently, was what the seemingly disconsolate were wanting to hear. In Scheidemann's words, they found the will to cheer, but Ebert did not share their joy. He turned furiously on Scheidemann, declaring that he had no right to proclaim the republic. In the ensuing period, the men were to work closely together, but this altercation was symptomatic of the deep-seated structural weaknesses inherent in the new 'ruling' party. They were to bedevil it for years to come. Ebert, furthermore, had played a card—unwittingly perhaps—before the game had properly begun.

Down the road, on what is now Marx-Engels-Platz, hundreds more waited that same day outside the Royal Palace. Inside, Karl Liebknecht, just out of prison, was on the political rampage. He had already found time to distribute leaflets calling for revolution; now he was romping impetuously with his supporters about the Kaiser's quarters, at one moment even trying the Kaiser's bed.

A couple of hours or so after Scheidemann had made his declaration, Liebknecht went out on to the balcony from which the Kaiser, four years before, had declared that he knew 'no parties, only Germans'. He too managed to draw rousing cheers when he declared, not for a 'German Republic', as Scheidemann had done, but for the 'free, socialist republic' of Germany. The balcony, as a consequence, has been preserved, grafted as a centrepiece on the front of the East German State Council building nearby, which dates from the early 1960s.

However, the differences between Liebknecht and the avowedly anti-Bolshevist Scheidemann group were already unbridgeable. This was a moment which confounded still further the confusion over precisely who was running and who was going to run the disarrayed country and its capital.

If this was revolution, the omens were distinctly mixed. The cafés and dancehalls, for instance, went on with their normal business, and the dancing only stopped for a matter of minutes if there was shooting outside. The city had not lost its aristocratic, notionally ruling class—though the actual business of 'ruling', in the sense of governmental administration, was in the hands of only forty or fifty people. It also still had a rich capitalist class, whose economic success, up to 1914, had somehow qualified them to marry aristocrats. It was the latter's thinking that they would echo in often feudal attitudes towards their employees. Nowhere was this clearer than in Berlin: when war broke out, after all, the capital epitomised the power that Germany had achieved as Europe's leading industrial producer.

Things were very different once the war was over. 'Among the civilians,' wrote Theodor Wolff, an acute observer of the Berlin scene, 'many are frightened and apprehensive, hiding their money, providing themselves with little acetylene lamps with their horrible stink, so as to have light whatever happens. Some of the people I know who have villas in Grunewald or on the banks of the Havel are shutting them up, feeling too isolated and unprotected there, and coming back to town. They are all afraid of the Spartacists, and their one hope now is in Social Democracy, which they know is sensible and will not smash up everything at once....'

Wolff also pondered for a moment on the 'costumes' of this revolution. 'In November, 1918,' he said, 'the only dress was the worn and shabby coat of the little man; nobody was in search of the picturesque and where indeed could it have been found amid the grey destitution of that day?... After four years of war there was no creative energy left ... too much of tragic reality had been lived through.... Nor did there beat, except rarely, any fervently revolutionary hearts in the tired frames beneath that November drabness....'

The politicisation which was in the air had become erratic. The molecules would not cluster. There were instances when soldiers streamed out of their barracks to join the crowds in the streets, men greeting each other fraternally, girls sticking flowers into the soldiers' uniforms and kissing them, while their hesitant officers looked on. But there were also instances, in the Chaussee-Strasse, for example, when officers opened fire on advancing crowds and killed people. The returning Prussian officers, who had enlisted in the cause of the Kaiser, were by no means always on the side of 'the little man'.

'The three who died in Chaussee-Strasse,' says a recent East German history, 'were victims of the first shots fired by the forces of reaction in Berlin.' On that day, 9 November, a total of fifteen 'revolutionaries' are known to have died—and almost as many others. There were to be thousands more. It was a day which saw red flags raised over the royal palace and the Brandenburg Gate, but it also saw armed police patrolling the city streets, guarding the more vulnerable public buildings.

Early next day—a Sunday—Chancellor Ebert made telephone contact with the Kaiser's command post on the Western front. He spoke to General von Groener who told him that Field Marshal von Hindenburg, still beyond question a hero-figure of the Berlin establishment, was expecting the new government to fight against 'Bolshevism'. The officer corps, von Groener added, would place itself at the disposal of the government for such a purpose. Ebert replied that von Groener should pass on the thanks of the government to Hindenburg, and, with this reply, painted himself and Germany, into a corner from which there was to be no escape.

Von Groener was a dour but realistic general who had done much to persuade the Kaiser to go. Later, he was to maintain that, because of 'the danger' then presented by the Bolsheviks, a total of ten army divisions had at that moment been earmarked to march into the city to take power. Ebert, astonishingly, had agreed to this. But Ebert, wrote the painter Grosz a little while later, was beginning to look more and more like a managing director.

Germany's first serious foray into revolution began and ended in a matter of days. Protests and demonstrations were to go on for years, up and down and around the Linden, but even at this early stage there was a disenchanted tiredness about the fervour. The zest, for the moment, had gone.

'Endless processions of workers and soldiers,' Wolff now wrote, 'were passing through without a break ... Most of the workers were middle-aged, with grey-bearded faces ... they had trade unionists' corporate spirit and marched conscientiously, in order. Some were carrying rifles, everyone had a red badge in the button hole or on the breast; the marshals were distinguished by the red arm-bands.... Great red flags were carried....' But it was not always so orderly: military vehicles moved about the city, wrote another eye-witness, full to overflowing with soldiers and sailors waving red banners and uttering ferocious shouts. Every so often, they leapt from the vehicles to tear the badges of rank from the soldiers or officers standing among the crowds. Men with the Kaiser's commission were not amused.

Ebert was in a no-win situation of his own making. He was obliged somehow to control wildly disparate elements which surrounded him in the city streets, and he was drawing increasingly on the willing help that was available from the long-experienced (imperial) forces of law and order. These were often officers and otherwise unemployed men who had served the Supreme Warlord in a wretched war and now sought, without him, to enforce a ragged peace. On Sunday afternoon of 10 November a noisy, urgent meeting was called of 3000 workers and soldiers in the Busch Circus, a structure which has long since gone, but was then sited on the north bank of the Spree close to the Marx-Engels-Platz S-bahn station. Ebert was first to speak and claimed that the formation of government was the first step towards unity and the victory, as he saw it, of the revolution. But there was confusion. A group of soldiers stormed the platform, urging the imposition of military rule.

Amid this semi-uproar, Liebknecht intervened with a controlled anger: he declared that Ebert was in fact a menace to the revolution. This is a sentiment readily echoed in East Berlin today where, at the Institute of Marxism-Leninism, they say that he 'betrayed' the revolution. But Ebert survived, and although the dim, November days had momentarily 'turned into spring', as one writer put it, and 'faces laughed', they did so only briefly.

Out of the stormy scenes at the Circus meeting, Workers' and Soldiers' Councils were elected—with an executive for the city of Berlin and for local government throughout the country. But the general coincidence of views with the central Ebert administration was not high. The Independent Social Democrats, the mainstream SPD, and the Spartacists still went their three separate ways. The people remained bewildered and cold—and always hungry. Food, even though it was severely rationed, was for most a more persisting preoccupation than revolution. The street traders—including the prostitutes—did their utmost to carry on business as usual.

For many in the city, the meetings, the marches and the demonstrations—and the steadily proliferating strikes—were often self-defeating, going nowhere identifiable, achieving little but further conflict and frequent bloodshed. Today one does not need to walk far in central Berlin to find one or more of the several silent backyards, doorways, and broken down walls, with and without memorial plaques, where for still unexplained reasons workers or their opponents were lined up and shot.

Indefatigably, Rosa Luxemburg and Karl Liebknecht, supported for the time being by a much smaller band than today's East German schoolchildren are led by their history books to believe, fought on. Those politicians who sat in the Reichstag, said Luxemburg, were sitting in 'a counter-revolutionary fortress erected against the revolutionary proletariat. Our task is to take this fortress by storm and raze it to the ground.' She had spent much of the war in prison in Niederbarnim and there is a memorial in Barnimstrasse, five minutes' walk from Alexanderplatz, unveiled in 1977, marking the site.

Ebert took her threat seriously, and thought of leaving Berlin. He told von Groener that if 'the Liebknecht mob' should seize power, he would set up a new government elsewhere in a matter of days. Von Groener counselled otherwise; and Gustav Noske, an SPD man who had become Defence Minister at the end of the war, took charge of the Army as a ruthlessly suppressive force. Somebody, he is now reputed to have said, has to be the bloodhound. The brutish and unsubtle Noske remained in this role for almost eighteen bloodthirsty months, setting up headquarters in the Luisa Convent, in the leafy suburb of Dahlem. He was to continue living in Germany throughout the Nazi period, dying shortly after the Second World War.

He brought a sergeant-majorish lack of equivocation to a dangerously fraught situation, frequently acting unilaterally or, at best, after consultation with Walter von Lüttwitz, who had been made general in command of the Berlin area. While Ebert talked, Noske acted, making arrests and suppressing rioters and demonstrators with the sort of single-minded, thoughtless efficiency which a dozen or so years later was to become routine. Noske's most active forces were drawn from the officer corps, often Prussian, which had found itself without a role. His irregular *Freikorps* (free corps) were the precursors—in content, allegiance and purpose—of Hitler's stormtroopers.

With only occasional interludes, this turbulence persisted throughout the winter. Ebert had taken the salute at the Brandenburg Gate in early December as tired but 'undefeated' troops, returning at last from the war, marched past. But otherwise, it turned into a winter in which meetings organised by the SPD would be broken up in disorderly mêlées—one, at the Philharmonic Hall, having been disrupted by a young chauvinistic air force commander called Hermann Göring. Despite an agreement reached in mid-December that there should be a general election a month later, the city's tensions and uncertainties, its violence and blood-letting continued.

An untidy climax came in the battle of Christmas Eve which took place near the Royal Palace. The royal stables (known then and now as the Marstall) which were an imposing and relatively new building adjoining the Palace, on the banks of the Spree, had been made the headquarters of the newly formed People's Marine Division. This was an ill-equipped, ill-organised unit of revolutionary sailors and unemployed ex-infantrymen, who were now camped in the home, of sorts, of otherwise homeless families of the servants of the former imperial household.

Ebert, by subsequent accounts, was confused by a situation which had been complicated by the sailors' decision to hold as hostage Otto Wels, a Social Democratic former upholsterer who was now a military commanding officer in the city. After much argument and procrastination, a pro-government guards unit was sent in. Shelling, shooting and hand-to-hand fighting followed and at least sixty-seven died, most of them guardsmen.

This incident was to be another nail in the coffin of the revolution. Wels, a spent force after his captivity, was deposed, though years later he was to resurface briefly as a vociferous opponent to Hitler in the Reichstag. Noske, the bloodhound, on the other hand, was firmly ensconced in the government.

Hugo Haase was a staunch critic of Noske's methods and was emerging as a popular leader of the Independent Social Democrats with an anti-war record. He had joined the six-strong Council of People's Commissars, the revolutionary core of Ebert's government. His view was that the battle for the Marstall had momentarily 'broken' Ebert, Scheidemann and Otto Landsberg (the SPD trio in the Council) and that this was the opportunity which should have been seized by the Independents. 'We would have taken with us the masses who were backing us,' he said.

But Hasse, like the revolution itself, was to be snuffed out. He was assassinated only a few months later on the Reichstag steps. Great crowds gathered for his funeral.

Rosa Luxemburg saw 24 December as marking the end of 'the first stage of the revolution', but she also spoke of 'the uncertain character, inadequacy, the half-heartedness and the aimlessness' of the movement, saying the need was first to undermine, then overthrow, the Ebert-Scheidemann administration.

The Communist Party of Germany was born on New Year's Eve at yet another stormy meeting of a hundred or so Spartacists, Independent SPD members, and Revolutionary Shop Stewards. This took place in a small room of the Prussian parliament building in Leipziger-Strasse. Once again Rosa's caution was not acceptable to all on the Left, and splits developed which were inevitably exploited by the Right. But a new party had been formed. Noske was once again ready, while elsewhere, Adolf Hitler, a thirty-year-old corporal recovering in a military hospital from a gas attack on the eastern front, was beginning to marshal his thoughts.

On Sunday 5 January, despite the bleakness of the winter and a 'flu epidemic which was claiming thousands of lives, Berlin was swallowed up in one of the biggest demonstrations the city had yet seen. Following plans which had been made at cold, open-air meetings held in gardens at the city end of the Prenzlauer Allee, swarms of people converged on the Mitte area, from the Tiergarten to the Alexanderplatz.

The government's fear, that buildings in the Wilhelmstrasse might be occupied and its administration crippled, proved unfounded. Militant elements in the crowd turned their attention instead to the police headquarters by the railway bridge on the Alexanderplatz. If these elements had been more determined and clear-headed, Noske was to recall, they could have had control of Berlin in a matter of hours. In fact, factories, department stores, transport and public utilities all struck. But once again there were uncertainties, procrastination and prevarication—over a period of days—at the highest level.

On 8 January, revolutionaries managed to occupy administrative offices in the city, newspaper premises, food distribution centres, railway stations, the main post office, and at one stage were even able to have a machine-gun team on the top of the Brandenburg Gate. They had broken into their own former barracks and an arsenal at Spandau, and had taken over other strategic buildings around the Royal Palace.

Wilhelmstrasse became impassable, and Ebert, after a series of confrontations in his office, was finally convinced by those around him that force was the only way. Surprisingly, perhaps, many of the buildings were retaken without much effort. This was partly because the revolutionary occupiers were, even at this critical stage, divided among themselves and partly because they had been infiltrated by government 'agents'.

A few days later, the workers were called upon by Ebert, and some of their own leaders, to return to their factories. Law and order had somehow to prevail, and economic life had to go on. Troops by the thousand began parading through the city centre; this time, however, they were pro-government men. Noske himself led a unit of 3000 up Potsdamer-Strasse into the Wilhelmstrasse.

Spartacus leaders went into hiding. With Liebknecht and Luxemburg, there was Wilhelm Pieck, already a central committee member. Thirty years later, in East Berlin, he became president of Germany's first socialist state. Luxemburg's evasiveness at this moment is suddenly tinged with a certain piquancy. She had written in *The Red Flag* that the German working class was not ready for office. It would be a criminal error to seize power, she said.

In Noske's eyes, she was right. On the evening of 15 January she and Liebknecht were seized by members of the *Freikorps* from their hiding place at No. 43 Mannheimer-Strasse in the Wilmersdorf district, and driven to the now demolished Eden Hotel, next to the Zoo. A credit bank now stands on the site, but the then hotel had become a temporary billet of one of the pro-government Army divisions. Here they were cross-examined by one Captain Waldemar Pabst, beaten by attendant soldiers and then taken away one at a time, through a side door of the hotel, ostensibly for transferral to the Moabit prison. In fact, Liebknecht was shot, 'while trying to escape' said the official version, in the Tiergarten, while Luxemburg was shot some minutes afterwards, still in her transit car, and her body dumped from the Liechtenstein Bridge into the Landwehr Canal in the Tiergarten. A small plaque marks the spot today.

In February 1962 the West German Government press office was hamhandedly to announce that both had been 'executed in accordance with martial law'. Liebknecht's widow, Sonia, living in East Berlin when this announcement was made, announced that she would sue the West Germans in court for 'glorifying murder'. The man who personally authorised the killings, Captain Pabst, meanwhile, was to survive until 1970—with further roles to play in German public life, as a member of the *Freikorps* and, later, in the active ranks of the Nazis. Franz Mehring, one of the communist leadership of that time, died only a fortnight later from pneumonia and, it is said, a broken will. Six weeks after that, Leo Jogiches, Rosa's sometime lover and perpetual comrade, was also murdered by the *Freikorps*.

Ebert expressed regret at these deaths and expected further massive demonstrations, but in fact the procession which gathered for the funeral of Liebknecht and thirty-two others on 25 January was quiet and orderly. Four months later the bloated, disfigured body of Luxemburg was washed up at a canal lock, and it too was buried by stunned supporters at the Friedrichsfelde Cemetery (now in East Berlin).

At this cemetery, in 1926, a gaunt brick memorial designed by Mies van der Rohe was unveiled by Wilhelm Pieck to commemorate them all. Seven years later, this memorial and the cemetery were both to be ploughed into the ground by the Nazis, but after 1945 the place was to become a political shrine. In June 1946, twenty years to the day after the first unveiling, a crude copy of Mies's memorial was unveiled, on the same site, by the same Wilhelm Pieck. Five years later, as President Pieck, he participated in a ceremony, beside the graves of Liebknecht and others, to dedicate a massive granite boulder bearing the inscription: '*Die Toten mahnen uns*'—'The dead remind us'. Pieck, who died in 1960, is now buried there himself.

On the day that Liebknecht and Luxemburg were finally arrested, a very different set of people had met in the city to erect their own notional barricades. These were the men whose industries were the mainstay of Germany's relatively new economic power. On the land, the old aristocracy of Junkers and estate owners clung to what they could of the *kaiserlich* past; the industrialists, however, sought to temper their nostalgia with a measure of adjustment to the fait accompli. Representatives of the Krupp engineering group, of the Vögler steel-making family, and others, decided to form an Anti-Bolshevist League. To this body each of them pledged several million marks, from which substantial sums were taken to arm and equip the *Freikorps* and other approved nationalist organisations. An implausible end apparently justified the same old means.

Yet still the revolution staggered on. Four days after the deaths of its two main protagonists, elections were held. They were boycotted by the Communists, and this led to the Social Democrats going into coalition with two parties of the centre. On 11 February, with the Reichstag obliged to meet in the National Theatre in Weimar (for its own safety), after heated debate, Ebert became first president of 'the German Republic' (as opposed to 'the German Socialist Republic') and supreme commander of the armed forces. Scheidemann was appointed Chancellor.

In the workers' councils of Berlin, where Communists and Independents outnumbered Social Democrats, another strike call went up for 2 March. Despite the new 'freedoms' enshrined in the Republic's first constitution, this call stemmed from general dissatisfaction with the 'new' political environment. The strikers' aim was to take over the city's gas, water and electric power supplies, but once again they were up against the ruthlessness of Noske and his men.

Noske's orders were unambiguous: 'Anyone found with arms fighting against government troops is to be shot instantly.' Up to two thousand are now thought to have died in pitched battles which went on for over a week in many parts of the city, as Noske's troops set about executing his order, often on the flimsiest of evidence. Makeshift barricades went up at strategic points, but hundreds were shot, others lynched or killed after brutal hand-to-hand encounters.

Noske proclaimed martial law on 9 March but not before one of the bloodiest shoot-outs had taken place on the Alexanderplatz outside the same police station which had figured in the earlier incident. Soldiers for revolution engaged with others fighting for Ebert, in a contest continued in a bitter struggle for the offices of the SPD's newspaper, *Vorwärts*, in Schützen-Strasse (now renamed Reinhold-Huhn-Strasse), a few hundred yards to the south of the Leipziger-Strasse, and for other strategic buildings in the city.

Executions were ordered. When later, in the Reichstag, Noske was accused of having gone too far, he replied: 'In such dangerous circumstances, it is not the paragraphs that count, but results.' For Berlin, at least, it seemed that the protracted and painful and somehow doomed exercise in revolution had finally been crushed. It had reached failure at this stage for the simplest of reasons: because it lacked leadership and lacked coherence. There was an inherent untidiness, in large measure the result of the city's being such a cosmopolitan place. Scars left by the struggle are still visible: one plaque on the wall of the printing works which now functions next to the Marstall commemorates the death of nineteen revolutionaries who were shot in a rear courtyard. Other plaques, rarely obtrusive but quietly eloquent, can be found elsewhere. Berliners, and especially those in charge of East Berlin, cannot and will not forget.

Until the events of 1918–19, political power in Germany had consistently been in the hands of the few. 'The Reichstag,' wrote a centrist deputy, recalling the last phase of the Kaiser's reign, 'is composed of three dozen clever and skilful manipulators and three hundred and fifty idiots who are indifferent to the progress of business. Our leaders endeavour to surround themselves with mediocrities in order to have no rivals ... we are a nation of lackeys and slaves whose minds have been prepared for all forms of servitude by intellectuals who have been domesticated by the government and are greedy for honours and distinctions. ...' For the specifically Berlin flavour, one might add the sentiments of a Bavarian academic of approximately the same period. 'This type of humanity,' he wrote of the Berliners, 'is composed of Prussian precision and energy, Jewish intelligence and tenacity, and Slav suppleness and keenness. It will dominate always everywhere where a central regime is established. ...'

Continuity rather than change was Ebert's preference, but he was doomed, in the words of a contemporary, to choose 'the road back'. When a red flag was unfurled over the Foreign Ministry in honour of those who died for their revolution in November 1918, and the diplomats walked out in protest, Ebert was one who understood. He it was who had approved the fact that most of them stayed in office, and who had authorised pro-government troops to have machine guns at the ready on the roof of the Reichstag.

While rioters and demonstrators milled about the streets, government bureaucrats did their utmost to carry on as before. Most of the Kaiser's old ministers kept control of their departments, though sometimes with political functionaries at their elbow. The administration remained largely in the hands of Prussians and conservatives, people who by nature were resistant to the ill-assorted aims of the revolution. With idiosyncratic dependability, the civil service somehow held together—even though at one time or another the country which it served was without a constitution, was hit by revolutionary disorder at every turn and, if not leaderless, certainly rudderless and with no clear sense of forward movement. Even the fact that the SPD coalition, which came into being after the national election of January 1919, fell apart irretrievably with further elections eighteen months later, did little to alter the bureaucrats' disciplined posture. Noske's *Freikorps*, broadly sympathetic in political outlook to this establishment, also continued to grow. It had reached an estimated 400,000 by mid-1919.

At city level, elections in February 1919 brought victory for the SPD. They took almost two-thirds of the 144 seats, divided equally between the Independents and the SPD 'majority' group. Women—twenty-five of them—were elected to the council for the first time. Unemployment in the city at this time was then a quarter of a million (about one in ten of the entire population) and increasing. In addition, there was the ever-present painful reminder in the streets and elsewhere of the large numbers who were incapacitated through the war—limbless, perhaps, or maimed. They were to be depicted in the works of George Grosz. There was to be no shortage of sympathisers when it came to the bloody demonstrations of March 1919, nor for the displays of anger and resentment which filled the streets after the terms of the Treaty of Versailles became known.

The food shortage remained serious, with only the rich, paying exorbitant prices, able to eat well. The big hotels continued to do good business too. But three things were necessary for the suppression of Bolshevism in Germany, said a British observer of this period: food, food, and more food.

Karl Radek, representing Soviet interests in Berlin, was arrested and imprisoned at Moabit for his part in the events of March. But even from his cell, he urged that German nationalists and Soviet Bolsheviks should join forces against Western capitalism. However, violent revolution, the head of the British Military Mission, General Neill Malcolm, wrote from Berlin, was no longer to be feared in the city as much as 'a general dissolution of the central authority'. The general also warned that there would be a slide into what he tellingly called 'passive anarchy'. The prevalent feeling was that things had to get worse before they could get better.

Even before war had broken out, the city—looking as usual half-enviously over its shoulder at what Paris was up to—had developed a range of entertainments. A taste for cabaret and revue was well-rooted, with the kaleidoscopic political situation presenting an inexhaustible supply of material; there had been avant-garde theatre, offering early productions of Ibsen and Strindberg, and circuses; there were vast beer halls and wine 'palaces'; tango competitions and cycle races. War and attempts at revolution had of course convulsed all these things, and further disoriented an already perplexed population. Kurt Weill, later to collaborate with Bertolt Brecht, was studying music in Berlin, and men like George Grosz, Max Beckmann, Otto Dix and the theatre director, Erwin Piscator, who had all—with varying degrees of bitterness—served in the Imperial army, were frenetically seeking ways of expressing their anger.

One result was the birth in the capital of the Dada movement. Dada anti-art 'evenings' were held at a city gallery owned by one I. B. Neumann from February 1918. In November, a week into the confusion which followed the abdication, a Dada 'happening' had even been staged in the Cathedral. Johannes Baader, an extravagant exhibitionist who believed, according to some followers, that he was Jesus Christ 'returned from heaven', shouted interruptions to a sermon to such effect that he had to be hustled out of the building.

Swirling uncertainties in so many areas of thought and activity had created a vortex in the city which had no outer limits and which sucked in anyone, of whatever taste or proclivity, who wanted to participate. The city happily fostered the bizarre and all-embracing reputation which remains a source of pride to many of its citizens to this day. Grosz shouted for all who cared to hear that this was (already) 'crazy, degenerate, fantastic' Berlin. Staid officers sitting in the Hotel Belle Vue on the Potsdamer Platz, fulfilling their role as the Inter-Allied Military Control Commission appointed by those nations which had defeated Germany in the war, were as perplexed as everyone else.

Ebert was to die six years and three weeks after assuming the presidency. Throughout those years, something happened almost every day in Berlin to justify the epithets that Grosz and others threw at him. Nine chancellors served under him, one ominous putsch took place in the city, as well as literally hundreds of political murders, almost all committed by known right-wing groups. Apart from Scheidemann, who resigned rather than accept the terms of the Versailles Treaty, and Gustav Stresemann, a monarchist who was to become one of the republic's most respected statesmen, the chancellors were not memorable. Men of extraordinary quality who did emerge as likely leaders (such as Walther Rathenau or Matthias Erzberger) were assassinated. These two were said to have connections with 'Bolshevist' plotters. But many others who did not were elbowed to one side in a game which, it was already clear, had no rules.

The putsch was not unexpected, and was attempted in almost Ruritanian style. It started in the small hours of 13 March 1920. Wolfgang Kapp, a provincial civil servant and, as a supporter of the Pan-German League, a fervent nationalist, had the backing of General von Ludendorff. The general had returned, incognito, to live out a low-profile retirement in Viktoriastrasse, just south of the Tiergarten. He was joined this time by General von Lüttwitz, an autocratic disciplinarian who had assisted Noske the previous year in putting down the Spartacists. Their combined threats of non-cooperation, and even of putting members of the government under arrest, were enough to force Ebert and his closest advisers to flee the city during the night and, after a negative reception in Dresden, to establish themselves for the time being in Stuttgart.

A brigade of the *Freikorps* under a ruthlessly anti-communist naval captain called Hermann Ehrhardt, which had disobeyed orders to disband, took the swastika as its emblem and marched at Ehrhardt's instigation into the city from the west. They were met at breakfast-time in the Tiergarten by Ludendorff and Kapp. The former was a willing collaborator and had at one stage talked of hanging Ebert and Scheidemann. There were other collaborators, of very high rank, in the Army. Kapp, unaware surely of the magnitude of what he was taking on, was quick to assume the title of Chancellor. He attempted a few unrealistic decrees—such as banning examinations for Berlin University students, confiscating matzo flour from Jewish shopkeepers—but in the end he was to be defeated almost as quickly by paperwork he could not cope with and by an extraordinarily effective political strike. This had been called by Ebert himself and it paralysed factories, shops, offices, transport and public utilities everywhere. There were no newspapers to be had in the city streets, therefore no 'news' of what Kapp was up to. Only Kapp's machine-gunners, and his nagging wife, appear to have kept him in Wilhelmstrasse for all of five days, before he threw in the towel, took a taxi to the Tempelhof field, still to be developed as a rudimentary civil airfield, and climbed into a plane which whisked him away to Sweden.

One fellow nationalist who had flown into Berlin to monitor Kapp's progress was Adolf Hitler. It was one of his first visits to the capital. But he only had time to shake hands with Ludendorff before the latter was obliged to flee to Munich. Lüttwitz escaped to Hungary, while Kapp, an oddity to the end, eventually gave himself up, only to die in prison while awaiting trial.

Some flavours of this brief period—more theatre than putsch—are fascinating. Ex-officers were suddenly found to be dusting down their *kaiserlich* uniforms and 'swaggered about the streets', according to a British diplomat, 'apparently imbued with the idea that the good old times had returned'. There was talk, ill-founded, of the Kaiser's imminent return. But the strikers, led by Independents and Communists, jeered and taunted and finally humiliated the troops.

When the five days of the Kapp putsch were over, the sullen and angry troops were obliged to set off back whence they had come. As they passed through the Brandenburg Gate, some of them fired into the crowd of onlookers, killing and wounding several in the panic. Ebert responded by appointing General Hans von Seeckt, a seasoned soldier and thoroughbred old-school

Prussian, to take charge of the country's Army. For six years, until his resignation in 1926, this man was to play a key role in building up the Reichswehr.

Few in the military were to be punished as a result of the Kapp venture: another small pointer to the shape of things to come. While chancellors, ministers and officials played musical chairs, it was the city's poor who continued to suffer.

Inflation was beginning to bite, and bite hard. 'The depression and low vitality of the common folk,' wrote the British Ambassador's wife benignly, 'would be evident to the least observant spectator. Morally, mentally and physically they all look "down and out". At dusk and as early as 4 a.m. one sees—going to and from their work—the drawn faces and bent shoulders, the thin clothes and ill-shod feet of underfed men and women. A skeleton of a boy has just passed the window, slowly dragging a cart full of some miserable merchandise. . . .'

Political murders were common enough, but the city was shaken by two assassinations taking place within twelve months of each other. Both were to have an irremediable, if unquantifiable, impact on political life. In August 1921, Ebert's Finance Minister, Matthias Erzberger, who had earlier been a signatory both to the armistice which ended the finally unwanted war and to the Peace Treaty which consolidated its humiliation, was murdered as he walked in the Black Forest. He had been publicly vilified during the preceding year for fraudulent business deals and his capability of leading Germany towards what one of the old Kaiser's former aides, Dr Karl Helfferich, declared would be 'total destruction'. A libel suit brought by Erzberger only served to highlight his own lack of judgment in commerce—for all his acumen in matters diplomatic—and he resigned.

Then, in June 1922, Berlin and much of Germany was stunned by the news that one of the country's best brains, Walther Rathenau, who as Foreign Minister had negotiated and signed the Rapallo Treaty with the Russians only a few weeks before, had been gunned down just a few hundred yards from his home at 65 Königsallee, by members of the same group which killed Erzberger. Rathenau, a deep and original thinker, had done much for the Kaiser's war effort before throwing his weight behind the Republic. He belonged to one of Berlin's most accomplished families, and his father had founded AEG, one of the city's biggest and most prestigious businesses. Between hours devoted to the business of government, he had written widely-read works on social theory and also distinguished himself as an aesthete, linguist and bon-viveur. His last night out ended at the Espanade Hotel, now a cracked and broken-down shell of its former self not far from the Potsdamer Platz.

After his death, Rathenau's body lay in state in the Reichstag for two days. Ebert, in his funeral oration, said the assassins had this time struck at 'the whole German nation' (which proved to be true enough). Despite steadily falling rain, a million people paraded through the city streets in his honour. Students at Berlin University refused to pay their respects, but the city's trade unions, in rare homage to a born capitalist, announced a day of mourning. This assassination did much to polarise political activity into an unequivocal Left versus Right pattern, and Germany's history would surely have been different had Rathenau lived. He was buried at what is today a little known cemetery in East Berlin, but a granite monument stands at the bend in the Königsallee where he died. His assassins, meanwhile, were in due course to be honoured by a procession through the city in 1933, organised by the Nazis and led by Heinrich Himmler.

At the end of April 1920, by a narrow SPD-dominated majority, the Prussian State authorities gave reality to the inescapable de facto situation which confronted them on the ground. Out of the conurbation which now sprawled so unevenly about the banks of the Havel and Spree rivers, as well as the several busy canals in between, they created the new municipality of Gross-Berlin, or Greater Berlin. This brought under one administration a total of nearly 3.9 million variegated souls, who had hitherto been living in seven separate towns (Charlottenburg, Köpenick, Lichtenberg, Neukölln, Schöneberg, Spandau and Wilmersdorf) or in any one of nearly sixty identifiable village communities. Some had worked on the estates which were now embraced by the 'new' area—there were nearly thirty of them—or on one of the several farms, which were likewise consumed. Parish churches, small 'high streets' with a very green and distinctly rural air, as well as locally-oriented bureaucracies, and determinedly proud local populations, are testimony that those smaller towns and communities linger today, in East as well as West. There are still working farms within the city boundary.

Transition was not easy and the vote in favour, after months of intense debate, was close. Demonstrations in the streets against amalgamation had led to fights the preceding January in which forty-two people died and more than a hundred were wounded. Social divisions in the city became even clearer. The 'haves' became vociferous about whether they wanted to live cheek by jowl with so many 'have-nots', but in the end gave up the unequal struggle. Today, there are some separately identifiable 'well-to-do' areas in both Berlins, notably in the outer suburbs, characterised by large villas built in another era, but the conurbation has evolved for the most part into a city that is unquestionably—and now without much choice—one of the most socially mixed in Europe.

If there are cells of local pride within the city context, they are formed by the people of one *Bezirk* (borough) trying to prevail over another. Twenty of them were created by the 1920 ordinance, each with its own mayor, council and accompanying bureaucracy. These twenty still exist. Their irregular boundaries are still in force and account for the wiggly nature of the lines which divide East and West Berlin as well as the boundaries of the four different sectors.

Elections to the new municipality were held two months after its formation, but bitter arguments persisted. Finally, State officers declared that invalid voting papers had been used, and ordered another poll to be held in October 1921. This resulted in a left-wing victory, with forty-six seats (out of the 225 total) going to the SPD, forty-four to the Independents (half as many as before) and twenty to the Communists, who were participating for the first time. The right-wing parties mustered 115 seats altogether, and formed the majority.

In late 1920, the city's Lord Mayor, Adolf Wermuth, resigned only a few days after being confirmed in office. The reason was violent disagreement over his handling of a strike by electricity workers, who for five days in November kept the city in darkness and without trams or electric power. In January 1921, Gustav Böss became Lord Mayor. He was a member of the Liberal-inclined German Democratic Party (DDP), which had been formed at the end of the war, and he was to hold the post down until forced out in 1930 for alleged involvement in one of the city's several financial scandals of the 1920s.

In two of these scandals, one centring on the Barmat brothers and the other on the Sklarek brothers, prominent politicians and business people were inveigled to participate in a whole range of 'protected' enterprises, which ranged from racehorse breeding to banking, from metalworks to textile manufacture. The brothers made their respective fortunes by lending in the days of hyper-inflation to smaller companies which could not repay, and which they then took over; and by importing cheap food for hungry Berliners willing to pay comparatively high prices. Often, it was the SPD, including at least one former Chancellor, and a son of President Ebert, who were involved and therefore besmirched by the various brothers' shady efforts to appear respectable. It is this sort of 'business', on a smaller scale, which was so vividly portrayed in Döblin's panoramic novel, published in 1929, *Berlin Alexanderplatz*. This tells of the poignant attempts of Franz Biberkopf, a reformed murderer, to retain his integrity in the seamy environment of the then Berlin underworld.

An immediate preoccupation for Böss, who came to the mayoral seat with the reputation of an able administrator, was the feeding of the city. Suddenly, there were rumours that murderers and butchers were in league to furnish fresh meat supplies. Children in Berlin in 1922 were coming to school not having eaten and often in clothing inadequate to cope with the city's bracing air. Some were staying at home because they had no underclothes. 'The only thing that matters to these people,' said Böss's report for that year, 'is the fight against cold and hunger.'

'In the small back room of a basement,' wrote Viscountess D'Abernon, the British Ambassador's wife, in her well-meaning diary,

'we found, totally idle and drearily seated on a deal box, a young woman and child, without furniture or fire. The husband had been a shoemaker and, during his absence with the army, she grew poorer and poorer. Prices rose continually and order to get food for herself and the child, she had gradually sold everything she possessed. We found her living in this bare, tiny little room, the six-year-old boy clinging to her torn dress, which she said she had no longer the spirit nor even the needle and thread to mend. The bed was a paliasse, thrown down in a corner, and had no covering but an old shawl...'

How much, one wonders, had changed since Rosa Luxemburg was writing in much the same vein a whole generation before? The same observer, whose views have some validity if only because she is so detached from what she describes, depicts other scenes that could have been lifted wholesale from a pre-revolutionary diary. The first 'big' official party by the British since before the war, for instance, was held on 30 October 1920 at the British Embassy: 'About three hundred people ... the white and yellow ballroom was open ... the servants were arranged in gorgeous buff and scarlet liveries ... at the entrance, two old German retainers, Fritz and Elf, enjoying the recovery of their cocked hats and egregiously long, gold-laced coats ...'. On 1 November 1920, Princess Radziwill, back in Berlin to regain possession of 'some wonderful jewels' held in a government safe, threw a dinner party in private rooms at the Hotel Adlon next door. On 13 December 1920: 'it is a pretty sight to watch old-fashioned sleighs gliding smoothly and silently across the ice-blue Tiergarten ... the occupants, often smothered in furs'. And so on, to 8 December 1923, when a crowded Benevolence Ball was held in the Adlon, with some 1500 people assembled, clearing well over £1500 for the various 'Hungerhilfe' soup kitchens, etc' in various parts of the city, set up to feed the hungry.

A few weeks before this ball, the same lady was riding in the Tiergarten with an American friend, while members of the Reichswehr, 'only a few streets away', were firing on crowds who were reportedly looting local shops and beating up local Jews. But apparently the misery and deprivation around her did not do too much to hinder the organisation of an inter-Embassy tennis tournament on five reserved courts in Wexstrasse, Schöneberg.

The 'pretty country club' at Grunewald was unavailable to British subjects—even diplomats, since they were representatives of the enemy, and even the Grunewald golf club (still in use today, mainly by the 'occupying powers') was temporarily out of bounds. The city's poor, who went to the woods for firewood, could turn 'nasty'. In the evenings, the glittering dinners and balls carried on at the embassies and the palatial hotels, though sometimes with the shutters closed in case restive crowds of the less privileged outside became angry enough to throw stones. The ritual of riding, however, had to be restricted for fear of 'something unpleasant' happening in the Tiergarten.

As inflation took off in early 1921, hunger and destitution in the city increased with dismal speed. Prices rose daily, soon hourly, and within months even essentials were beyond the means of large sectors of the population. Milk and sugar were still virtually unobtainable, bread and potatoes were rationed, and though meat could be had, it was at extortionate prices. Long queues formed at the ubiquitous soup kitchens—one of them inside the Reichstag itself—while shops selling food had empty shelves or were forced to close down.

The appointment, by Ebert of all people, of a 'businessman's Chancellor', in the shape of Wilhelm Cuno, a company director and one of the new breed of German leaders, was found to be controversial. It underlined the fact that there was no SPD participation in the Government.

Increased poverty among the already poor became more visible with inflation. Emaciation, threadbare clothes, joblessness and begging were its most potent symbols. Among the middle classes, it took a different, less visible form: servants were laid off, furniture, jewellery and clothing were sold, and a previously varied diet became one of bread and weak tea. Streets were not swept, and the fabric and services of buildings on all sides deteriorated. Smaller businesses went to the wall or were swallowed up by bigger ones which had the resources to play the international currency markets. Inflation, said a British observer in 1923, destroyed the balance of society, and 'ruined' the middle class.

The banks of Berlin responded by printing more and more marks, billions of them. By the end of 1923, a worker who ten years before was surviving on a 25 marks a week wage was measurably worse off on a wage of well over 500,000,000 marks. A stage was reached where bank notes that had been made by the Ullstein Press in Kochstrasse were bought and sold—by the boxful—as waste paper just a few hundred yards away, for a price which was less than half that paid for old rags. It was a time, not surprisingly, when the city's suicide rate climbed sharply.

Nevertheless, there were Berliners who salvaged what they could in the way of pride, however misplaced. They laid much of the blame for their current distress on iniquitous demands from the Allies for war reparations. Despite Germany's public unwillingness to acknowledge 'war guilt', the Allies had demanded that all the country's military hardware be handed over, three quarters of its merchant fleet, a quarter of its fishing fleet, several thousand locomotives and lorries, all in addition to a finally agreed total of

132,000 million gold marks. This was a sum which more perspicacious economists (such as Keynes) said was at least three times greater than the Germans could hope to pay over the allotted time-scale. This time-scale, even with later revisions, would have had the Germans still paying instalments until the year 1988.

It was a situation only retrieved over a period of years, after French occupation of the Ruhr (which further damaged German pride) and after painstaking negotiations to rephase repayments according to a plan devised by a New York banker called Dawes. This plan led through a complicated juggling of earnings, repayments and further borrowings to a net gain for the country, and after 1929, as a result of the debate surrounding a successor plan, the Young Plan, repayments were shelved altogether.

Inflation of the absurd and horrendous proportions endured by Germany in the early 1920s was not only an economic disaster. It was also a further psychological and social blow to mores and standards which had already been so severely dislocated by war and attempts at revolution. Berlin was the old empire's, now the republic's, financial and commercial centre, and Berliners, for all their capacity to improvise, set great store by money. As the mark lost its meaning, so too did social criteria lose theirs. The process of governing was seen to be pointless; there was no clear objective, no leadership, and total disorientation.

Deaths in the city as a result of deprivation and hunger became as grotesquely unexceptional as death at the hands of political hit-squads. It is understandable that against such a hopeless backcloth, the shadowy figures of lurking extremists, whether communist revolutionaries or still disgruntled old members of the Kaiser's officer corps, should become more and more substantial.

Intriguingly, Franz Kafka lived the last winter his life in the city at this time. He was attracted, he told friends, to 'the dirty Jewish streets' of Berlin, but once there, with his last girl friend Dora Diamant, was made miserable by the city itself and chose rooms successively in Steglitz, Grunewald and Zehlendorf. Years before, he had become unofficially engaged to Felice Bauer, acting out that relationship in tormented walks in the Grunewald and the Tiergarten. Now with Dora, his health failing disastrously, poverty and inflation were such that they couldn't afford to go to the theatre or to pay the rent, and were at one point reduced to cooking with candles.

One of the city's most trenchant commentators to write about this ferment was Kurt Tucholsky. He remains widely read in both parts of the city today, an acerbic yet romantic writer who could distil what reflective Berliners see as the essence of Berlin when it was most chaotically vibrant. Looking at the social and ideological disarray around him, Tucholsky suggested the place resembled 'a fourth-class waiting room full of misfortune'. Later, he was to ask whatever happened to 'the spirit of November', and later still, to emigrate for good. His columns encapsulated the human misery which prevailed in many parts—though in comparison with the expressionist and, increasingly, post-expressionist explosions from the arts generally at this time, they often read like modest understatements.

From a vantage point late in the same century, it now seems that a process had been started of self-laceration, a sort of political exorcism. Creative people in the city who had ideas, in an environment which only a few decades earlier had consciously distanced itself from mainstream Europe, were engaged in a struggle to break through, to tear apart, at all costs to start again. Many, inevitably, were politically inspired but not politically motivated. If they were communist, it was in many cases because this was the most sympathetic camp in which to pitch a tent. Grosz, who at one stage had been to Moscow and talked with Lenin, and Brecht, to name but two, were to have their differences with the ideologists, despite their unambiguous commitment at this time.

For years, the favourite meeting place of the city's artists was the Romanisches Café at the corner of Tauentzien- and Budapester-Strasse. Kitsch art shops, part of the massive Europa shopping and entertainment centre, stand in its place today.

In 1924, a small group of artists was formed, calling itself simply 'The Red Group'. The members sought, according to one of their spokesmen, John Heartfield (born 1891 in Berlin as Helmut Herzfeld) to make people aware of 'the servitude, unworthiness and inhumanity' of their situation, and to shake off the chains of their class. Otto Dix, who moved to live in Berlin a year after the group was set up, signed an early manifesto which said: 'We can't stand silently by and watch human rights being trampled underfoot.' Max Beckmann, who had lived in the city before the war, announced in 1920: 'We must participate in the whole wretchedness that is to come. We must sacrifice our hearts and our nerves to the awful crying pain of poor deluded humanity.'

The Kaiser had gone; the generals remained ... but the city

over which the generals, through the *Freikorps* and the emerging Reichswehr, thought they and their values might yet prevail, was changing tectonically under their feet. For the poor, urged on by the strident Left, nothing had displaced the disenchantment of being exploited in the Kaiser's war, and the city had not reached out to help them. At the other extreme, there was also disenchantment, but there was a certain loose political cohesion and, anyway, the cushion of wealth. Somewhere in between these two extremes, the middle class looked to the city fathers, bureaucrats and politicians-in-office to steer a ship which was apparently fast getting out of control, while they themselves clung as best they could to their fragmented standards of living.

People were drawn to Berlin from other parts of Germany and from outside. The traditional facility for welcoming and absorbing foreigners, always a very tangible asset, was as strong as ever. Incomers joined a mad throng (or, in Grosz's words, a lunatic asylum). 'Within the city,' Klaus Mann recalled in 1952, 'millions of underfed, corrupt, sex-starved and pleasure-hungry men and women writhe and totter in a jazz-induced delirium. Dance had become a mania, an obsession, a cult. The Stock Exchange hops like a frog, ministers sway on their feet, the Reichstag does a jig. War cripples and profiteers, film-stars and prostitutes, former monarchs (with princely pensions) and retired schoolmasters (with no pension at all)—all twist and turn in gruesome euphoria.'

A guide to *lasterhaft* (or dissolute) Berlin, published in 1920, noted that transvestites favoured Puttkamerstrasse (just south of today's Checkpoint Charlie), that lesbians met in Kleiststrasse (half a mile from the Kaiser Wilhelm Gedächtnis Church), and that male homosexuals preferred Skalitzerstrasse, close to today's Oberbaum Bridge crossing point. Revue and cabaret, of varying tastes, styles and quality, could now be seen at every turn; a nihilism, which was sometimes diluted into mere cynicism, was the chief commodity. The venues may have changed, but the tastes, overtly advertised in West Berlin, remain—with more than a hint of desperation—the same.

Other arts, too, began to flourish vigorously at this time. The Universum Film Group (UFA), originally formed by the nationalist politician, Alfred Hugenberg, out of ideas floated earlier by General Ludendorff, had set up studios in the south-east of the city at Neubabelsberg. The Berlin Philharmonic Orchestra took on Wilhelm Furtwängler as director and conductor—a position he was to keep even under Hitler because, he claimed later, he misunderstood the true ramifications of Nazi Germany. This was in spite of the fact that his concert hall was regularly used, between musical performances, for political meetings.

In the theatre, one of several names to conjure with was Erwin Piscator, whose first productions in Berlin were in the city's beer houses, in the slums. Then he moved to the Volksbühne, a plain and strangely mute building still standing in what was the Bülowplatz and what is now called Rosa-Luxemburg-Platz. Later he came to the Nollendorfplatz, at the western end of Kleiststrasse. His theatre here—which still bore his slogan, 'Art for the People'—is now appropriately used by the city's ethnic minorities for the showing of their own films.

Another name was that of Max Reinhardt who took over the Deutsches Theater (built 1850, rebuilt 1872 and 1883 and still in use) in Schumann-Strasse, just north of the Spree and west of the Friedrichstrasse, before moving soon after the First War to what he called the Grosses Schauspielhaus (the Big Playhouse). This building, demolished in the mid-1980s because its foundations were deemed unsafe, started life in the 1860s as Berlin's first market hall, before conversion a few years later into premises for one of the city's half-dozen circuses. Three months or so after the second war, bomb damage repaired, it resumed life as a music hall, and then as a variety theatre. A new Friedrichstadtpalast was opened with great fanfare in May 1984 as an entertainments centre by the East German leader, Erich Honecker. It is a simultaneously gaudy but staid affair, describing itself as a successor to the Reinhardt theatre. In the sense that seats are hard to get, it may be a justified description.

Later in the 1920s, Piscator and Reinhardt were joined by the irascible Bertolt Brecht: he took over the nearby New Theatre on the Schiffbauerdamm, built in 1892, converted during a brief period under Reinhardt, and later to be adapted further during rebuilding after 1945. This theatre saw the premiere of *The Threepenny Opera* in the critical year of 1928—*Baal* had opened in 1924 to a rowdy reception elsewhere. The building is now known as the Brecht Theatre, a proud if overworked possession of the East Germans who choose not to highlight differences between Brecht and the Communists of his time.

*   *   *

The year 1923 saw the dramatic attempt by Hitler, in November, to force a putsch in Munich. It was also the year in which the Communists in Berlin most seriously reconsidered the feasibility of revolution. In July, plans were made to hold a massive anti-Fascist rally in the city. All went well until the planners conferred in Moscow with Soviet policy-makers. Then Heinrich Brandler, who had become leader of the German party, agreed the protest should bow to the law and be an indoor affair. Some 200,000 Berliners are believed to have attended these meetings.

Stalin's interest in the German party's progress was careful and studied, but there was unabashed enthusiasm from Grigori Zinoviev for an uprising. Karl Radek, now executive secretary of the Communist International, had been in and out of Berlin, always watching hopefully for real movement, for several years. He now took a large measure of control of the German party, and waxed suitably enthusiastic.

The feelings of the 50,000-strong Russian community in Berlin—with its own newspapers, magazines, theatres, restaurants—at this time can only have been mixed. Many, after all, were fugitives from Moscow rather than avid supporters of the cause of 1917. But Carl Zuckmayer, a wayward playwright in the city at the time, had no hesitation in declaring that the Russian influence was 'much more stimulating and productive' for Berliners than what the West could offer. There were plenty of takers for such an argument. A 'Friends of the new Russia' society was formed in Berlin. But there were also some friendless Russians: a suicides' cemetery, with mainly Russian graves, can be found in the Grunewald.

In the summer of 1923, Trotsky summoned the German Communist Party leaders to Moscow. After several weeks, they were urged to make that October into Germany's '1917'. Brandler was again hesitant, as Rosa Luxemburg had been nearly five years before. In 1918–19, he told a Berlin meeting in September, around 20,000 'troops' had been lost; this time round, confronted by a million or more organised opponents, they could lose many more. So, on 21 October 1923, the uprising was cancelled in Berlin, though there were pitched battles for the cause resulting in scores of deaths in Hamburg and in Lower Saxony. Ernst Thälmann, a former dockworker who is today a revered figure in East Germany, came out of the turmoil of Hamburg as a leader of potential.

At the other end of the spectrum, Hitler was sentenced in April

1924 to five years in prison for his part in the Munich putsch, though he was released the following December. While inside, he embarked on the writing of *Mein Kampf*. The work has little to say about the city. Hitler never particularly liked 'red' Berlin; nor, for that matter, did many of the people of Munich.

The second half of the 1920s is today remembered as the 'golden twenties'. For Berlin as an innovative cultural and entertainment centre, this makes some sense—though there was in fact a marked decline in theatre audiences as well as experimentation among the directors. For Berlin as a still growing social and economic organism, it makes less sense. The acute hardship which followed the war, exacerbated so often by the great inflation, coincided with the entry into the city, and its consciousness, of ulta-conservative forces who thrived on intrigue, conflict and confrontation. These were hardly the ingredients of any golden era.

When the seventy-eight-year-old war hero Paul von Hindenburg became president, brought back to serve the nation as he had been ten years before, there was restored to many Berliners a sense of hierarchy and order, even a feeling that the Kaiser might yet be reinstated. The city and the country were, after all, still being run by men whose careers had started, and often progressed, under the Kaiser. The values and the sense of order of his time were their benchmarks for progress. The communists, readily urged on by their Moscow standard-bearers, saw these benchmarks as anathema, but their own leadership was still unable to coalesce. Incipient splits in the Kremlin did nothing to assist their cause.

The political Right slept relatively easy at nights, reassured that the Reichswehr was once again being reconstructed by the conservative but practical General von Seeckt and that, anyway, some of the city's barracks now housed police units who could be armed and in action at a moment's notice. New scapegoats were targeted. Several leading communists were Jewish, and thus 'Jewish Bolsheviks' or 'Bolshevik Jews' became the subject of violent verbal or physical abuse. 'Anti-Jew feeling', said the Military Control Commission, was endemic in the city in the same way that persisting poverty and distress were endemic. The Berlin which had placed no obstacles in the way of the birth of the Anti-Semitic League half a century before, had not changed.

In August 1923, Gustav Stresemann, the monarchist but Liberal-inclined son of a Berlin brewer, became the Republic's eighth Chancellor since the war. This tenure was brief—about a hundred days—but climacteric throughout. Morale when he took over was at rock-bottom. A US dollar was changing hands for 4,200 million German Marks, and the French had occupied the country's industrial heartland in the Ruhr. Stresemann introduced a new *rentenmark*—each one of which was to displace 1,000 million of the old ones. He also ordered an end to passive resistance to the French occupation. The first measure savagely dislocated cash flows, and bankrupt company directors joined displaced workers on the city streets. Those with money, or something left to barter, formed queues; those without turned to looting. Strikes and demonstrations intensified.

Even so, Stresemann—though soon rejected through an SPD no-confidence vote over his attitudes to regional political developments—made an important impact. Morale began to pick up and the message that such a durable city could not remain downtrodden indefinitely began to get through. The Dawes plan radically revised reparation payments procedures and finally saw the French off German soil. But Mr Parker Gilbert, an American banker, who came to Berlin to monitor the financial implementation of the plan, found a city still without any strong corporate sense of direction. This was in spite of the fact that elements in the Republic were retrieving a sense of unity and self-respect. When Dada activists, proclaiming themselves to be German Bolsheviks, converged, with a symbolic hearse, on government offices in Wilhelmstrasse, they were turned away.

The year 1924 saw the death of Ludwig von Hoffman, Berlin's chief architect since his appointment by Wilhelm II in the early 1890s. His concern with public buildings (especially around the turn of the century) gave way in his successor, a dynamic young architect called Martin Wagner, to a radically different concern, at least, for quality housing. Shortly after the departure of Hoffman, the retirement, long overdue, was announced of Wilhelm von Bode, for many years the arbiter of public taste under the Kaiser. He had built up the Museum Island complex opposite the City Palace and had acquired works of art that are among the most precious possessions of museums in both parts of today's city. Wilhelm Wartzold, an art historian, became the city's museums director in 1927.

In February 1925 Friedrich Ebert died in the West Sanatorium of Charlottenburg Hospital. He was only fifty-four, a man who had risen from an unlikely background to preside over the birth pangs of post-imperial Germany, but who at the end of his life was surrounded by wider political uncertainties and personal doubts about his own achievement. By his own lights, he had sought and often found a middle way. For some, the middle way remained visible after his death, but it was still fundamentally the old order that carried on, in the form of old Marshal Hindenburg, who won the presidential elections the following May. The evening before Ebert died, Adolf Hitler, in a Munich beer cellar, was making his first major political speech.

In the winter sunshine Ebert was given an elaborate funeral. After his body had lain in state at the Potsdamer station, there were solemn processions through the streets crowded with sceptics as well as the genuinely bereaved. There were orations from the politicians who had argued with him, disapproving of his facility to turn vacillation into compromise, and there was silent respect from hundreds of thousands who must, in their heart of hearts, have been disappointed by his achievement. It was not *reason* which brought Field Marshal Paul von Hindenburg back to Berlin, Germans say now, it was *feeling*: he was a father figure who would serve the nation.

The former Kaiser, in exile in Holland, had counselled him to come to the aid of the people. Berlin, with him around, recovered some lost pride. It was once more a capital city to reckon with. As he was driven in state through the Brandenburg Gate and into the Linden this man, whom some British had wanted to put on trial as a war criminal for his alleged share in killing so many British troops in the war, was cheered and fêted all the way.

For the second time, though, it was for the most part a hungry, troubled and leaderless city which had drawn him out of retirement. One of his first acts was to allow the Kaiser's officers back into the Army, and the Kaiser's senior officials back in to key government departments. Nevertheless, he earned himself a reputation in the Wilhelmstrasse as one who would dutifully and rigorously uphold the republic and its constitution. . . .

*   *   *

On a grey November evening in 1926, young Joseph Goebbels arrived as *Gauleiter* (district leader) to set about the nazification of 'red' Berlin. It was just a year after Ernst Thälmann, who had run against Hindenburg for the presidency, had become the communists' leader. Goebbels was still in his twenties, starry-eyed but intelligent, highly articulate and wildly ambitious. He arrived, alone, at the now demolished Potsdam railway station and headed a few hundred yards south to find the city headquarters of his party. He was appalled by what he found. 'The Berlin section,' he later recorded, 'had its "office" in a dirty basement at the back of Potsdamerstrasse. A kind of manager was based there with an exercise book in which he would enter debits and credits as best he knew. Masses of paper cluttered up the place, and in the ante-room several unemployed party members would hang around and kill time. We used to call the place "the opium den".'

Potsdamerstrasse—Goebbels was at No. 109—has not greatly changed over the years. It was, as its name implies, a main tree-lined artery from the city centre to Potsdam. But today Potsdam is in East Germany and the northern end of the street which bears its name is cut off at the incongruously quiet Potsdamer Platz by the wall. The street itself is tired and run down, a favoured haunt for the city's prostitutes and drug peddlers. There are small shops and businesses, trading in cheap or second-hand goods laid out on ill-kept uneven pavements. Whatever post-1945 reconstruction was carried out here already has an almost redundant look, and the crumbling façades of the last century, encasing dirty windows, are somehow surprising but melancholy reminders of more affluent times.

The area is today one of the most ethnically mixed in the whole city, dominated by an upstairs Turkish bazaar which straddles the rusted overhead railway line at Bülowstrasse station. Geopolitical realities mean the railway itself has nowhere to go, but this bazaar is a late-twentieth-century city landmark in its own right, as worthy of attention as the Siegessäule, for instance, or a disused church.

Goebbels, despite his small stature, his clubbed foot and his comparative youth (or perhaps because of all three), was a relentless taskmaster. He immediately sacked his predecessor as *Gauleiter* and threw out nearly half the one thousand membership as useless to the Party cause. Berlin's 600 members, he told his staff, would have to become 600,000 in six years. Within weeks, he had found new 'offices' round the corner at No. 44 Lützowstrasse. They might still seem 'extremely modest and primitive', he wrote, but they did represent a step forward.

He set out to conquer the city by way of 'the street', ordering his activists to stop passers-by and engage—or provoke—them in conversation. This he saw as 'the only road to political power'. Soon, exchanging insults and blows became routine. Usually these were with the newly formed Red Front brigade of the Communist Party, and the exchanges soon escalated into organised street fights and structured demonstrations. In no time at all, the Nazi Party, about to be reformed as the NSDAP (the National-Socialist German Workers' Party), was receiving precisely the kind of attention that Goebbels intended.

On 11 February 1927, he hired the Pharus Hall, in a mean little street called Müllerstrasse, in Wedding. The hall was next to a beer-house and was where the local Communist Party held many of its meetings. The Nazis brought their new banners and the Communists brought invective, calling Goebbels a murderer and a bloodhound. It was not long before fighting broke out: chairs were hurled, knuckle-dusters were used, and water-bottles were thrown from the platform. The Communists departed only after the police intervened, but Goebbels stage-managed the meeting so that it could continue with the injured Nazis dramatically laid out on stretchers on the platform. From this moment, the 'Unknown Stormtrooper' became a favoured Goebbels theme; so did the Jewish origins of Bernhard Weiss, Berlin's deputy head of police.

On 1 May, Hitler made his first big speech in Berlin under Goebbels' aegis. For this occasion, the *Gauleiter* chose the Clou dance hall in another poor part of the inner city. Stormtroopers and police merged again with the crowds, one side fomenting disorder and fights, the other forced into fighting to restore order. This confrontation occurred despite the fact that Goebbels had said it would be a 'private' meeting (since Hitler had been barred from making public speeches). Four days later, the Party itself was banned—an order treated by Goebbels with predictable contempt, and to which he retaliated, in July, with the launch of his own weekly Berlin-based newspaper, *Der Angriff* (*The Attack*).

★   ★   ★

Gustav Stresemann, though his time as Chancellor was brief, remained until his premature death in 1929 a dominant figure in German politics. He was determined, through diplomacy which grew into statesmanship, to capitalise on what he called 'the moral experience of the German people'. How he managed to reconcile this 'experience' with the palpable moral uncertainties of the capital city around him is an intriguing matter for debate. However, as Foreign Minister, he saw Germany into the League of Nations (September, 1926) and witnessed, nearer home, mass protests around the Siegessäule and the Bismarck statue over France's continued occupation of the Ruhr. The Allied Control Commission was at this time beginning to clear its offices in the hotel it had taken over on Potsdamer Platz, prior to final departure in January 1927. But for many participants at this protest there was a gnawing frustration, almost twenty years before it happened, that their city was already a capital without a country.

Between 1924 and 1928, Germany's military budget crept up steadily, and weaponry was accumulated from the least likely sources abroad. But midway through that period von Seeckt was sacked as Defence Minister for over-reaching himself when he invited the Kaiser's 'heir' to watch Army exercises. His successor, Otto Gessler (a former friend of Ebert's), did not stay long: he was soon deemed to be mismanaging Army finances. General von Groener, who had been close to Hindenburg during the war and had played such a key part in ordering the transition from empire to republic, then took charge.

The succession of these three, helped by the occasional collusion of a retired field marshal as head of state, lends credence to the notion that Adolf Hitler achieved power on the back of the Army, appropriating for himself the Kaiser's stamp of (phoney) authority. Certainly he managed, during this same four-year period, without effective hindrance from the Army, to consolidate his control over the new party. And it had been the Army, after all, which had given him his first political job at the end of the First World War.

Cultural life in Berlin in the second half of the 1920s, despite checks and hiccoughs, remained at least as buoyant as any European city in this time. The cinema was coming into its own, and queues formed for a whole year to see Eisenstein's film, *The Battleship Potëmkin*. It had its première in Berlin, at a small variety theatre in Kreuzberg, and was shown despite vehement protests from General von Seeckt who declared the film to be subversive. It needed a police viewing before the public could see it. There were queues, too, to see the works of Charlie Chaplin. At street level, the Tauentzienstrasse and the Kurfürstendamm, said one 1927 observer, had all the characteristics of a Paris boulevard, and at the time of day when Unter den Linden would be respectably subsiding into evening somnolence, it was these two thoroughfares which started to teem with life. Their cafés and restaurants, their multifarious places of entertainment, their shops and stores were, and are, all magnets. The quality may have changed with the years but the variety and the versatility remain.

In the Wilhelmstrasse, meanwhile, there were now only two buildings—a 'palais' and a bank—which were not concerned with German or Prussian government affairs. At the centre, No. 73, the Reichspräsident, Field Marshal Paul von Hindenburg, presided—and quietly declined. For all his efforts, the sun was gradually setting on the Reich which he had known, and which, of course, was no longer a Reich.

In July 1928, a Goebbels newspaper, the *Völkische Beobachter* gave its readers its own view of the 'golden twenties'. The city, it said, was 'a melting pot of everything that is evil – prostitution, drinking houses, cinemas, Marxism, Jews, strippers, negroes dancing, and all the vile offshoots of so-called "modern art"'.

Just a few weeks later, Bertolt Brecht made perhaps his most deeply felt impact on Berlin when *The Threepenny Opera* opened at the Schiffbauerdamm theatre. It was not a work set in the city, but it managed with a certain wistfulness to evoke the underside of city life at the time, dwelling paradoxically on the same elements that had been singled out by the Nazi journalist. The show was to have one of the longest popular runs the city has known, despite the initially hostile reception. The political Right condemned it as 'class-conscious bolshevism' or as 'bolshevism gone mad'. Although this was surely something Brecht and his composer, Kurt Weill, must have anticipated, its effect was to isolate the author, plunging him deeper than ever into political argument with supporters and detractors alike. Ordinary Berliners, meanwhile, whistled the show's best tunes.

For intellectual succour, Brecht turned to the Marxist-oriented Workers' School, where he took formal lessons and book-learned his Marxism. For argument, he laid with great energy into all and sundry, even including the composer, Paul Hindemith (then professor of composition at the Berlin Hochschule für Musik) with whom he was collaborating on a political oratorio. On the streets, he created as many enemies as admirers, haring around at reckless speeds in an open car.

The close of the 'golden era' is readily identifiable. It came with a succession of events in 1929. Within the space of its first few months, Berlin's unemployment nearly doubled to more than 500,000, and by the end of April, the city authorities were forced to deploy armoured vehicles and water cannon to put down regular demonstrations and Left–Right clashes. These occurred mainly in the working-class areas of Neukölln (around Karl-Marx-Strasse), the Scheunenviertel (near Alexanderplatz), and in Wedding (notably in the congested and then barricaded area around Köslinerstrasse and Nettelbeckplatz). On 1 May there were Communist-led attempts to hold a May Day rally. They resulted in the police firing on the gathering crowds, killing thirty, wounding hundreds more, and arresting no fewer than 2000. Wedding, where there had been a pitched battle between police and demonstrators, suffered most of the casualties.

The Young Plan of that year, which under American auspices sought once again to reschedule reparation payments until 1988, stood no chance, meeting only fierce antagonism from the Right. Hitler and some well-placed supporters organised a referendum to have it rejected. Nationally, they drew more than four million opponents to the plan, each one of whom must have contributed to Stresemann's death, from a heart attack, in October. Right up to the night before he died, he was arguing for acceptance of the plan with members of the Reichstag. This did not stop the city from re-enacting a now familiar ritual, and mourning him with a state funeral. It was one of its most ceremonial occasions since the death of Walther Rathenau.

Three weeks after Stresemann died, Wall Street crashed. Whole tranches of life-support capital were withdrawn from the city overnight, assets wasted, prices fell through the floor, trade collapsed, and unemployment climbed at an unprecedented rate. The city administration, tossed about uncontrollably by such economic forces, then heard its Lord Mayor, Gustav Böss, tender his resignation as the Sklarek affair caught up with him.

Even in this twilight time—some might say, especially—the city continued to draw the prurient and the curious. By way of complement to the gains and encroachments of the intolerant political forces within, there was a unique competitive drive to divert and entertain the most wayward of tastes. The drama in the streets was vivid enough; that which went on in licensed, and unlicensed, places of entertainment was, when it came to sexual explicitness, almost too vivid for words. Restraint was cast to one side, and while so many Germans elsewhere (for instance Thomas Mann) agonised over the virtues of respectability, Berlin sought with a prodigious, amoral, yet somehow anxious, burst of energy to cater for anyone who needed to be tantalised and who had the means as well as the stamina to satisfy that need.

W. H. Auden came to Berlin for a year (1928–9) abroad, after graduating from Oxford. The contrast with that city's gleaming spires can only have been traumatic, but he wrote poetry (even in German) as he drank in what he saw before his very impressionable eyes. 'The Berlin climate,' he said with a precise but beguiling ambiguity more than forty years later, 'is the best in the world.' The apathy which he claimed this climate induced, however, was something he deplored.

Some months later his friend Christopher Isherwood, whose father had been killed by a German bullet at Ypres in 1915, came to Berlin. His books have done more than almost anyone else's to depict and convey the almost tangible and rapidly increasing tension in the air at that time. But they also described the fabric of the city. 'The courtyard,' he wrote in *Mr Norris Changes Trains*, 'was narrow and deep, like a coffin standing on end. The head of the coffin rested on the earth, for the house-fronts inclined slightly inwards.... Down here, at the bottom, ... the rays of the sun could never penetrate.'

More dramatically, in the same novel, Isherwood describes a Communist meeting: 'The hall was very full ... what struck me most was the fixed attention of the upturned rows of faces; faces of the Berlin working class, pale and prematurely lined, often haggard and ascetic.... They were attentive, but not passive. They participated, with a curious, restrained passion ... at intervals they applauded, with sudden spontaneous violence....'

He stayed at Nollendorfstrasse, just off the Nollendorfplatz. There was an American church nearby, though this has now gone. Stephen Spender was a frequent caller: 'The bridges, arches, stations and commanding noise of the overhead railway had taken possession of the square and the streets leading ... eastward to the ever more sordid tenements which never quite lost some of their claim to represent the Prussian spirit, by virtue of their display of eagles, helmets, shields and prodigious buttocks of armoured babies. A peculiar and all-pervading smell of hopeless decay (rather like the smell of the inside of an old cardboard box) came out of the interiors of these grandiose houses now converted into pretentious slums.'

Spender seemed to scent very clearly the political shape of things to come. 'There was a sensation of doom to be felt in the Berlin streets,' he said. 'The feeling of unrest went deeper than any crisis. . . . Berlin was the tension, the poverty, the anger, the prostitution, the hope and despair thrown out on to the streets. It was the blatant rich at the smart restaurants, the prostitutes in army top boots at corners, the grim submerged-looking Communists in processions, and the violent youths who suddenly emerged from nowhere into the Wittenbergplatz and shouted: "Deutschland, erwache!" '*

Among those who were watching the progress of the young Goebbels was Alfred Hugenberg. He was more than twice the *Gauleiter*'s age, but he had resources which admirably suited the *Gauleiter*'s intentions. There was a network of several hundred newspapers—including a number in Berlin—a majority stake in the UFA film production and cinema management group, and a great deal of money. He had been executive director of the Krupp engineering group, and as an entrepreneur had profited while others suffered during the great inflation. He also had a hugely domineering personality, an unquestioning devotion to the nationalist cause, and a bigoted intolerance towards anyone, however democratically inclined, who did not share his views. He became leader of the German Nationalist Party in October 1928, in time to provide Goebbels and Hitler with the sort of assistance, in manpower and finance, which they were quite content to exploit.

Those ex-servicemen's organisations and others which were anti-republican gravitated towards Hugenberg and counted on him for leadership and financial backing. He also found other industralists and not a few senior government functionaries to

* '*Germany, awake!*'

join discussions which went on into the small hours in private clubrooms.

One important group which turned to him was the Stahlhelm. This was an unambiguously right-wing paramilitary organisation, which even in 1920 had claimed to have 300,000 armed men at its disposal. When the SA stormtroopers began to operate, it was the marauding, single-minded and invariably well-equipped Stahlhelm which vied with them for members and crowd appeal. Although they were at one point dismissed by Tucholsky as less dangerous than the phalanx of men at the Stock Exchange whose 'uniform' began with a top hat, they became in their way a serious early threat to the unity of the Nazis themselves. This was most evident when their leader, Franz Seldte, entered into acrimonious argument with Hitler, standing against him in one poll as an anti-Nazi candidate.

Finally, after a series of police raids on Stahlhelm premises and arrests, they were incorporated—at the end of 1933—into the stormtroopers, and disbanded altogether in 1935. But this was only after more than a dozen years, during which their military presence on the streets of the city was becoming increasingly recognisable as a portent of a bigger, and more intractable, presence which was to follow.

Under Hugenberg's auspices, the Stahlhelm were frequently joined by such organisations as the intellectual and anti-semitically inclined All-German League and the League of the Fatherland, as well as handfuls of displaced generals (including von Seeckt and Lüttwitz), disoriented industralists and financiers, and Junker landowners still living in, and on, the past. It all amounted to a very substantial foundation for Hitler and Goebbels to build upon. The Young Plan—and the opportunity it gave the nationalists to push through their cunningly orchestrated referendum—marked the earnest beginning of that building process. In April 1933, the Stahlhelm leadership was passed to Hitler.

Ranged against the Stahlhelm and their allies was the Reichsbanner Schwarz-Rot-Gold, which had been started—forced to start, one might say—in early 1924, despite a heartfelt resistance amongst many in the SPD at the time to paramilitarism. Within a year from provincial beginnings (in Magdeburg) the Reichsbanner claimed more than a million members, nationwide, and its banner-carrying processions of loyal, uniformed Republicans were satisfying a need of the Left. Frequently during the 1920s, they would gather at the Halle Gate, and set off in formation to rallying points along the Linden or in the Lustgarten. Frequently too, there would be Communists marching with them on one side, and Stahlhelm/Nazi supporters on the other. It only needed a provocative word to be met with a suitable retort for a fight to develop which often turned into a full-scale street battle.

Reichsbanner support came mostly from youth groups, trade unions, workers' clubs and the ranks of the unemployed. Some elements within the organisation were deployed into officially approved defence units, primed to take emergency action in the case of a coup by the stormtroopers. The organisation's most resolute core was the Iron Front, formed in December 1931 as a 'last-minute' move against National Socialism, but the core was not the whole, and eighteen months later, it was the SPD's non-militaristic solution to abide by the letter of the constitution which ended in their capitulation.

The Reichsbanner in Berlin was a mixed lot. Initially, it consisted of ex-servicemen, but any 'golden' haze that some might detect even in this era of twilight was not reflected by them. 'When one looked closely at them,' wrote Theodor Wolff a few years later, 'one saw that in this vast army the battalions of strong young men, the daring youngsters with muscles of steel and a determined spirit, were only a minority. So many in these crowds bore the marks of the long privation of the economic crisis; hunger and cold, the unending vain search for work, the misery of homelessness, of fusty "lodgings for single men" and crowded refuges, had robbed them of vitality and courage. Alongside the young men stood or marched the old party members, decent and loyal, but apprehensive and without hope, and silent under the crushing burden of their anxieties....'

To their political left, the Rotfrontkämpferbund—the Red Front of the Communists—constituted a presence which was spirited in principle but, in the late 1920s anyway, dispirited in its physical manifestation. A march through Berlin in the spring of 1926 drew around 30,000 supporters. They were addressed by Ernst Thälmann, but there was as much tedium and tiredness in the air as there was excitement. The crowds were reported to be disciplined and well-behaved, but also travel-stained and exhausted. The fire, it seemed, had gone out of the revolutionaries' belly.

*　　*　　*

79

Some who were children during the 1919 upheavals were students by now. In 1927, a poll was organised by the Prussian Students' Association on who could or could not join. Three out of four, it emerged, were against Jews being members; three out of five were Nationalists or pro-Nazi and ready, even then, to fight for their beliefs. By this time, too, the national youth movement had grown quietly, assertively but not aggressively German-oriented, into the Wandervögel. This had started as a totally non-political, fresh air-loving group at the turn of the century. By the late 1920s, it was taken over by the Right, and progressively infiltrated by anti-semitism.

Young people in some parts of the city were attracted to the paramilitary units, or even to the stormtroopers themselves. But the strictly military flavour was sometimes hard to discern. District units were often more akin to street gangs than the constituent parts of a disciplined army. In Wedding and in Neukölln, for instance, there was a distinct element of thuggery and MacHeath low life about their activities. Prussian State orders halting rallies and outdoor meetings, intended to stop street fighting, had little effect.

The student Horst Wessel, son of an Army padré, was a leader of one such SA gang. He lived in poverty with a girlfriend who was a prostitute, spending his spare time writing marching songs for the SA. This brought him to the notice of Goebbels, and when Wessel was shot and fatally injured in a fight with a young rival, Goebbels took to issuing bulletins on the young man's failing health. Since the rival who fired the fatal shots was also a Communist, Goebbels had all he needed to create a political martyr.

When Wessel died, there were suitably ostentatious ceremonials. Streets were cordoned off for the occasion (it was January 1933), around the Bülow (now Rosa Luxemburg) Platz, and armed and mounted police were deployed in strength. Armoured vehicles, with mounted machine guns, were also in evidence, backed by several more lorryloads of police. In the Nikolai cemetery on Prenzlauer Strasse, after a peroration by Goebbels—comparing Wessel to Jesus Christ—a monument was unveiled by Hitler. Wessel was buried six weeks later. The Horst Wessel song had been sung publicly for the first time; and a district of the city was named after him.

Other Berliners showed their patriotism in different ways. December 1930 saw the local première of the American-made anti-war film, *All Quiet on the Western Front*, written by the Berlin-based journalist, Erich Maria Remarque. It was scheduled despite earlier euphemistic warnings from the licensing authority that it was defeatist and could offend German sensibilities. The showing was at the Mozart Hall in the Nollendorfplatz, the audience protected by police from the encroachments of screaming Nazi demonstrators. Some, however, managed to get into the cinema, where they let off stink bombs and released little posses of white mice. 'Hate,' wrote Christopher Isherwood later, 'exploded suddenly.'

Unemployment in the city had been climbing steeply in the months before the Wall Street crash. The first eight weeks of 1929 saw a jump from 300,000 to 450,000, many having been laid off as the final phase of the electrification of the city's extensive railway network came to a close. Then misery in many homes was increased by the decision to shut down local schools for a week on account of the extreme cold. There was no shortage of people willing to join demonstrations, usually focussing on joblessness and ending in violence. At the same time, however, the profit motive remained strong, as the Karstadt department store, at the head of Karl-Marx-Strasse, opened its doors, joining Wertheim, in the Leipzigerstrasse, and KaDeWe, in the Wittenbergplatz, as the city's biggest. Two of these three still stand, enlarged and rebuilt.

It was a piquant moment for some in the city to note the death of Heinrich Zille, the popular artist who had managed to depict, even to caricature, the characteristics of the poverty in the city without causing offence. Though he may never be considered a great artist, his works are regarded still, by many on both sides of the Wall, with great warmth and affection. He has tended to reach a wider audience than the more solidly, ideologically motivated Käthe Kollwitz, but a memorial to her has also been erected in East Berlin. Both artists expressed extraordinary compassion for the predicament of the 'average' Berliner, the 'little man' and his family.

In the municipal elections of November 1929 the Communists and the Nazis were the gainers. The SPD, with sixty-four seats, remained the largest party, with the Communists—up thirteen to fifty-six—second, but the National Party (forty) and the Nazis, in the Council for the first time with thirteen seats, ensured that there would be perpetual confrontation in the debating chamber. Joseph Goebbels became leader of the Nazi group.

While Nazi stormtroopers marched, without much hindrance, up and down the city streets, shouting slogans, singing and picking fights, the Communists held their twelfth Congress at a hall in Wedding. The SPD coalition government was denounced from the platform as 'a form of social fascism', paving the way, according to one speaker, for fascist dictatorship. It was a label which was never, in the pre-Second War years, to come unstuck. It was also a theme which was to persist among Communist-led strikers and agitators for several months and which was enough to cause Communist-led trade unions to break away from the central union organisation. Ironically, at West Berlin's trade union headquarters in Joachimstalerstrasse, off the Kurfürstendamm, the plaque on the wall today is to Friedrich Ebert rather than Ernst Thälmann. In East Berlin, it is Thälmann who has museums and parks named after him.

Political skirmishing in the streets was accompanied by a depression which began to bite ever more savagely. Once again, the suicide rate rose dramatically, crime increased, and after a too-brief lull, deprivation and destitution once again became an unquestioned norm. Men and women roamed the streets, often well enough heeled but with placards round their necks, pleading for work. Sometimes they had chairs and card tables set up for playing cards to pass the time. Others begged in order to keep alive, others joined ad hoc camps set up, as they had been generations before, just outside the city boundary. Farmers were once again obliged to mount round-the-clock pickets to prevent theft from their potato fields. But the camps—'tent towns' as they were known—tended to be very orderly. In the Grunewald, nude sunbathing was the popular pastime—the obverse to the climate of desperation—while at the Sportpalast, just off the Potsdamerstrasse, six-day cycle races became a big draw. In the same hall, a few years later, the oratory of first, the city's leading communists, later Hitler and Goebbels, was to supplant the cyclists. It was pulled down in 1974.

Politically, as in a host of other ways, Berlin was no longer Germany and Germany was not Berlin. In the Reichstag elections of September 1930, the Nazis, against even their own expec-

tations, swept in to a position of stark and unmistakable pro-
minence with 107 seats, making them the second power after the
SPD, with 143, and well ahead of the Communists who had
seventy-six. Massive demonstrations followed outside the Reichstag building. But six months or so later, the Nazis were the ones
who abstained in the City Council chamber as Heinrich Sahm, a
moderate right-winger from Danzig, became Lord Mayor.

One in four of the city's population when he took over was
dependent on some form of public financial support. Much of the
Council's time was spent debating the sale of city assets, properties
as well as utilities, in order to meet growing obligations and debts.
Soon, the banks themselves were in difficulties; some collapsed,
while others had to close down periodically. Anterooms and offices
in the City Hall tended to be busier than the debating chamber,
where what might have been important discussions were often
turned very quickly into useless slanging matches. One of the
first big sales of this time was that of the city's electric power
corporation—which occurred just three months after the opening
of the first German broadcasting station in the Masurenallee in
Charlottenburg.

The late evening of 9 August 1931 saw one of the city's biggest
street flare-ups since 1919. Close to the national headquarters of
the Communist Party, in Bülowplatz (now Rosa-Luxemburg-
Platz) a scuffle, possibly started by the Communists, broke out in
which three policemen were shot. Two of them died instantly,
and feelings immediately ran high. A general mêlée, quickly
spreading to surrounding streets, ensued, and hundreds, if not
thousands, of people were soon engaged in bloody hand-to-hand
fighting. The party's offices were raided and ransacked by the
police, and the scars they inflicted there and in the streets are still
nursed by the older generation of Party followers in East Berlin.

Today, the square is of course quiet. It is used as a starting
point for organised rallies and demonstrations but otherwise little
visited. The old Party building, strangely anonymous and undis-
tinguished, was knocked down after further raids by the Nazis
once they were in power, but it was rebuilt along similar lines
after the Second War. It is now called Karl-Liebknecht-Haus,
and has rooms and a small rather austere exhibition devoted to
Thälmann.

One month later came the first big anti-Jewish riot. On the
evening of the first day of the Jewish New Year, hundreds of

Nazis swarmed into the Kurfürstendamm, apparently looking for, and setting on, anyone who looked Jewish. The Reimann Café, a frequent haunt of film stars and actors, was a prime target. Only after half an hour were the police able to restore some sort of order, arresting about sixty of the instigators. Less than half of these were later given prison sentences by the courts.

When Chancellor Hermann Müller, a tired and sick man, stepped down from public office in March 1930, it was the beginning of the end of parliamentary rule in Greater Germany. He had filled a gap earlier, after the Kapp coup attempt of 1920, but this time round was too weak to cope with daily mounting economic and political pressures. Less than a year later he was dead, and despite the state of emergency throughout the country, which had been declared the preceding Christmas, he was also given a state funeral through the city centre. A year after that and the city was again agog as Hindenburg, now in his eighty-fifth year, was re-elected the country's president.

The heat in the city refused to die down. Two days after this election, the stormtroopers were banned. But six weeks after that, Franz von Papen, seen by many as a well-meaning fool of little real competence but by Hindenburg as 'a friend', became Chancellor. He lifted the ban on the stormtroopers, and played into their hands as he denounced what he called 'culture-bolshevism'. Goebbels was delighted. Brecht at this time was in Moscow; Grosz was in New York. While von Papen was still engaged in pointless discussions about reparations in Lausanne, the city of Berlin, at odds politically with the rest of the country, edged towards collapse.

Clashes in the streets, almost always Nazis versus Communists, continued to spread. In the seven weeks between 1 June and 20 July 1932, there were well over 300 recorded street battles in Prussia (where April elections had given the Nazis a massive overall majority), and most of these were in Berlin. More than seventy people died and 500 were injured in those few weeks, a period in which countless other battles were fought and not officially recorded.

Berliners could only watch as the fabric of their capital disintegrated before their eyes. The university was closed because the students were out of control; the Prussian Parliament was forced to adjourn in uproar; newspapers were ordered to cease publication; the Army was given further exceptional powers;

thousands of new arrests were ordered. The great emigration of Berlin's creative talent, so much of which had taken the world by storm in the years just passed, began.

Reichstag elections were held at the end of July and gave the Nazis nearly 40 per cent of the seats. Paul Löbe, a respected parliamentarian who had been president of the Reichstag throughout its brief heyday since 1920, was displaced by the flamboyant Hermann Göring. The Reichstag met on September 12th. The Nazi deputies—there were 230 of them now—could not wear their uniforms into the Reichstag, so—not for the first time—they took them with them and changed into them once inside.

Klara Zetkin, a senior deputy and veteran Communist, opened the debate, denouncing Hitler and Nazism. It was a courageous act because she was sick at the time (and died soon afterwards). Uproar ensued in the chamber. When Chancellor von Papen requested the floor, Göring chose to ignore him. It was a gesture which changed the course of Europe's history.

THREE

1933-1945

Lieber Gott mach mich stumm
Daß ich nicht nach Dachau kumm

Lieber Gott mach mich taub
Daß ich nicht am Radio schraub

Lieber Gott mach mich blind
Daß ich alles herrlich find

Bin ich taub und stumm und blind
Bin ich Adolfs liebstes Kind[1]

There is a meanness about the east wind that blows round Putlitz-strasse, and apart from local shift workers, not many people seem to use the station there. It is situated between the overcrowded district of Wedding to the north and industrialised parts of Moabit to the south and west, and is dominated by waterways, inland docks, factories and power stations, meat and vegetable markets. Berlin would never have grown if it hadn't been for the trans-actions conducted at such places as these, light-years though they may be from the Kurfürstendamm or Friedrichstrasse. Today, the whole adds up to a bleak and grimly functional city-scape— though not everything is now functioning. Some of the cars at the cobbled roadside are rusty wrecks, long since abandoned by their owners. There seems always to be dirt in the air.

It was from the Putlitzstrasse goods yard, and from Grunewald station to the west, that tens of thousands of Berlin's Jews made their last journeys. Today, the lines which head away in the direction of the then concentration camp at Terezien (Theres-ienstadt) or the extermination camp at Oswiecim (Auschwitz) are overgrown with silent weeds. In the year or two before the Second

[1] Dear Lord, make me dumb, so to Dachau I won't come. Dear Lord make me deaf, so I can't hear the radio. Dear Lord, make me blind, so that everything seems fine. If I'm deaf and dumb, then I'm Hitler's favourite child.

World War, and during the course of that war, they carried trains of cattletrucks, often open to all weathers, bearing 500 to 1000 Jews at a time to either of these, or to some other of the many camps set up to receive them.

When these transportations took place, the stations were cordoned off by armed guards. Those Jews who had been forced out of their homes or hiding places were either marched in ragged groups across the city to 'assembly points', or herded for the purpose into furniture vans with whatever belongings they could safely carry. The most notorious assembly points were at No. 26 Grosse Hamburger-Strasse, Oranienburgerstrasse and No. 2 Rosenstrasse. The first of these, originally an old people's home, has been demolished and the Jewish cemetery behind it was destroyed—by the Nazis. A simple memorial stone stands at the roadside.

The Rosenstrasse centre was the focal point for a protest in 1943 by some 6000 'Aryan' wives whose Jewish husbands had been rounded up with a view to transportation to the camps. For hours on end, the women shouted defiance at the SS guards, some of whom had machine guns at the ready. Eventually their men were freed.

Former French prisoners-of-war, working on the railways, and other eye-witnesses have told since how, on some occasions, there were not many visible stormtroopers or SS men on duty at the stations. Orderlies who appeared to be Jewish themselves were given the tasks of supervision. Those who awaited their final journeys did so in what Walter Laqueur, a survivor, has since called a mood that was 'subdued, a mixture of resignation and faint hope'. People stood around in small groups, he noted, a few sobbing, but being comforted by others. There were children as well as old people, some of these stretcher cases. When a few of the youngsters suggested singing, they were told by the guards that this was 'unseemly' and was anyway inconsiderate towards local residents.

But how is a representative of the post-war generation, however conscientious he or she may be, to convey the full horror and inhumanity of what the Nazis were doing in these now quiet corners of their capital city? Laqueur again:

'The transport which left on 29 May (1943) was different from the preceding ones: for the three hundred who left on that day did not walk but were carried. These were the inmates of the nursing home in the Auguststrasse (off Oranienburgerstrasse), and they were bedridden almost without exception. It was a scene such as I had never witnessed: very old people, incurably ill men and women, some very quiet, others agitated and shouting as if delirious, they were carried in a long and orderly procession from the vans and ambulances to the platform of the railway station. They had to wait several hours for their train, and there was a great deal of moaning and crying; some were asking for water or for their medicines.

'These old people were not intimidated by the shouts of the SS guards. Old people are obstinate, used to getting their own way, and they are no longer particularly afraid of anything. And so the SS guards were quite helpless: they did not know how to silence these incurables, short of strangling or shooting them, which clearly would not have done at all in a Berlin railway station. How relieved they were when at last the train came in. . . .'

A little over ten years before, the persecution had not yet become institutionalised. One in three of the working population of Germany was unemployed, and in Berlin, nine people out of ten lived in five-storey buildings. Wages were kept artificially low and when, in early November 1932, the city transport department announced that it would have to cut the pay of its 20,000 employees by a few pfennigs a week, a strike was called. The call did not come from the local SPD union leaders, who argued for negotiating with the bosses, but from the Communists led by Ernst Thälmann.

Somewhat surprisingly, they were joined in this exercise by the Nazis, but Goebbels, who made no secret of hating 'red' Berlin— 'a monster city of stone and asphalt', he called it—was delighted. Berlin looks dead, he wrote in his diary, and 'our people' had seized the initiative. But he also wrote: 'If we had withdrawn from this strike, our firm standing among the workers would have been shaken.' The Nazis had gained an important foothold. The strike lasted four days, and when the elections took place on 6 November, voters had to get to the polls under their own steam.

These elections showed the Communists were still the strongest party in the city, taking more than 869,000 of the votes. The Nazi vote fell from 757,000 in the previous July to just over 720,000, and Goebbels wrote that the Nazis had suffered 'a setback'. But there were posters in many of the city streets with the legend, 'A new Germany must be forged', and these were of his devising. By now he was operating out of a newly built headquarters office, in a building known as the Adolf-Hitler-Haus, situated in Voss-Strasse, just round the corner from Wilhelmstrasse.

Nationally, the Nazi Party had lost two million votes. Financially, it had to be rescued by big business once again, with groups like Krupp and Thyssen to the fore. The 'rescue' was in part an insurance policy to halt the advance of the Communists, and was a gesture which could only serve Hitler's interests. He therefore demanded full power from President Hindenburg. The latter, in tears it is said, may have relieved von Papen of the Chancellorship, but he still despised Hitler. On 2 December General Kurt von Schleicher became the Weimar Republic's fifteenth and last Chancellor.

Von Schleicher's time as Chancellor was to last only eight weeks, but it was long enough to drive Hitler into impotent rage at some of his appointments. It was also long enough to earn von Schleicher the gratitude of the ancient president and, apparently, to give the city an incident-free Christmas. But it was, of course, the lull before the ultimate storm. Within eighteen months of stepping down, unsuccessful in his endeavours to divide the Nazis and rule the Reichstag, von Schleicher and his wife were murdered on Hitler's orders by plainclothes SS men who raided their house by the Wannsee.

Hitler's headquarters during the fretful weeks before he achieved full power was the Kaiserhof Hotel. This establishment, completed in the early 1880s, was one of the first and the grandest of all Berlin's luxury hotels. It stood immediately to the south of the present Thälmannplatz underground station, overlooking what was then the Wilhelmplatz. The American Embassy at that time was on one side, and both were very close to what later became Goebbels' Ministry for Enlightenment and Propaganda. This was erected just to the north of the Wilhelmplatz. On the opposite side of the Wilhelmstrasse the Reichschancellery was to be built.

The departed Kaiser had said the Kaiserhof Hotel was better appointed than his own palace. Its pedigree was such that officers from the Imperial Army would regularly hire its ballroom for big events, while Berliners and others who could afford it went there for some of the best food (prepared by Parisian chefs) to be had in the city. Hitler is said to have liked the Kaiserhof because it employed his favourite dance band.

Today, all this is gone. It is another of those spots in the city where there are few people about and not much traffic. Here, the only sounds are probably coming from the music school further up the street. This school occupies premises which previously housed the Nazi Party's central administrative offices.

The most graphic account of the night of 29 January 1933—the eve of taking power—is in the highly subjective pages of Goebbels' diary. 'We sit up until five o'clock in the morning,' he wrote. 'We are ready for everything, and have considered the thing from all angles. The Führer paces up and down the room. A few hours sleep and the decisive hour will strike. . . .' In fact, not long before, Göring had been seeking to strike some sort of deal with von Papen, while General von Schleicher, in Hitler's view, was preparing to seize total power and proclaim martial law. When Goebbels spoke of being 'ready for everything' he meant that six battalions of stormtroopers had been placed on the alert, if the need arose, to take over the whole of the Wilhelmstrasse.

On Monday morning, 30 January, the summons from a reluctant Hindenburg reached Hitler at the Kaiserhof just before noon. The president had been convinced that, as head of a coalition administration, Hitler would be controllable.

The summons was the end of a road that Hitler had elected to take many years before. In the words of Alan Bullock, he had been 'jobbed into office by a backstairs intrigue'—through cajoling and pressure exercised in drawing rooms in Charlottenburg and Dahlem. Peripherally, rather than centrally, Hindenburg and his son, Oskar, had been involved; so had the exiled Kaiser, whose second wife Hermine made frequent trips to Berlin. And on to these manoeuverings, the old Right—including the aristocrats who had been elbowed to one side by the events of 1918 and 1919—grafted the best construction they could. Many did not like 'Corporal' Hitler as a person; others could not stomach what they knew of his policies. But they could all clearly see that he had taken the initiative and was offering leadership out of present political and economic uncertainties. Others, though they had not yet moved into positions of outright opposition, were simply uneasy about what was unfolding in front of them.

Any chance the stormtroopers might have had of taking over

Wilhelmstrasse, had the order been given, would have been seriously impeded that Monday morning by the great crowds which filled the Wilhelmplatz. Many had been drafted in by the Nazi machine and their silence gave way soon after noon to what the *Gauleiter* described as 'wild uproar'. It was not until ten years later—to the very day—that such uproars could be stopped. That was the day on which the Nazi army was destroyed by the Russians a few miles south-west of Stalingrad.

Hitler's rule, like that of Wilhelm II, began with, and was regularly sustained by, acts of theatre. By the early evening of his first day in office, having formed his Cabinet and presided over its first meeting, he was fêted with one of the most dramatic processions the city had yet seen. Column after column of troops emerged out of the darkness of the Tiergarten, marching in time to synchronised drumbeats and martial music, through the Brandenburg Gate and down Wilhelmstrasse, past the presidential palace (where Hindenburg, leaning on his stick, and apparently much moved, looked on) and past the Chancellery into the darkness beyond. Each man carried a flaming torch.

'These torches,' wrote the French Ambassador, M. André François-Poncet, some years later, 'form a single river of fire, and the waves of this swelling river build up to advance with great power into the heart of the capital. And from these men in brown shirts and high boots, marching in disciplined ranks and singing warlike songs as loudly as they can and as if with one voice, there comes a new enthusiasm, a dynamic force. The spectators are seized by this enthusiasm, and they break into long and continuous shouts which coincide with the pace of the march and the rhythm of the men singing. . . .' The parade went on until well after midnight. It was, the Ambassador added, an occasion which filled him with a certain dark foreboding.

In all this, where stood 'the little man' who had unsuccessfully attempted a revolution a dozen or so years before? As recently as late 1932, the Communist Party had maintained the time was—once again—ripe for revolution and, a few months before that, it was one Walter Ulbricht who, in the name of the Berlin area of the same party, was calling for a massive anti-Fascist demonstration. But in 1932, party numbers were increasingly being made up from the ranks of the unemployed. In most parts of the country, it was to lose a disconcertingly large proportion of its members to the National Socialists. Ulbricht himself, who had been running the Communists' Berlin operation since 1929, was to leave soon for exile in France. After the war, he was to take over the political leadership of Germany's 'first socialist state'.

Unemployment, in Berlin as elsewhere, had brought back the spectre of hunger for many people. One workless man's wife of this time reported that the family diet consisted of 'bread and potatoes, but mostly bread'. When the dole money came, it meant giving in, once a week, to the 'temptation' to have a little meat, probably sausage. 'But,' the same woman reported, 'the last two days of the week, we go hungry.' If there was meat in the city's less salubrious restaurants, it was often horsemeat. The restaurants were rarely more than half-full.

The city's population was four and a quarter million by now. More than half of them lived four to a room. Government estimates spoke of a shortage of nearly half a million dwellings and said that 300,000 of those which were standing should be pulled down. Eight people out of every ten in the city were stated to be living in 'negative' environments which dulled their senses, while hundreds of thousands of children had nowhere to play except the streets. The city, according to Werner Hegemann, a town planner, was 'a stone coffin'. There were proportionately more suicides in Berlin than anywhere else in Europe.

In voting habits over the years, Berliners had often fallen just short of producing a natural advance guard for the country's Left. And when Hitler took power, the guard was politically once again in disarray. As at previous critical moments in their history in the not too distant past, its hyperactive members had shown they were capable of decisive voting, of organising industrial action, of demonstrating in the streets—but apparently incapable of throwing up a leadership which was not in the end divided, incoherent and painfully indecisive. January and February 1933 in Berlin were critical months for Germany and for Europe and would have presented such an advance guard with amazing opportunities. Because of the cunning of a small handful of keenly motivated men—and because these men acted together—the guard failed to materialise and the opportunities were lost.

A week before Hitler took power, the Communists suffered an irreversible blow. Ten thousand Nazis were ordered to demonstrate in Bülowplatz, outside Karl Liebknecht House, the Communists' headquarters. It was a further planned move, in Goebbel's words, 'to win back the streets of Berlin for the German nation'. A counter-demonstration, called by the Communists, was restricted to the surrounding side streets. As the police looked on, some of them from surrounding rooftops, the stormtroopers took over the square *en masse* and posted themselves as 'guards' outside the House. Their blockade was strengthened with the presence of armoured vehicles and carefully deployed machine gunners. 'The Bülowplatz,' said a jubilant Goebbels, 'is ours.'

A month later, the truth of these words was irrefutable. A posse of police was sent in to ransack the now deserted offices. The Party's leadership had either gone undergound or had left the country, in some instances seeking sanctuary in Moscow. Papers were produced after this ransacking and advanced as proof that the Communists were on the point of launching a revolution. Three days later, the Reichstag was on fire and the Communists were inevitably blamed.

Before Hitler, the city's Communists, on advice from Stalin, had been more interested in breaking the SPD and taking over the unions than in halting the Nazi advance. The Communists were single-minded, where the SPD argued for compromise. But the Communists had mounted pickets, after all, alongside the Nazis in the recent transport strike. The SPD, in the same period, had taken to invoking some of the hopelessly outdated slogans they had used against Bismarck. One of them was to the effect that 'our enemies will perish through our legality'. There was to be little chance of that.

The SPD newspaper, *Vorwärts*, had called for a fight against Hitler immediately after he was installed, but then the Nazis retaliated by banning the newspaper and extending the ban to 'all attempts to produce a new paper which might represent the opinions of the old one or replace it. . . .' Within weeks, most of the SPD leadership had also left the city and the country, to set up offices in Prague. Their leader at the time was Otto Wels who, in November 1918, had swung Berlin's wavering soldiers over to revolution. The few SPD members who remained actually went along with some Nazi policies; others withdrew from active politics altogether.

George Grosz, once a militant communist, had returned briefly from exile in the US to 'taste' Berlin only a few months before.

For a while, he and his wife Eva lived in their old flat in Trautenau Strasse in Wilmersdorf, round the corner from his studio in Nassauische Strasse. But finally they were obliged to give in, and to leave. His wife wept as they flew out from Tempelhof. The masses, he later reported, had not lifted a finger against Hitler. 'Far from it,' he added, rather exaggeratedly, 'they flocked to him in their thousands.'

Three men among several—Hitler, Goebbels and Göring— were now to play crucial roles in Berlin, seeking whenever they could to control the levers of the city, and to make it work for them as a capital. All three were provincials and relatively young, and all had records of failure behind them. But all cherished notions of their own artistic and architectural capabilities. Tangible traces of their projects for the city are there today, although these traces bear little or no relation to the grandiose pretensions that accompanied the projects' conception.

The places most closely associated with Hitler in office—the Sportpalast, the various chancellery and government buildings, the last bunker—were all to be virtually obliterated, either by the war or by zealous occupying powers afterwards. The refurbished and renamed underground station of Thälmannplatz, a rundown multi-storey block of flats, a car park, and some huge jutting lumps of impenetrable and seemingly indestructible concrete are all that can be seen above ground—who knows what lies beneath— at these places.

A short distance away from this central government area, Goebbels, who was *Gauleiter* of Berlin until the day he died, was to occupy luxurious accommodation in the rebuilt former Leopold Palace. Hitler was a frequent visitor and though he was usually a very frugal eater, he was much taken, it seems, by Magda Goebbels' cooking. Göring, perhaps the most gluttonous of the three in his appetite for opulence, occupied in turn a sumptuously appointed flat on the Kaiserdamm in Charlottenburg, the 'palace' of the President of the Reichstag, and a house he had built next to the new headquarters of the Gestapo. These headquarters were in the former School of Applied Arts, on the corner of Prinz-Albrecht Strasse (now a bleak and overgrown Niederkirchner Strasse) and Saarland-Strasse (now Stresemann-Strasse). For his last city 'palace', Göring took over land belonging to the Berlin Applied Arts Museum, and for a while had Saarland-Strasse renamed Hermann-Göring-Strasse. The open space adjacent to the late nineteenth-century Martin Gropius House is close to the razed site of where Göring, for some of the time lived.

On 10 February 1933, the last 'free' election that Germany was to have until after the Second World War was launched with a mass rally at the Sportpalast. The palace, usually used for boxing or other sporting contests, was packed. One eye-witness later described the event as a 'monster' rally, and said that Goebbels, in his speech introducing Hitler, had been able to whip the crowd into a frenzy. Hitler approached the task now confronting him with a certain feigned humility, invoking the Almighty himself to support his case. In conclusion, he uttered a quiet 'Amen'—and was greeted with deafening acclamation. His audience, furthermore, was countrywide: radio was being used at a political event for the first time. Goebbels had done his homework.

A week later, the more staid SPD sought to organise a cultural evening at the Kroll Opera House—across the Königsplatz from the Reichstag building and soon enough to have an historical role of its own. But once again, Hitler's acolytes and Goebbels' troops were prepared. When one Adolf Grimme took the stage to read out a message in favour of 'German democracy' from the writer Thomas Mann, these troops moved in and broke up the meeting.

The notoriously bizarre climax to the election campaign came on the evening of Monday 27 February, when the great Reichstag building was set on fire, an act which symbolised its dispensability as a seat of democracy for the men now taking control. Accounts of how the fire was engineered, and by whom, have never been conclusive, but a surmise that Göring was involved seems credible enough. Certainly a crazed young Dutchman, Martinus van der Lubbe, seized on the scene and executed almost a year later, was also involved. So, too, were a group of men thought to be wearing Nazi uniforms of some sort under labourers' clothes, who were seen running from the building and making off in a lorry which conveniently arrived as the confusion reached its height.

Göring's residence was then on the Unter den Linden side of the Reichstag (and now east of the Wall), connected to it by an underground passage. He was one of the first on the scene, and promptly ordered journalists who were present to leave the premises. At 10.15 p.m., an hour after the fire started, Hitler and

Goebbels arrived, as did dozens of fire engines from all parts of the city and hundreds of police, brought by the lorryload and on horseback to clear the streets.

The epicentre of the fire was the mainly wooden debating chamber underneath the central dome. Göring's own presidential seat was blazing furiously. According to *The Times* correspondent of the day, who happened to be passing as the fire began, the worst of it had been 'overcome' by the time Hitler appeared. Entrances and lobbies, he added, were unscathed, but the blazing dome presented all Germans who cared to look with a beacon which must have been visible for miles around.

Later accounts were to the effect that the building could have been restored for use without too much difficulty. Perhaps—but that would have nullified the wished-for significance of the deed itself. Hans Bernd Gisevius, at the time a senior official in Göring's Prussian Interior Ministry and later a repentant anti-Nazi, summed up the situation: 'Everywhere the old order was falling, and its relics bore a strong resemblance to the split and blackened pillars in the assembly hall of the Reichstag. They still stood, but they no longer supported anything. . . .'

Communists were blamed for the fire and several were tried. Van der Lubbe, who in the days before had apparently drifted about the city from lodging house to lodging house, and had at one stage tried to set fire to the Royal Palace, was executed. Karl Ernst, a former hotel doorman who had become a senior figure in the Berlin stormtroopers, and Rudolf Diels, one of the early heads of the Gestapo, were not touched—though later both were heavily and directly implicated. Ernst is said to have led a detachment of men along the passage from Göring's house and to have scattered petrol and inflammable chemicals at strategic points about the building, leaving van der Lubbe behind once the blaze started.

Gisevius swore to lawyers some time afterwards that the idea of the fire had in fact first come from Goebbels, while Diels claimed, also in a formal statement to lawyers, that Göring knew all about it in advance, to the extent that he was ordering lists to be drawn up of people who could be arrested afterwards as culprits. Years later, at Hitler's birthday party in 1942, Göring was to declare, according to a Nazi general who was present, that he was the only one who knew the facts 'because I set it on fire'. But this was a 'confession' he was to deny emphatically as soon as the war was over.

Three days after the fire, and two days before the March election, the leader of the German Communist Party, Ernst Thäl-mann, was arrested. He was to be detained for eleven years, before he was finally murdered in Buchenwald concentration camp in the summer of 1944. The election itself, as an exercise in democratic rights, was a farce before it even happened. Newspapers had been suppressed, meetings banned, or, if they were held, rapidly broken up. Almost no opposition posters were to be seen and according to the *Manchester Guardian*'s man in the city, it was only a brave and reckless person who would hang out a red flag in Berlin. The city's drearier working-class quarters, he reported, were even more dreary than ever. The inhabitants were 'grimly silent'.

Since the Nazis were only to secure 43.9 per cent of the vote in this election, with the Nationalists taking 8 per cent, it was unavoidable that the new machinery of fear should be trundled into action. In a matter of days, almost every individual who might conceivably have offered alternative scenarios of government had departed from the political scene. Organisations which had been household words were disbanded. Eighty-one Communists had been returned to the Reichstag, but many failed to take their seats: they had either been arrested or had fled the country. Oto Wels, the SPD leader, was to make one more defiant speech against Hitler before his party too was silenced. Some trade unionists hung on to a nominal independence for a while, trying to find a way of co-existing with the Nazis, but they did not organise a single day's strike as a protest.

Suddenly, almost overnight it seemed, the creative spontaneity of the political city—everyone and everything that had con-tributed so much to its 'golden twenties' sparkle and mythology—was being snuffed out. To the accompaniment of rehearsed cer-emonials, military music, torchlight parades and rabble-rousing speeches, Berlin found that it was about to endure, though not all acknowledged the fact, a very long night. And the men who now ran the city were doing so, as it soon became clear, with the reckless contempt of the psychopath.

There were different ways of capitulating. Hundreds of thou-sands of Berliners, adopting what they doubtless saw as a realistic posture, decided to join the National Socialist Party. Large numbers of these were civil servants, some of who had occupied government positions even since the days of the Kaiser. Now, they were implicitly swearing allegiance to a jumped-up little autocrat about whom they knew almost nothing.

Perhaps it was their patriotism, the sense of duty, of giving 'authority' its due; perhaps it was the fact that members of the aristocracy, including sometimes visible members of the Kaiser's own family, and big industrialists, as well as some senior echelons of the army, were siding with Hitler. Something had tipped the balance. Perhaps it was the fact that unemployment was quickly and visibly falling or that Hitler's forces were visibly suppressing an opposition which these people also found unacceptable. Their reasons why were not of immediate consequence to Hitler himself. Before the year was out, he had been imbued—mainly by Goebbels—with a quality not far short of infallibility. Certainly the passage of the Enabling Bill, in a Reichstag now obliged to meet in one of the city's opera houses, presented no real problems. Despite minimal, but embittered, opposition, this bill went through on 23 March. It gave Hitler and his party full powers. Now there was only negligible resistance from the SPD. Slowly but surely, the country, with Berlin the focus of a strange fascination from all parts of the world, was being overwhelmed.

A week after the election, Nazis took over the administration of the city. All SPD council members were sent on leave and the Mayor, Friedrich Lange, who had served on the council since the inception of Greater Berlin in 1920, prepared for the worst. On 14 March, he found a note on his desk to the effect that the Reichskommissar for Internal Affairs, Wilhelm Frick, had given instructions that he too should go on leave until further notice. He was replaced by Julius Lippert, leader of the council's Nazi group and one of the first editors of Goebbels' newspaper, *The Attack*. One of Lippert's first orders was to dismiss all Jewish doctors working in the city's hospitals. But he was to get his own come-uppance soon enough. He was sacked by Hitler for disagreeing with the latter's extraordinary plans which were then being formulated for the total rebuilding of the city centre.

Frick was a dreary, desiccated man and one of Hitler's more low-profile supporters. He had participated in the Munich putsch—to be charged with treason in the trial which followed it—and stayed with Hitler almost to the end. As the Bill of Rights was suspended after the Reichstag fire, he introduced imprisonment in makeshift, or 'wild', concentration camps. These were often factories which were standing empty because of the economic recession, or converted army barracks. As Frick did this, Göring drafted in tens of thousands of young Nazis, many of them unemployed, to join his newly formed *Hilfspolizei* (or auxiliary police). Its ranks were swelled with recruits taken from the stormtroopers and the old Stahlhelm, and many of them were armed and given authorisation—by Göring himself—to move freely about the city and to use their weapons without fear of reprisal. They could not interfere with Nazi events in any way; their targets were to be communists and socialists, who were natural political adversaries, and Jews.

In April 1933 Goebbels turned his attention to what remained of the trade unions, clearly anxious that their spokesmen should not become a source of opposition. His ploy was to make 1 May, a day widely celebrated with traditional solemnity by the communists and socialists as 'their' day, an exclusively Nazi festival. The chosen venue was the Tempelhof field and according to estimates which vary between 100,000 and a million and a half people (!)—all said to be 'workers' with their families—were brought in from all parts of the country. The old President sat next to Hitler on the platform and was presented with flowers by Goebbels' stepson. The Horst Wessel song was sung, and towards evening searchlights were dramatically brought into play. Hitler stirringly proclaimed the dignity of labour and declared that the class struggle was a thing of the past.

Next day, the main offices of the trade unions throughout the country, together constituting one of the biggest national workers' organisations in the world, were raided by stormtroopers and their funds seized. The operation, it has since been learned, had been at least two weeks in the planning stage. Many union leaders who had not already fled were arrested—even though they had promised, in some instances, to collaborate with the Nazis—and were accused of stealing workers' contributions for their own use.

Similar raids were staged throughout the country, and in the months that followed, machinery was set in motion to establish the German Labour Front (the DAF). This organisation aimed to give a new sort of sanitised beauty to work activity—but it also banned all industrial action. In the wake of the raids, by an insidious process of political osmosis, all professional and business associations were effectively reorganised along Nazi lines. Memberships were re-oriented accordingly, and even artists, actors and journalists were coerced into unaccustomed conformity. An artists' colony at Laubenheimer Platz in Wilmersdorf—a lingering small pocket of Berlin *bohème*—was broken up and its members publicly ridiculed, punched and kicked before being taken off by lorry to unknown destinations, some never to return.

Such developments, by all accounts, pleased Goebbels, and perhaps because he was a failed writer, he now turned his educated mind specifically to books. Students in every part of the country, but particularly in Berlin, were ordered by the Party to go into bookshops and libraries, taking from them all they could carry of the printed works of black-listed Jewish writers and other political undesirables. Marx and Freud were obvious targets, but so were such hitherto acclaimed writers as Heinrich and Thomas Mann, Stefan Zweig, Erich Maria Remarque, Erich Kästner, André Gide, Emile Zola, Marcel Proust, H. G. Wells and, from another era, Heinrich Heine.

On 10 May, a day of pouring rain, the books were gathered, either by lorry or by students and others in procession. Some of them marched to a musical accompaniment from their hostel in the Oranienburgerstrasse, to Kaiser-Franz-Joseph-Platz (now Bebel-Platz) on Unter den Linden. It was a carefully chosen site, opposite the university main entrance, and between the Opera House and the Old Royal Library (the Kommode). There, the great pile, as it soon became, was set on fire and the students, urged on by less literate stormtroopers, danced and chanted ritualistically round the flames. At a pre-arranged moment, Goebbels himself arrived by car and declared that 'the phoenix of a new spirit' would arise from the books' ashes. A Reich Chamber of Culture was set up almost immediately to be sure that this 'phoenix' did his bidding.

Earlier on the same day a revered figure in German art for half a century or more, Max Liebermann, aged eighty-five, who had been president of the Prussian Academy of Arts for the last twelve years, resigned in disgust from public office. He was forbidden to paint or to exhibit his work, but lived on another two years, a lonely and defiant old man. His wife was to commit suicide before the Nazis could kill her.

On the Bebel-Platz today the same elegant buildings surround a scrubbed and austere open space. Since the last war, it has been a place where the 'new spirit' has been symbolized by the hanging of giant portraits of the members of the Politburo of the Socialist Unity Party. But the amount of attention given to such portraits

100

was debatable, as was the amount of 'profit' to be derived from displaying them. After Erich Honecker became Party leader in 1971, they were returned to storage.

The Kroll Opera House, a few hundred yards across the Platz der Republik (formerly Königsplatz) from the fire-damaged Reichstag, had been rebuilt and reopened in late 1927 as a trail-blazing cultural centre. Stravinsky's *Oedipus Rex* had its first stage production here, as did new works by Hindemith, Milhaud, and others. By what can only have been a policy decision, the Wallot building was never repaired under Hitler and the Kroll, which had staged its last operatic performance in July 1931, now became the parliament building. A week after the burning, Hitler delivered a 'peace' speech in which he declared that war would be 'madness'. It won over many doubters to his side.

One of the first laws of this Reichstag, passed in July, 1933, was to make Germany a one-party state. How shattering such a law was to the easy-going Berliners can only be a matter for guesswork. The brutality had begun to spread. A few weeks before, in the south-eastern district of Köpenick, stormtroopers aided by the SS carried out their most systematic and violent purge yet of local socialists and communists. Hundreds were beaten up and tortured; ninety-one died.

At this time, however, the Church took on a new role and assumed new meanings in what had until now been a largely a-religious city. Quiet, deliberate church movements got under way which Hitler never quite came to terms with, as many Berliners who could not stomach Nazism and who had previously been undemonstrative in their beliefs now turned to religion. Personalities like Martin Niemöller, who had a parish in Dahlem—at St Anne's Church, on Pacelli-Allee, not far from Dahlem Village underground station—and Dietrich Bonhöffer, padre to the city's students, decided to organise. Even after they were arrested, as they were bound to be, these two, and their closest supporters, were to remain a thorn in the leadership's side until the end of the Second World War.

The summer of 1934 was a hot one in Berlin. In the dawn that preceded the last day of June, the new order consolidated its grip in grisly fashion. In Munich Captain Ernst Röhm, who had been nursing into life an anti-Hitler group in the Reichswehr, and his companions were shot in cold blood. In Berlin, Göring, now actively assisted by the ascetic Heinrich Himmler as head of the

SS, had 150 stormtrooper leaders lined up against a wall in the old Lichterfelde barracks and summarily executed. Hundreds of others, including the last Weimar Chancellor, several former ministers and generals, as well as a host of intellectuals, were also murdered.

Hitler later told the Reichstag that a total of seventy-seven had died, including thirteen who were killed 'resisting arrest'. Postwar estimates, however, had yielded a figure of well over 1000. The day after it was over, Hitler was host at a Chancellery garden party in the Wilhelmstrasse, and the following day, Hindenburg was able to congratulate him and Göring for having nipped treason in the bud and saving the German people 'from great danger'.

A month later Hindenburg, aged eighty-seven, was dead. When he was buried (with great pomp and ceremony, at Tannenberg, the scene of his First World War victory), more, much more, was being interred than a tired old general. A minute's silence was called for in the centre of Berlin and the city came to a virtual standstill as thousands—Nazis as well as anti-Nazis—bared their heads. Something of the old Germany, too big and too deep to comprehend in these confused times, had gone. The idea that somehow the Kaiser might be restored, persistent until the old man's death, went with him. And so did the last vestiges of constitutionality.

Hitler promptly took the title of Führer and Reich Chancellor, demanding an oath of allegiance to himself from all members of the armed forces. Colonel Oskar von Hindenburg publicly gave him his support, but the Junker class and the old aristocracy, even where they acquiesced, knew they had lost a guiding light. Today the descendants of these groups in particular remain politically disoriented, unable to come to terms with the 'new' Germans from capitals in Bonn and East Berlin, who now make up the country's ruling class.

In the summer of 1934 the Nazis constructed a new municipal council for the city, consisting mainly of Nazis and nationalists. Each district (*Bezirk*) was given its own new authority of up to a dozen members. By the end of the year the new city body was putting in hand plans for new Army barracks and quarters for the Air Force to be built on sites at Spandau, Gatow and Kladow—west of the Wannsee. By March 1935 the city fathers were able to put in hand a practice for the city's first 'air raid'. This entailed all but 1500 of the city's 120,000 street lamps being put out between 10 p.m. and midnight. The confusion, and the crime, which were to accompany total blackouts half a dozen years later remained beyond the horizon.

In the quarter century before Hitler's takeover, work on a variety of building projects in Berlin, many of them intrinsically exciting and highly innovative from the architectural point of view, had been halted only because of runaway inflation or scarcity of cash. Under the Nazis, however, architecture was to become a contentious issue. Hitler had his own ideas. 'It is not a real metropolis,' he said at an early stage, 'it is nothing but an unregulated accumulation of buildings.' And he enlisted a compliant team, not without talent, to see his ideas realised.

In the decade before Hitler, nine buildings out of ten in the city had been municipally funded, and the spirit of 'revolution' in design and planning, which had been born some years before the outbreak of the First World War, was largely unquenched. Once the First War was over, the 'inspiration' of Paris was discarded by men who had been more impressed by Chicago and New York. Skyscrapers were planned—though none materialised—after competitions for a new Friedrichstrasse and a new Alexanderplatz. One was intended to straddle a new main road which would cut across the Tiergarten.

Presiding geniuses in architecture who emerged at the end of the war rejected emphatically the old notions of 'elegance and good taste' and, in an effort to see their art developed as a 'sculptural' form, established the Bauhaus school in Weimar. In 1923, one Bauhaus protagonist, Walter Gropius, wrote of the need for what he called 'a clear organic architecture, whose inner logic will be radiant and naked, unencumbered by lying façades and trickeries.' A year later, with backing from the trade unions, a city-wide building association, to be known as Gehag, with the new city architect Martin Wagner as its first director, was established. Wagner was joined by Bruno Taut, and these two men—and Gropius—were in a short space of time to change the face of many areas of the city.

In the second half of the 1920s, Wagner and Taut, who was Gehag's chief designer, started work on the co-called *Hufeisen-siedlung* (Horse-Shoe Estate) on farmland bought by the city authorities in the Britz district, a few miles south-west of the Tempelhof field and just west of the 1961 Wall. Much of that estate still stands, unexceptional perhaps today with its clean lines and modest proportions, but a monument nevertheless to what in its time represented quite fundamental change. It is the plenitude of trees and green spaces which mark out this area, as they did at Taut's 'forest development', started a year or so later at Zehlendorf, a few miles to the west. In other urban contexts such areas have come to be known as garden suburbs.

In 1929, Gropius took charge of the plans and designs for Siemensstadt, a settlement for the workers of the great electrical equipment company which had, and still has, a number of factories just across the road (the Nonnendamm). The site is north-west of Charlottenburg, on the north bank of the Spree, and south-west of Tegel Airport. Some of Germany's finest architects were drawn to participate in this scheme, and it retains much of what Gropius might have called its 'sculptural' freshness to this day.

Gropius parted from the Bauhaus group in 1928 to work exclusively in Berlin. The group meanwhile had been harried into leaving its original home in Weimar for Dessau. From here in October 1932, pressure from Nazis forced them once again to move on to rejoin Gropius in Berlin. Their premises were an old factory in Birkbusch Strasse, in Steglitz. By this time, Nazi polemicists were saying that the 'new' style houses were fit only for animals, that they induced physical and mental stress, and therefore 'weakened the German race'. Terms like 'architectural bolshevism' were now used as a term of abuse for the work of Gropius—someone who not long before had declared that Bolshevism was 'probably the only means of creating the preconditions for a new culture'.

During the winter of 1932–33, those who remained with the Bauhaus, now under Mies van der Rohe, sought to keep their spirits up and their imagination flowing from their base in the old Berlin factory building. Then in early April 1933 the Gestapo raided these premises, arresting students for possessing 'illegal' Communist literature. Months of pleading from Mies van der Rohe proved pointless, and the school and the group were formally dissolved in August the same year. Gropius, Mies and Wagner left soon afterwards for London; Taut sought a new life designing cities in the Soviet Union.

Precisely what 'style' Hitler favoured architecturally, apart from what might be called the unsubtle monumental, is not all that clear. He authorised the Reich Chamber of Culture under Goebbels to lay down ground rules for what was 'taste'—echoes of the old Kaiser—and to carry out purges of architects and planners who did not 'fit'. This thorough-going organisation was divided horizontally and vertically, with associate chambers for each art discipline and with sub-chambers in selected provincial centres. German art, said Goebbels at the inaugural tone-setting ceremony, was in need of 'new blood'; he had the network to achieve it.

One person whose veins were apparently filled with just this sort of blood was Albert Speer, who was to become Hitler's architect in 1934 when he was still only twenty-eight years old. Not long before, Speer had been a student at the Charlottenburg Technical Institute, where his most influencial teacher was not, as he had wished, Hans Poelzig, a radical personality of the Weimar era, but Heinrich Tessenow. Tessenow was warmly approved of by the Nazis and, according to Speer, was 'a champion of the spirit of simple craftsmanship in architecture'. He moulded the ambitious young Speer into a creature who was generally only too pleased at the scope the Führer gave him. No pupil of Poelzig would have been so malleable.

When Hitler found himself irreversibly disagreeing with the city council, it was Speer, by his own account, who was entrusted with the great 'renewal' plan for Berlin. Often until the small hours, the two of them would discuss projections for the new city, to be called Germania and to be completed by 1950. The accounts of these discussions, and the projections, as seen by Speer, make fascinating—if tendentious—reading.

The Reichsbank and Treasury building, erected on a canalside site just south of the City Palace, dates from this time. The streets around it have since changed names or disappeared, but the austerely handsome, dark grey sandstone building, erected between 1934 and 1938, is today one of the most important in East Germany, housing the Central Committee offices of the Socialist Unity Party (the SED).

Otherwise, and apart from the Air Ministry buildings and barracks, there are few Hitler/Speer artefacts left in Berlin. Their era is now remembered by the widening of the Charlottenburg-Chaussee, so that it could be used in emergencies—as it was—as an aircraft runway, and in the still standing multi-storey concrete bunkers, taking up to 1000 fighting men when in use, which rise up with brutal suddenness in odd parts of the city. Some have been demolished, but only after using much more explosives than many had thought necessary—notably in the Tiergarten where a bunker which had sheltered several hundred people had to be blown up. Others were dotted about the forests in the city's outlying areas and some of these have been judiciously buried under mountains of rubble from the blitzed city centre.

One bunker, six storeys high, stands in Pallasstrasse, just off the Potsdamerstrasse. It rises up, strangely haunting and pointedly indestructible, grafted incongruously and quite unsuccessfully into the blocks of flats that have been built all around it. At levels that can be reached, its outer walls have been decorated with plaintive, and eloquent, anti-war graffiti.

According to Speer, there was no 'Führer-style'. But Hitler did give him bits of paper which, symptomatically, he had kept since his youth and on which, he said, he had sketched some ideas that he liked. These designs, it has since been suggested, represented the 'daydreams of a provincial megalomaniac', things that the upstart from Munich, very much a rival city, thought he could carry out to transform 'red' Berlin. They lacked an important element. Speer claimed that when he showed the Führer plans for humanising factories with flowers and lawns around them, there was little enthusiasm. Hitler's frustrated passion, he concluded, was for notions 'architectural' rather than 'social'.

Berlin today, even rebuilt Berlin, would have been a vastly different entity visually if even half of these notions had been realised. Speer was given powers to acquire any land and demolish any buildings that obstructed his designs. He therefore advised that the Anhalter, Friedrichstrasse, Lehrter and Potsdamer stations—with others—would have to go. He even asked for the Reichstag to be demolished—a request turned down by Hitler himself. And he requested that about 200,000 people, Jews in the first instance, should be decanted from the city centre so that the tenement blocks they lived in could be removed.

The projected new city was to have a population of ten millions. In its central avenue, according to Speer, Germania would spell out in architecture the political, military and economic might of Germany, of the thousand-year Reich. He was appointed, or rather designated, Inspector-General of Buildings for Berlin, and was installed in the former Academy of Arts next to the Brandenburg Gate. As the plans became models, the first demolition work was put in hand.

Almost no construction was to be done on the central showpiece area, to be known as the Adolf-Hitler-Stadt, but right up to the end of the Second World War, Hitler would go by underground passage to Speer's office to be transfixed by the shape of things to come, spread out on a big table in front of him. He saw a great avenue, the North-South Axis, several miles long, running from close to the Reichstag building down to a point close to the Tempelhof field. At the northern extremity he saw the world's greatest ever Congress Hall—sixteen times bigger than Rome's St Peter's and capable of holding 150,000 people—fronted by a huge plaza (Adolf-Hitler-Platz). This would be for holding May Day rallies and included also a large man-made lake for the city's recreation.

At the southern end, there was a massive Triumphal Arch in granite, some 400 feet high, and many times bigger than the Arc de Triomphe in Paris. It would carry the names of all 1,800,000 Germans—but not the Jews—who had died in the First War. Along the avenue, interspersed among the administrative head-quarters of the various Reichministries and big industrial concerns, there were an opera house, three theatres, two cinemas, a concert hall, a twenty-one-storey hotel, a Great Hall of the German Soldier, and there were some of the best shops in Europe, all backing on to peaceful courtyards.

Nor was that all. A new university area was planned for the city; the old university buildings (now the Humboldt University of East Berlin) were, said Speer, in 'deplorable' condition. A new complex of museums was planned to run along the southern bank of the Spree (from Kupfergraben to the Reichstagsufer). Two all-embracing railway termini, one at each end of the new axis, would be erected, the northern one flanked by a new City Hall, a War Academy and police headquarters, and the southern one adjoining a great amusement park which would outdo in all respects the Tivoli Gardens in Copenhagen. Four new airports were planned for north, south, east and west of the new centre.

These projections apparently excited Hitler no end, though for Speer they finally became 'not only crazy, but also boring'. Of the whole vast project for the reshaping of Berlin, he wrote later, some of the deciduous trees that he had planted, by the thousands, in the Grunewald, were to be all that remained. This was small consolation to those in the concentration camps who, on minimal rations, had been expected to break down great blocks of granite for the city's builders—much of which finished up as hardcore for the new autobahns.

However rich the dreams of Hitler, those of Göring were always more grand. He had muscled in at the planning stage to demand a fantastic administrative HQ-cum-pleasure dome at the very centre of the axis. It would include a theatre or two, a ballroom, ample facilities for entertainment, and all the office space that such an expansive, bombastic personality, with so many portfolios, might require. It was never actually started, but its centre is roughly beneath the feet of anyone who stands just across the Charlottenburg-Chaussee to look at the Soviet War Memorial.

Göring's marriage to the actress Emmy Sonnemann in April 1935 had been the great event of the year, the greatest street event, some said, since the Kaiser's time. A gala performance of Wagner's *Lohengrin* was held the night before, with a glittering reception, at the Opera House, and a fly-past was organised by Göring himself. The ceremony, under Reichsbishop Ludwig Müller, was conducted first at the City Hall (it was Göring's second marriage) and then at the Cathedral, followed by another reception at the Kaiserhof Hotel. Crowds lined the streets and bands played, while Nazi guards kept a careful watch.

The social welfare needs of the city of Berlin, which had always been apparent since it became the imperial capital in 1871, were not much discussed in *Mein Kampf*. The extent to which this was a matter of immediate concern to the unemployed, who now found under Hitler that they had jobs, or to the erstwhile hungry who suddenly found they had enough bread, is debatable. Where men could be used rather than machines, in the construction and refurbishment of autobahns, public buildings, or army barracks, for instance, this was done; women who had achieved some liberation during the heady 1920s were now encouraged to stay at home. That was until the late 1930s, when a general labour shortage meant that once again women were encouraged to return to work.

The German Labour Front directed labour. Homelessness, it was decided, was 'dangerous' to the state. Prices continued climbing and wages were frozen, in spite of longer working hours. The right to strike was non-existent. Obligatory deductions were made from wages for 'welfare' benefits—and Party projects. Small businessmen, often Jewish, did less well than their bigger brothers, and in that respect too Berlin was a changing city. Hitler's assertion that the economy was somehow 'for the people' soon began to sound hollow. For those accepting the political and economic orders of the day, however, Party-organised subsidised cruises and holidays to the Mediterranean and Madeira were not to be sniffed at.

All youth organisations were banned except, of course, the Hitler Youth. For those who enrolled, there was quick and early induction into programmed militarism. Camps were held in the Grunewald and parades organised to the accompaniment of newly formed young military bands. The Alliance of German Girls, designed in part to promote motherliness and motherhood, followed some years later.

Just as the entertainment and nightlife of the city became more restrained, so the café and restaurant life, while still brisk, became more orderly. The ambience of a district or a single street, or the decor of a room, would be changed with the unquestionable introduction of a picture of the Führer, a Nazi slogan or swastika flag. 'Empty theatres, bankrupt bookshops, starving authors, artists and composers,' wrote a British diplomat in 1936, 'are a constant reminder that the cultural life of Berlin is threatening to expire.'

At one level, jazz music of all sorts was officially frowned upon (though secret 'swing clubs' thrived); at another level, the music of Jewish composers (Mendelssohn, to name but one) was banned. Even the tango somehow lost its ubiquitous appeal. Berlin, it was clear, had begun to lose its zest. As emigration quickened, the colour began to drain, in more ways than one, from the city's cheeks. Women were discouraged from wearing make-up; 'the Aryan woman,' said the Goebbels machine, 'has a natural beauty and needs no artifice'.

A Reich food office was set up in October 1933, a gesture followed somewhat ironically by three successive years of falling grain and potato harvests. Soon, this led to food shortages. The ill-feeling of farmers and those responsible for marketing, who resented political interference in their routine activities (even where this included some black-marketeering) was compounded by resentment from the consumers themselves who now had to pay more for dairy products, eggs and meat. Even so, the average family managed to eat well enough, and certainly better than a few years earlier.

The *Eintopfgericht* (one course meal) was instigated in 1935. This was a means of appealing to the nation to eat simply once a month and to contribute the savings made to the Government's winter relief scheme which provided food, fuel and clothing for those adjudged in need. In selected centres in Berlin, on the chosen day, austere ladies in white coats would dish out a sort of stew. The citizens would eat at prepared tables to the accompaniment of military music from a small band of stormtroopers, perhaps sitting next to a presentation display honouring the Führer, with flowers and flags decorating his portrait; for many consumers, such a dish wasn't that much different from their usual; for others it was an exercise in ostentatious privation. The Irish stew at the Bristol Hotel became very fashionable; the stew at the Adlon, by contrast, was said to be 'tasteless'.

In December 1935, the Lord Mayor of the city since before the Nazi takeover, Heinrich Sahm, was forced to offer his resignation. He had started his career in Danzig (now the Polish city of Gdansk) but was not a Nazi and he had come to office on the back of Nazi Party abstentions. His room for manoeuvre had become increasingly limited and as he departed for the relatively minor post of Ambassador to Norway he was replaced by the more simple-minded but almost always acquiescent Julius Lippert.

Sahm was one of a small handful of people who had campaigned assiduously for the holding of the 1936 Olympic Games in Berlin. He shared this task with Dr Theodor Lewald, who had been chairman of the organising committee for the Games of 1916 which had also been awarded to Germany, and with Karl Diem, an athlete who at an early age had become Wilheim II's de facto Sports Minister. Although a stadium was purpose-built in the Grunewald, situated in the middle of a racecourse on land leased from the Berlin Racing Union, the games scheduled for 1916 had been lost as soon as the First War broke out. Germany was then precluded from participation in those held in 1920 and 1924, but now Lewald and Diem, backed by Sahm, persisted and persuaded an initially sceptical Hitler that such an exercise would in fact be worthwhile in 1936.

After some procrastination and altercation, the racecourse

stadium was demolished, and a great new one—to seat 100,000 spectators—erected in its place. This is still known as the Olympia Stadium. It was to rise into the air with more than seventy tiers of seating and to include more than fifty dressing rooms for the athletes. The stark, almost brutal simplicity of its natural stone design, reaching a high point with the cleanly vertical Bell Tower, was to be complemented by the May Field, a green expanse of more than 120,000 square yards, laid out on its western perimeter. Here mass meetings of up to 500,000 could be accommodated, and Hitler was to make much use of it for later rallies. One of the biggest of those, punctuated by a great thunderstorm, was to cement his alliance with Mussolini in September 1937.

The stadium was a project of heroic proportions, bigger than anything the city had ever seen before. The whole complex was constructed to the overall design of Werner March, an architect whose father Otto had devised the original smaller stadium within the racecourse. Of that stadium only a single oak tree at the main entrance survives. Some thousands of men were engaged on a 300-acre site, latterly toiling round the clock to complete on time for the 1 August opening.

German politicians and polemicists soon glorified sport and German potential to excel, at the expense of Jews, negroes and other 'inferior' competition. There was no place in German sport, said the viciously anti-semitic newspaper, *Der Stürmer*, for Jews. It was a sentiment which could only create tensions between the games' hosts and those drawing up the visiting and competing teams.

It fell to Richard Strauss, who was well past seventy, to compose and conduct the hymn for the grand opening ceremony. Like other distinguished musicians of this time, he was regularly in conflict with the authorities. His latest skirmish arose over his determination to collaborate with the Jewish writer, Stefan Zweig, whose words he used for the opera, *Die Schweigsame Frau*.

Once the Games got under way Hitler, sitting with representatives of European royal families as his main guests, followed events closely—and often tensely and angrily—from the tribune built to give him maximum exposure. His arrogant disregard for the achievements and evidently popular personality of the US athlete, Jesse Owens, belong to legend; at that time in Berlin, it symbolised the irreconcilable differences between the Führer's ideology and human values. For him, the whole exercise was an excuse to further 'evil patriotism'. But today there is a Jesse-Owens-Allee not far from the stadium entrance.

Great events were held in the city to mark the Games. Göring, in the garden of his ministry, created an entire village to delight his guests, and was host to a gala dinner and dance at the Opera House. Goebbels organised an 'Italian' evening on the Peacock Island (Pfaueninsel) in the middle of the Havel River—an evening which deteriorated at times into orgiastic frenzy as guests enjoyed the balmy air with the nubile 'nymphs' in the bushes. At his house in Dahlem, meanwhile, the ambitious and pretentious Joachim von Ribbentrop, sometime Ambassador to London and later to be Foreign Minister and a co-signatory of the non-aggression treaty with the Russians, was not be outdone. He held a party of his own: he had been a champagne salesman in his earlier life.

The stadium today is a public monument, but is still used for major sporting events—such as the 1974 football World Cup. Damage sustained during the war has been repaired, and for a nominal entrance fee visitors can see the greatest relic (in tangible form) of the Nazi period. The May Field is used for rugby and polo by the British occupation forces, and for the annual Queen's Birthday parade. Cricket is played a mile or so away to the north, near the German Sports Hall—of the same vintage as the stadium—which houses the head offices of the British garrison. The Olympic village of Döberitz, ten miles west of the Stadium itself and just outside the Berlin boundary, became a Reichswehr training area, but is now a Soviet barracks. In 1936, as many already knew but few acknowledged, it was a short distance only from the already busy Oranienburg concentration camp.

Visitors looking at the stadium these days tend to come only in small numbers. The man who runs the one hot-dog stall in the great forecourt—a nice Berlin touch—chats happily to pass the time of day. Looking down on the vastness of the stadium itself, immaculately maintained, from the seventieth tier up, one can only be struck by the daunting scale of it all. Other visitors on the far side may be almost audible—the acoustics are so good—but they look minute. Watching a drunk on the running track go through the motions of a sprinter at the starting block (as I did once in 1986), it is difficult to avoid the feeling that one is standing in a hugely expensive architectural folly.

★　　★　　★

Long before these Games were held, Berlin's Jews had learned to avoid the Kurfürstendamm and similarly crowded areas of the city centre at the weekends. The Kurfürstendamm had become a favourite haunt for stormtroopers and others wearing swastika armbands looking for a fight, and it had become unexceptional for Jews to be beaten up there. By March 1933 Jews were being arrested for 'political' offences, and consigned either to the new camps or the so-called 'brown houses'. The most notorious of these were at Nos 1 to 3 Columbia-Strasse, close to the present Platz der Luftbrücke (Airlift Square); No. 10 Hedemann-Strasse, the SA's Berlin headquarters near the Anhalter Station; and the basement of the huge former barracks building on the General-Pape-Strasse, nearer to the Tempelhof field. In the latter, it was not long before torture and 'executions'—hanging as well as beheading—became routine.

Other detention centres were at Gestapo 'offices' in Burgstrasse, in the Mitte area of the city, and in Grolmannstrasse, not far from Charlottenburg's Savigny Platz. The SS, meanwhile, occupied the former Hotel Prinz Albrecht and the Prinz Albrecht Palace.

The Jews had first preoccupied Hitler in his Vienna days before the First War. By 1923, Hitler was convinced they were 'ruining' the country, and he began to rationalise and formulate his hatred. Thus, one week after the 1933 Enabling Bill was passed, giving him full powers, a major boycott was instituted—initially for one day only—against Jewish shops and businesses in the city, Jewish doctors and lawyers, and Jewish goods. This was launched by Goebbels at a mass rally held in the Lustgarten.

In an interview in November 1935, Hitler announced that Germans' rights had to be 'protected against destructive Jewish influences'. Practically all Bolshevik agitators in Germany, he added, had been Jews. The exodus of the city's talented, and not so talented, 'offenders' quickened inexorably—though with only grudging assistance from, for instance, the US and British immigration authorities. Paradoxically, almost every day from now on was to bring an event or an impulse to strengthen the solidarity of the Jewish community.

An outstanding personality in this community was the city's de facto chief rabbi, Dr Leo Baeck. By any standards, he was a figure of great courage and dignity. By nature reserved, he came from a typical German-Jewish middle-class family, having first come to Berlin in the 1890s for its intellectual stimulus, when other Jews of that time gravitated towards commerce and the professions. In such company, however, Baeck attended the Jewish High School in its then run-down premises in Unter den Linden.

In 1912, the city's Jewish population, which he was soon to lead, was highly organised and close-knit, with its own sophisticated administration and taxation system. The High School, at which he became a teacher, moved in 1907 to No. 14 Artilleriestrasse (now No. 9 Tucholskystrasse, a street which cuts at right-angles across Oranienburgerstrasse) and was to remain operational, through all the traumas that were to follow, until June 1942. Baeck attended—with Albert Einstein—an inaugural meeting, in 1927, of Berlin's pro-Palestine committee; soon after that, the German Zionist Federation opened its head offices at No. 10 Meinekestrasse, off the Kurfürstendamm.

In early 1933, Baeck warned his friends that 'the end of German Jewry has arrived' but when, some months later, the National Council (*Reichsvertretung*) of German Jews was formed, he accepted the leader's role. When uniformed Gestapo men began to stand in at Council meetings, or when there were policy differences with Heinrich Stahl, leading the city community, Baeck pressed on. In the First War, he had gone to the front as a rabbi to the Jewish troops; when the Second War came, though he was nearly seventy, he vowed to stay in Berlin until the last Jew had left. However, as prisoner No. 187984 he was taken to Theresienstadt, to leave it only in July 1945 when he was flown to London. Here, he took up British citizenship and died unknown. But he is remembered in Berlin.

The April 1933 boycott had displeased the ancient Hindenburg and some of Germany's allies. Berliners as consumers disliked it: after all, many of the city's most popular department stores were, and are still, Jewish-owned. For a while in mid-1935, anti-Jewish demonstrations along the Kurfürstendamm were such that detachments of special police had to be posted as a token precaution outside many of its cafés and restaurants. Then, in the confusion of demonstrations and riots which followed, the guards were removed. This allowed the boycotts to be stepped up and to become more thorough. Notices were posted across the windows of Jewish premises, warning Germans not to enter. Armed stormtroopers stood at doorways barring entry.

As Jews were increasingly harassed and ridiculed in the streets, the arguments that these people had been willing to fight and die for Germany in 1914–18 lost their force. So, in due course, did the view that Jewish-owned concerns in the city were submitting viable tenders for big government contracts and easing the lingering unemployment problem. After the death of Hindenburg, for whom the Jews held their own memorial service in Berlin, the so-called Nuremberg laws were enacted to protect 'German blood', denying Jews the right to marry Germans and stripping them of German citizenship. By the time Göring's four-year economic plan got off the ground in 1938, the unemployment problem was more or less solved, and the bigger Aryan companies had bought out—often for a pittance—the many smaller Jewish enterprises which had been forced to go to the wall. The Jewish community experienced its own unprecedented levels of unemployment.

Jewish judges, lawyers and civil servants were removed from public office, and doctors, dentists, chemists, artists, journalists and other professionals were debarred from practising. The university, colleges and schools, clubs and associations, even public parks and bath-houses, began to close their doors to Jews. Such organisations were increasingly run by thoroughbred Nazis. Even the Jews' own community associations were wound up. The synagogues became their main meeting places. Jewish paintings and books were removed from galleries and libraries—when they had not been burned in the Opernplatz inferno—and their works dropped from the repertoires of the city's many theatres, concert halls and cinemas. Cemeteries and synagogues were consistently desecrated, and streets named after celebrated Jews systematically renamed, though not for the first or last time. Jewish names were chipped off war memorials. (About 12,000 Jews had died for Germany in the First War out of 100,000 who enlisted.)

The chillingly violent climax to this process was reached on the night of 9 November, 1938. It was billed as a 'spontaneous' (Goebbels's word) reprisal for the shooting of a German diplomat in Paris, by a seventeen-year-old Jew called Herschel Grynszpan. Squads and sometimes lorry loads of men in civilian clothes and armed with clubs set about a systematic ransacking and destruction, usually by fire, of all Jewish property. This included 400 synagogues throughout the country, among them the two biggest—out of a total of twenty-four—in the capital. One was in Fasanenstrasse, not far from the Zoo Station and between the Kurfürstendamm and Kantstrasse, the other halfway along Oranienburgerstrasse, about ten minutes walk from Alexanderplatz. Only the Levetzowstrasse synagogue, one of the most-used Jewish community centres, was not destroyed.

Jewish businesses and homes were smashed up without mercy, and at least 12,000 of the city's Jews rounded up and despatched to concentration camps, mostly to Sachsenhausen, to the north of the city. One aim was to expunge the (very considerable) Jewish presence from the country's and the city's economic life. The police did not interfere. In Berlin this meant a brutal and abrupt halt to the activities of 17 per cent of the city's bankers, 16 per cent of lawyers, and 10 per cent of doctors, as well as—still—a number of small shopkeepers. Nearly 40 per cent of all Germany's Jews, in 1933, had been located in Berlin. The ninth of November was, said Leo Baeck with feeling, the night of 'the great blasphemy'.

Albert Speer passed the still smouldering ruins of Berlin synagogues on his way to work on 10 November and wrote that it was one of the 'most doleful' memories of his life. The 'disorder' he saw on Fasanenstrasse, he said, represented in charred beams, collapsed façades and burned out walls, were 'anticipations' of a scene that during the war to come was to dominate so much of Europe.

The Jews themselves were ordered, amazingly, to pay millions of marks in compensation for damage caused, but Göring was furious at what he saw as Goebbels-directed sabotage of his newly launched four-year plan. Products and services which he had incorporated into this plan had been looted or no longer existed; warehouses and production units had been destroyed; German marks and other required foreign currencies were being used up by banks and insurance companies in compensation payments.

'To the credit of the people,' wrote Hans Bernd Gisevius in his memoirs, 'it must be said that the overwhelming majority had no part in this hideous affair.' On *Reichskristallnacht*, Speer suggested, though it was not immediately obvious, Hitler had crossed a Rubicon for the fourth time in his life. Jews today say it was not so much the destruction which was the tragedy, but the collusion of the Government in allowing it to happen.

Recent research has shown that reactions to the *Reichskristallnacht* exercise were not what Goebbels and others expected. 'The actions against the Jews in November were very badly received,' wrote a member of the stormtrooper security services in his report. 'Many believed that they had openly to stand up for the Jews. The destruction of the synagogues was declared to be irresponsible. . . .'

Berlin's Jewish population before Hitler came to power was at least 160,000; by the beginning of 1939, it was 75,000. But questions about the '*Nacht*', which led the US to withdraw its Ambassador from Berlin forthwith, did not stop the persecution. Within a few weeks, Jews were told that there were certain streets, notably in the Wilhelmstrasse government area, where they could not go. They were also told they could no longer go to public theatres, concert halls or cinemas, and Jewish children were told that they would no longer be able to continue at state-run schools.

It is deeply disturbing to walk about Berlin looking for synagogues that are no longer there, for meeting places and homes that were removed by other means than Allied bombing or post-war bulldozers. In Fasanenstrasse, a Jewish community house has been erected (in 1959) to replace what was one of the great architectural glories of all Germany's synagogues. The Kaiser himself, and his Army, had been represented at the original grand opening ceremony in 1912. Now only a few fragments of the old building remain, including the old portal which has been retrieved and re-erected around the entrance. Inside there are some rather ascetic meeting rooms, a library and a simple memorial to those who died. A trickle of people come and go, and although it is not a very busy place, there is a constant police guard. Anti-semitism is by no means dead in today's Berlin.

At Oranienburgerstrasse, the huge and ornate brick facade remains, but the rusted gates are locked. This cathedral-like structure dates from the 1860s, and represented, according to later Jewish commentators, 'an elegance which lulled Berlin Jews into believing they were secure in Germany.' There is a Jewish community house two doors along but once again there seem to be very few people about. On three visits to this spot I have never seen anyone else lingering to read the memorial stone which stands by its main entrance, erected by the Jewish Community of Grossberlin in 1966. 'It must never be forgotten' is the message, and in 1986 there was talk of the possibility of rebuilding this synagogue.

Synagogues in the city which were not set on fire or otherwise desecrated during the *Reichskristallnacht* rampage were often destroyed in Allied bombing raids. The *Reichsvertretung* office in Kantstrasse has been replaced by business premises, but is remembered with a plaque. The Jewish High School, attended by Baeck and so many others, is now an apartment house with a children's nursery on one floor. A playground covers the site once occupied by one of the city's bigger Jewish places of worship; a car park has taken the place of another. The Levetzowstrasse synagogue might never have existed.

Berlin's fragmented opposition to Hitler ran more or less true to form. Less than twenty years before, its forebears had compromised their own revolution through an inability to coalesce; they had remained persistently and quirkishly at political odds with the Prussian or prevailing 'German' administration, albeit with a sense of humour. Now they were, as they had always been, an assorted agglomeration of people.

But then, even what was offered in entertainment in Berlin's golden era was compartmentalised, catering just as eagerly for individual tastes as for the collective need. Hedonists may make natural oppositionists, but they don't often work together to formulate policies.

As Germans, many Berliners nursed the thought, at least in the early 1930s, that Hitler, like the chancellors who preceded him, would not last long. While there was some relief that the new leader was creating jobs and making efforts to fill stomachs, there was also resistance almost from the beginning. His notion of *'Ein Reich, ein Volk, ein Führer'* was always a non-starter. From the shopfloor, there were grumblings about working conditions, food prices and, for example, Nazi building priorities at a time of acute housing problems.

Opposition came in many forms, and the objective varied: some wanted to seize Hitler by force, even to have him assassinated, others wanted to see an end to his policies: others to see the restoration of a 'just' society. A dozen years after the Second War, Golo Mann described the resistance as 'a shining light' in the darkness; at the time, Reinhard Heydrich, the icily brutal head of the SS, spoke of all symptoms of 'disease and germs' having to be removed 'by every suitable means'.

Plötzensee Prison, one of several used by the Nazis in Berlin, is in the north-west of the city, between Charlottenburg and

Wedding. A small, outwardly innocent red-brick outhouse, in the grounds of what is now a juvenile corrective establishment, served as an execution chamber until the very end of the war. At least 2500 German and non-German men, women and children were hanged here—sometimes eight at a time—or guillotined. A memorial erected by the City Senate in 1952 recorded that 'Berlin honours those millions of victims of the Third Reich who, because of their political convictions, their religious beliefs or racial origins, were vilified, abused, deprived of their freedom or murdered'.

Even when there was bomb damage to the prison and the execution chamber, the executions went on. Invitations to witness them were counted as an honour by local Nazis and sometimes brandy was served to spectators. Films were made of some plotters' final moments and shown for the Führer's pleasure. The hangings continued even as Soviet troops converged on the prison buildings at the end of April 1945. Many prisoners, it is now said, were shot dead by SS men after the moment of liberation.

By the time the Second War broke out in September 1939, more than 225,000 men and women had been through the courts and imprisoned for political reasons. Another 75,000 were in political custody. By the end of the war, well over a million Germans had spent time in prison or in camps. Tens of thousands died; others survived to become public figures, in East and West Berlin. Erich Honecker, who has led East Germany since 1971, joined the Communist Party as a boy of sixteen in 1929. By the end of 1933, nearly 150,000 Communists were in camps or in prison, and Honecker was in prison from 1935 until the war's end. In Berlin, Tegel and Moabit prisons, as well as Plötzensee and others already mentioned, were in full use. The SS frequently used their barracks at Lichterfelde, previously a billet for the Kaiser's army, as a place both of imprisonment and of execution.

The resistance shown by the military later in the war was obviously important but it was by no means the only source of opposition from within government. Pastor Dietrich Bonhöffer, the churchman who opposed Hitler (even from the ranks of the Army), declared in 1942 that there was 'an organisation representing the opposition in every ministry'. And certainly within the Foreign Office and the home civil service, still staffed in large part by Prussians and 'tamed' aristocrats, there was simmering discontent. Equally certainly, in the established Church, there were many ill-fitting and highly vociferous elements. From the beginning, there were Catholics as well as Protestants who never ceased to support the State of Emergency which the Church itself had declared after a meeting of clergymen in Dahlem in October 1934.

In government industries, absenteeism became a measure of dissent, and strikes were not infrequent. Anti-Nazi trade unionists and other agitators did what they could to sabotage output. Herbert Baum, for instance, was employed at the Siemens factory and with his wife, Marianne, organised a many-pronged and highly effective opposition operation from their flat at No 3 Stralauer Strasse, to the south-east of the Red Town Hall. Wilhelm Leuschner, a Bayreuth joiner, ran a nationwide network of support from his home (which he called a 'factory') at No. 84 Bismarkstrasse, in Charlottenburg.

Among the city's intellectuals, one of the outstanding personalities was Carl von Ossietzky, forthright editor of a thinking person's journal called *Weltbühne* (still produced in East Berlin). He was awarded the Nobel peace prize in 1935 and, despite intense personal pressures from Hermann Göring himself, refused to turn it down. He remained till the last, when he died in great pain from tuberculosis in a Gestapo hospital, unyielding in his criticisms of the Nazi regime.

Among the city's students a resistance movement calling itself White Rose bloomed for a while, to be followed when it faded by another called the Edelweiss. School groups got together to produce and distribute anti-Nazi leaflets.

Stickers would go up overnight, some with impassioned appeals, some with the one word: NEIN. The same word would be chalked up on walls and hoardings where it could be seen most clearly. Rumours were manufactured and disseminated vigorously: that the Führer's government had been toppled, that a truce had been proposed, that Stalin was flying in for urgent peace talks.

Most poignant of all, there were countless acts of spontaneous, personal opposition: medicines or other supplies for someone in hiding; a food parcel for a persecuted Jew (though kosher meat became virtually unobtainable by anyone in the war); a seat offered on public transport.

A number of conspiratorial groups planned their activities on a geographically limited basis in different parts of the city. Today, in the various *Bezirk* (borough) town halls, local cemeteries and elsewhere, they are not forgotten. The East Berlin authorities, for understandable reasons, seem to have done more than their West Berlin counterparts, to encourage the writing up of the activities of these groups.

Hitler's greatest example of architectural self-indulgence, and Albert Speer's greatest architectural achievement, was undoubtedly the Reichschancellery which was completed at astonishing speed at the beginning of January 1939.

When he first moved into the quarters occupied by preceding Chancellors, between the Foreign Ministry at No. 75 Wilhelmstrasse and Voss Strasse to the south, he declared contemptuously that they were 'fit for a soap company' but not, by implication, fit enough for him. In January 1938 he called in Speer and said he was placing the whole of the Voss Strasse at his disposal, to clear the site, design, build and equip—'cost immaterial'—a new Chancellery, within one year.

Speer, apparently undeterred by the enormity of such a task, had the north side of Voss Strasse, which had included Adolf Hitler House and Goebbels' earlier offices, demolished immediately. He then ordered large quantities of carpeting and rugs, since they would take longest to deliver, and worked out his design around them. This design incorporated 'great gates' at the entrance and a staircase surmounted by doors seventeen feet high. These opened into a reception hall done throughout in mosaic which led into a marble gallery 160 yards long, twice the length of the Hall of Mirrors at Versailles. Heroic figures sculpted by Arno Breker were used for decoration. 'It was architecture,' wrote Speer, 'that revelled in ostentation and aimed at startling effects.' Hitler, he added, was delighted.

Thousands of men worked in shifts to complete the job. Addressing them at a special Sportpalast ceremony, Hitler said each had contributed to a structure that would last for centuries, 'the first architectural creation of the new, great German Reich'. Little did he care about the 'evil omen' which worried Speer: a bust of Bismarck for the entrance hall lost its head when dropped by some of the workmen. Breker was quietly drafted in to make a copy.

In this extraordinary environment, Hitler held his cabinet meetings and, later, his wartime strategy meetings. He then went on to draw up plans for an edifice that would be even more extraordinary: a palace that would serve as his residence on the proposed North-South Axis. This would also be completed in 1950 and would be more than a hundred times bigger even than Bismarck's official residence—not counting offices. More to the point, it would be twice as big as anything envisaged by Göring.

If this was the sort of 'art' of which Hitler approved, the art of which he disapproved went up in flames on 20 March 1939. For some three years, with his and Goebbels' approval, appointed experts had been scouring the country's galleries and museums for 'unacceptable' works of art. As many as 20,000 had been collected. Some went to make up the exhibition of 'decadent art' which opened in Munich in July 1937 and then toured the country. Others were stored in a commandeered warehouse at 24a Köpenicker-Strasse and were inspected by Hitler personally in early 1938. He decreed that those which could not be sold abroad for the war effort were unusable and should be destroyed. Thus, in a ritual bonfire in the yard of Köpenicker-Strasse fire station, which was unavoidably reminiscent of the Opernplatz book-burning nearly six years before, more than 1000 oil paintings, 4000 water colours and a host of prints were burned.

The American Embassy in Berlin was in a state of near chaos on Thursday morning, 31 August 1939. Would-be refugees and other displaced persons, many of them Jewish, were besieging this and other Western embassies seeking visas or, in some cases, simply protection. There was the same sort of chaos at the main-line railway stations; here, those who were so anxious to leave included representatives from the same embassies where others were looking for sanctuary. Though the mood of the city, for weeks and months past, had been one of general anti-war gloom, the accoutrements of war were being got ready. There were more Army vehicles about the streets than usual and gun emplacements were being prepared on selected rooftops. Turrets on the out-of-use Reichstag building were brought into play.

In his address to the Reichstag in the Kroll Opera House a few months before, Hitler had gone to great lengths to spell out his achievements in and for Germany, attained 'without the misery of war'. But from that date, what he knew of what was going on in the capital was learned second-hand; he spent most of his time at Berchtesgarten.

As the summer wore on, the sullenness seemed to increase. The impression gained, and later recorded, by the British Ambassador of the time, Sir Neville Henderson, was that the mass of German people were 'horror-struck' at the whole idea of war. 'The whole general atmosphere in Berlin,' he wrote, 'was one of utter gloom and depression....'

If, as Speer suggested, Hitler was 'initially stunned' by the British and French moves towards declaring war, he can have been little comforted as he drove on 1 September to break the news to an emergency session of the Reichstag. The streets were emptier even than usual, there was little enthusiasm for the Führer or his motorcade, no shouting or cheering. 'From now on,' he told the Reichstag, 'I am just the first soldier of the German Reich.' But his calm, when he received Göring and others in the Chancellery that morning, was only skin-deep. Within minutes it had cracked into uncontrolled excitability and bellowing. Göring, equivocal at this stage about the idea of going to war, was embarrassed. And as the reality became clearer, even Goebbels was to become 'downcast'.

A guidebook published that year described Berlin as 'the world-city of the future', but that night the streets of that city were subjected to their first more or less necessary blackout. What might be called 'rehearsal' blackouts had been held intermittently for two years already. These involved everybody, at work or at home, stopping what they were doing, and taking 'shelter' in cellars, halls or garages singled out for the purpose.

Yet still the general depression, if that is what it was, had its manic aspects. Berliners flocked to fill their drinking houses, cafés and restaurants that night; there was much drunkenness in the streets. The rationing of certain foods—as well as clothing, fuel and petrol—had yet to be felt. Though the word 'war' was prohibited in German newspapers at this stage, and though newspapers from abroad were unobtainable and listening to foreign broadcasts was suddenly a punishable offence, the pretexts for such a bout of escapism were clear.

On Sunday morning, 3 September, when 'a state of war' between Germany and the Allies was formally announced, about

250 people stood outside the new Chancellery. They listened closely as the announcement was conveyed through loudspeakers, but when it was over they had nothing to say. They seemed unable to comprehend the road that had now been embarked upon. A generation before, the parents of these people had heard of the outbreak of the First War; then they had erupted into singing and dancing in the streets. Now, the marching songs which suddenly started blaring through the loudspeakers plunged many into a knowing despair. From Berlin, the prospect of the war seemed somehow unreal. William Joyce, who had recently arrived with his wife from Britain to fill his propaganda role as Lord Haw-Haw, had difficulty in getting a job.

For Goebbels there was unreality of a different sort. By January, he told his diary, Hitler was 'spoiling for the fray'. A rally was organised at the Sportpalast. 'Overflowing,' said Goebbels. 'A seething ocean of humanity. Frenetic rejoicing. Fantastic storms of applause even during my introductory speech. Then the Führer speaks. Withering attacks on London and Paris. Resolute will to victory. Most unshakable confidence. . . .'

Such orchestrated rejoicing did little to halt the decline into a brutish and self-interested cynicism. Hunger returned to the city as potatoes became scarce. Funds for the *Winterhilfe* relief scheme to help the poor in winter-time were collected by members of the Hitler Youth and went, it was widely believed, straight into arms procurement. Items like shaving soap and toilet paper became intermittently unavailable, as did shoelaces, electric wire and candles. Supplies of gramophone records, typewriters, clothing and furniture became erratic, and elastic bands, paper clips and buttons could not be found. Demand for things that were readily available—leather goods, books, theatre and concert tickets—was intense. The search for necessities was of more importance to the average Berliner than the progress at the front.

By the end of August 1940 and the first anniversary of the war, saucepans were regularly being rattled in many of the big houses of Berlin as a warning to the inhabitants to take shelter in their cellars. For the first time, bombs actually fell on the city, something that Göring, as head of the Luftwaffe, had maintained would never happen. The city's anti-aircraft defences had been penetrated, and the leadership had been proved fallible. Morale was severely shaken at all levels. Churchill was ridiculed by Hitler in another orchestrated Sportpalast event, and a sustained bombing campaign was launched against London. But Goebbels' tune was changing 'The whole of Berlin,' he noted, 'has to get out of bed and into the shelter. Terrible! ...'

The damage inflicted in those first raids was not great. The first bombs were dropped on Pankow and Lichtenberg; two days later they fell around the Görlitz station in Kreuzberg and the count was twelve dead and twenty-eight injured. The minimal distress caused by such casualties had been counter-balanced by the display of joy along the East-West Axis and Unter den Linden when a parade was held to celebrate victory in France. It was, in part, the route taken by Wilhelm I after the victory of 1870–71, and now as then there were flags and flowers in profusion, bands playing and children throwing confetti. Hitler became for a moment 'Gröfaz', an acronym for the German words, Greatest Military Leader of All Time.

It was seen as an occasion for pure and spontaneous joy—but it was a joy which came to pieces almost overnight, as quickly as the viewing platforms could be dismantled. When, on a dark and drizzly day in November, talks broke down between Hitler and the Soviet Foreign Minister, Vyacheslav Molotov, it was all suddenly clear the war would not be over for quite a while. This failure somehow meant more than the earlier 'success' in uniting Germany, Italy and Japan, and the big party at the Soviet Embassy that evening deceived no one; Hitler had stayed away.

Talk of the possibility, however remote, that Germany could lose this war was already audible in Berlin at the end of 1940. Diaries and other accounts from this time show irritability punctuating the exchanges of the Hitler–Goebbels–Göring triumvirate. There were 'serious problems', Goebbels acknowledged, in evacuating the city's children, and the Nazis' welfare organisation was not equal to the task. Göring was forced to concede that some air defences were mismanaged and warning sirens had sounded by mistake. Provincial *Gauleiter* began to complain that the leadership in Berlin did not understand their problems and was anyway too highhanded.

Within months, the air-raid mistakes were rectified; bombs started to fall on the Brandenburg Gate area and along Unter den Linden. As the screws tightened on morale, the scapegoat of 'the Jews' was revived. *Jew Süss,* a contrived anti-semitic film, was shown and party members were urged to go and see it. In early 1941, it was decreed that no Jew over the age of seven could appear in public without the mark of the star of David, depicted in black on a yellow background, the size of a man's hand, displayed and clearly visible on the chest. By October of that year, the city's Jews managed to hold their last public Yom Kippur service in Berlin. The first 'transport' of Jews to the east was authorised.

The problem of the availability of everyday items grew worse during the summer of 1941. Coal, for instance, was so short that even factories producing for the war effort were threatened; the city was virtually out of shoes; the food supply situation was growing more critical each day; beer and cigarettes became scarce; potatoes and other vegetables were unobtainable. Readily available, by contrast, were cinema seats: Berliners remained avid filmgoers, even when Goebbels' bureaucrats were telling them what they could see.

On 22 June 1941, the Barbarossa campaign was launched against the Soviet Union. It was a massive offensive against an enemy which had been in Hitler's sights ever since he first formulated a political philosophy, but it was also an offensive against a country whose emissary had been solemnly received in the city only a matter of months before. Thousands of Russians, furthermore, still lived in Berlin; they regularly crowded the Russian Orthodox Cathedral of the Resurrection in Ruhrstrasse, Wilmersdorf (which still functions today); many were without sympathy for Hitler or Stalin.

On the night of Barbarossa, Goebbels drove out to his villa at Schwanenwerder by the Wannsee to see the sun rise and hear the dawn chorus. An hour or so before, he had left Hitler at the Chancellery. 'The Führer's mood,' he recorded, 'is very solemn.... An oppressively hot day. Our soldiers will not find the fighting easy.' Small wonder that the Kaiser's death, reported a fortnight or so earlier, had caused scarcely a ripple in the city where he once meant so much.

Across a wide stretch of the river Havel from Goebbels' villa, in an equally pleasant semi-rural setting, stands another large house, with the address Am Grossen Wannsee, No. 56–58. It was then known as the Villa Minoux and contained the German offices of Interpol. (Until very recently, it has been used as a recreation centre for schoolchildren from the less well-off Neukölln area of the city, but there are plans to make it a memorial centre for Jews who died at Nazi hands.)

On 20 January 1942 senior officials gathered here from the Ministries of Justice, Foreign Affairs and the Eastern Territories, together with others from Hitler's own staff and the party machine. The meeting was under the chairmanship of Reinhard Heydrich, a still young but ruthlessly ambitious naval intelligence officer who was now head of the SD security police. He had been a leading organiser of the *Reichskristallnacht* of 1938; now he assumed the role of presiding genius in shaping the 'final solution' of the Jewish problem.

The aim of the conference was to organise a way of clearing all Jews out of Europe, 'from West to East'. To the extent that six million of them died before the war ended, the aim was achieved. The house itself, undamaged by the bombing, stands today as an accusing monument to the worst excesses of Nazism. But the insidious ripples remain: long after the end of the war, a memorial plaque which had been erected at the gateway to the drive of the house was daubed with Nazi slogans, and later stolen. A replacement plaque, fixed to the wall of the house itself, cannot be seen from the road. As for Heydrich, he died within six months of holding the meeting—assassinated in Prague where he was the acting Reich 'protector' of Czechoslovakia. Five hundred Berlin Jews, and countless others in Germany and Czechoslovakia, were immediately executed in response.

As Heydrich's death was being planned in Prague, Goebbels mounted an exhibition on the theme of 'the Soviet Paradise' in the Berlin Lustgarten, where at this period there were billets for members of the Reichswehr and which was used by them as a parade ground. The intention was to win support for the war against the Soviet Union, something which could not be stomached by the communists associated with a group of Jewish resistants who were soon to become known as the Baum group. Half a dozen of these went to the site and planted incendiary and explosive devices at various points, burning down one of the barrack huts and killing five Nazis. A week later, 250 Jews were shot at the Lichterfelde camp as a reprisal and the Baums and friends arrested. A month afterwards, the authorities said Baum had committed suicide; friends say he was tortured to death.

The year 1943 began badly in Berlin. On successive nights in January, British bombers were able to destroy the popular (morale-helping) sports venue, the Deutschlandhalle, built in 1935 on the exhibition grounds near the Radio Centre, as well as residential areas situated in Tempelhof and Dahlem. Then, at the end of the month, after an historic battle lasting several months, newspaper reports appeared with black borders around them telling of the Sixth Army's defeat at Stalingrad. It was the decisive turning-point in the war and, despite the outright rejection of Allied demands for Hitler's unconditional surrender, there was a creeping sense of panic in the city. A deep-seated fear of the Russians took a firmer hold on many of its people. Posters went up ordering all Berlin men between sixteen and sixty-five and women up to forty-five to report for 'defence' duties. School-children from the age of fifteen were drafted to learn anti-aircraft searchlight drill. New dimensions of anxiety and uncertainty were introduced into already dislocated family lives.

On 18 February Goebbels brought together several thousand of the party's most committed supporters for a rally at the Sport-palast to proclaim 'total war'. His ten rhetorical questions to weed out any lurking doubters drew an affirmative frenzy of shouted support for Hitler and Nazi policies. But from the provinces came reports of an inherently subversive disenchantment. Goebbels himself was becoming the butt of popular jokes. Songs were being sung urging '*lieber Tommy*' to go ahead and bomb Berlin. Deteriorating food supplies and further cuts in strictly controlled rations sharpened the cynicism still further. An increasing number of black marketeers came into their own, often forced to operate in the city's streets and parks as many bars, cafés, restaurants and dance halls—but not yet the theatres and concert halls—were closed.

The raids did not let up. In a matter of weeks, well over 20,000 houses were damaged in the inner city area. Hundreds of people died or were injured and thousands made homeless. 'In March 1943,' wrote Joel König, a Jew who had stayed on illegally in the city, 'a number of districts of Berlin became great wastes of rubble. It was like a miracle that the tram system was largely spared. When the tramcar went through a destroyed part of the city, the passengers crowded to the windows and let their gaze wander over disgorged trams and row after row of hollow-eyed house fronts. . . . But none of them said a word of anger or horror. They did not even exchange glances, but just looked out and were silent. It was an uncanny silence, filled with anxiety and bitterness. But bitterness against whom? . . .'

Demolition squads and firemen, stretcher bearers and odd-job men, fixing and refixing supplies of electricity, water or gas, became permanent features of the landscape. Sometimes little knots of people would gather round someone who was weeping, but more usually the atmosphere was one of calm. The streets seemed always to be full of people, some going places, some standing and staring. At one point, when the Zoo was bombed, there were wild animals going quietly berserk in the streets. But the incongruous had ceased to be abnormal. There was an acid smell in the air after the bombs had fallen, dropped, as Goebbels put it, by 'cowardly terrorists'.

The evacuation of all Berliners not engaged in the war, and especially women, children and old people, was now given priority. Posters appeared in every street. Between the beginning of August and the end of October, 700,000 people were taken out of the city, and by the end of the year half as many again. There was chaos once again at all main railway stations, intensified by the influx of thousands of refugees who had been blitzed out of their homes in the big raids on Hamburg.

The removal of the Jews also continued, and towards the end of the year Goebbels announced that Berlin was *judenfrei*—clear of Jews. By this time, the Gestapo had closed down all Jewish offices except the hospital (which still stands) in Iranische Strasse in Wedding. The Jews who remained here were officially described as inmates of the Jewish Police Prison; there was a Gestapo office in the grounds.

In the operational sense, it has been suggested that the Battle of Berlin—initiated by the RAF from mid-November 1943—was 'more than a failure, it was a defeat'. Berlin, it is argued, won because it was 'too tough a nut to crack'. Maybe—but in the space of two weeks, more than 3000 died as a direct result of the bombing and as many were hurt. A quarter of a million people lost their homes, more than doubling the number of the city's homeless. And the bombing went on, with few interruptions, until the end of March 1944.

Eye-witnesses later spoke for themselves. On Monday 22 November 1943, Konrad Warner wrote: 'I ran first to the Zoo Station which, clearly, had not been hit. But round about, all the buildings were burning. The Kaiser Wilhelm Gedächtnis Church was in bright flames, the Ufa-Palace (cinema complex) by the Zoo was a mere ruin already. I went on, through Joachimstaler Strasse to the Kurfürstendamm. Here too houses were burning, the sky was red, but because of heavy cloud and dense smoke, one couldn't see far. I looked into the side streets, but could not see through the impenetrable black curtain out of which bright red flames darted every so often. I ran into the Kaiserallee, where a great draught of air full of sparks gushed towards me from the buildings burning on both sides. Trolley-bus cables lay on the ground, trees had been torn down, branches ripped off. The road crunched under my feet, because it was completely covered in broken glass. I rushed and stumbled on, a handkerchief over my mouth and eyes, my hat pulled well down and my coat collar turned up. . . .'

The next morning, Hans-Georg von Studnitz reported: 'Around the destroyed Alexanderplatz S-bahn station, the big department stores are blazing [though the police headquarters was still serviceable!] . . . In the city centre, Schlüter's splendid castle, one-time residence of the Hohenzollerns, still stands in the middle of a great storm of smoke and sparks. Huge flames rise up out of one wing. We cross the Spree and see the banking quarter is ablaze. The Armoury, the university, the Hedwiga Cathedral, the 'Kommode' and the National Library are already reduced to ashes. Clouds of smoke obscure the view from Unter den Linden into the Friedrichstrasse and the Wilhelmstrasse. On the Pariser Platz, the IG Farben building is in flames. The Adlon, opposite, seems unharmed. The French Embassy, the Friedländer Palais, the casino, the guard houses built by Schinkel on either side of the Brandenburg Gate, show for the last time the graceful lines of their design against the fiery background. . . .

'Of the hotels, only the Esplanade, the Adlon, part of the Kaiserhof are still standing. Almost all ministries, almost all banks, the old Chancellery, the Palace of Wilhelm I, the Palace at Charlottenburg, the area around the Lützow Platz are all rubble. The embassies and diplomatic missions have with few exceptions been reduced to ashes. The Italian and Japanese embassies have suffered terribly. In Ribbentrop's palace, the roof has been burnt out, and the upper floors of No. 74 Wilhelmstrasse. . . . Thousands of lorries are blocking the streets; an army of soldiers, prisoners-of-war, convicts are fighting fires, humping furniture, leading people to safety. Everyone is amazingly calm.'

'We started out,' wrote Marie Vassiltchikov of 26 November 'dragging our luggage through the mud and ashes of the Tiergarten. The houses on all sides were black and still smoking. The park looked like a battlefield in France in the 1914–1918 war, the trees stark and gaunt, and broken-off branches everywhere over which we had to clamber. I wondered what had happened to the famous rhododendrons and what it would be like in the spring. As transport was non-existent, we had to walk all the way.... The whole neighbourhood (around the Potsdamer Platz station) was one smouldering mass of ruins....'

But Berlin being Berlin, and Goebbels being the *Gauleiter* he was, the show had to go on. There was a pointed lack of tragedies included in the repertoire of what could still be seen in the theatre, for understandable reasons, but there was still a cabaret for the soldiers in the Behrenstrasse, and the theatre on the Nollendorfplatz, for instance, still offered singing, dancing and laughter even as houses in the neighbourhood continued to burn in the November gloom. People's faces, meanwhile, were pale— 'unhealthy white as flour, except for red rings around their tired, lifeless eyes'.

Women in lurid make-up prostituted themselves—they still do—along the Kurfürstendamm. They and fastidiously elegant 'swingboys' picked their way among the crowds of the bombed-out or shell-shocked homeless and the hopelessly bewildered. Had George Grosz returned, with the same eye that he had ten years or so before, he would have had great scope for depicting the half-life Berliners were now living. Cigarettes became a sought-after currency, and a sophisticated underworld flourished. All sorts of clothing, food and drink changed hands; an unknown quantity had been taken from homes or shops now exposed to the four winds, but deserted by their owners. There seemed to be even more foreigners in the city than normal—drawn from countries now occupied and collaborating with the Nazis, or from the ranks of their prisoners-of-war. One estimate is that the 2.8 million Berliners were at this time complemented by 800,000 foreigners.

By the end of March 1944 well over 6000 of the civilian population had died in raids, 18,000 had been severely injured, and more than one and a half million—equivalent to one in every three of the population—were homeless. Of just over 100 manufacturing companies directly involved in the war effort, more than thirty had been hit, and half of nearly 600 other producing companies in the city had been badly damaged. But then, on 6 June, came the Normandy landings, furtively and illegally followed on the radio. The swastika seemed suddenly to be less in evidence in the city streets.

The 20 July plot of 1944 was the strongest sign yet of a growing resistance to Hitler among the military. It was Claus Schenk, Count of Stauffenberg, who planted the fatal briefcase and came nearer than anyone to killing Hitler. Four of the protagonists were shot at night, in the light from the headlamps of an armoured car, at the offices of the Reichswehr in Bendlerstrasse. Since 1955 Bendlerstrasse has been called Stauffenbergstrasse in memory of the Count. The rest of the plotters were held and often tortured at Plötzensee, tried, and then executed in the small outhouse. Today, this outhouse is kept clinically clean. Bus tours of the city include it in their itineraries, but otherwise it is rather off the beaten track. A busy motorway nearby breaks the silence, though during the drawn-out process of the executions, if there was any silence then, it tended to be broken by the 'jokes' of the hangman or the agony of those who died. Piano-wire was used and some deaths could take twenty minutes.

One of those executed was the high-living Count Wolf-Heinrich von Helldorff, who had had a chequered career as a distinguished officer in the First War, then as a *Freikorps* commander, participant in the Kapp putsch, exile, and devoted Nazi. Röhm, before he was murdered, had made him head of the stormtroopers in Berlin, and he was president of the city's police force from 1935. He had also been a member for a while of the Reichstag, but became disillusioned after the excesses of the 1938 *Reichskristallnacht*. Differences with Hitler and with Goebbels pushed him towards the plotters, even though, because of his weak character, he was not always trusted. On more than one occasion he openly declared that Hitler was a menace to Germany and had to go, and at the end, he was forced to watch the other plotters being executed before he himself, as last in the queue, took his turn.

The July plot led to the execution of at least 200 people and, according to SS figures, the arrest of 7000 others. Central to the plotters' success would have been the so-called Valkyrie Operation, which entailed the military occupation of the whole of Berlin. This would mean, in the first instance, sealing off the Wilhelmstrasse government area, reminiscent of the similar act carried out by Goebbels in January 1933. Army loyalists would then take over the affairs of state, having first immobilised the SS and the Gestapo, and dissolved the Nazi Party. They were also to shoot Goebbels.

The operation failed for a number of reasons. First, Colonel-

General Fritz Fromm, a senior Army staff officer in the Bend-lerstrasse, refused to co-operate; second, no account had been taken of the energies and resourcefulness of Goebbels (who was able to rally and organise the counter-plotters with a rousing speech made in his back garden the very next day); third, most importantly, Hitler though maimed was still very much alive.

Streets in Berlin and elsewhere have since been named after the men of 20 July, but as Golo Mann has asked, who remembers today who these people were? The Bristol Hotel on Unter den Linden, where the might-have-been Chancellor, the enigmatic Carl Goerdeler, stayed under another name, was bombed out of existence. His written thoughts were recovered from a hotel safe which was dug out of the rubble. Stauffenberg's house, however, at No. 8 Tristanstrasse, in Zehlendorf, still stands, as does the home of General Ludwig Beck, once Hitler's Chief of Army General Staff and the likely head of state had the plot succeeded. He was said to be the 'heart and soul' of the opposition, and lived at No. 24 Goethestrasse in a quiet corner of Lichterfelde.

In August 1944 Goebbels was appointed *Regierungspräsident* (government leader) as well as police chief, for Berlin. Having not long before called up all pensioners for active service, he now proceeded to intensify the local war effort by declaring that all arts 'events' such as theatre festivals and new exhibitions, all theatres, music halls and cabarets, all orchestral performances, should be halted forthwith. Office working hours were increased to sixty a week in the national interest.

In mid-January 1945, Hitler, who was seen by those around him to be growing more and more remote and inaccessible, returned to Berlin. He went to tea with the Goebbels for the first time in five years, with his own vacuum flask, but he did not move beyond the precincts of the Chancellery, or the vast underground bunker behind it, again. He made his last radio broadcast, marking the twelfth anniversary of taking power, on 30 January. A few days later he was stunned to hear that the judge at the People's Court, Roland Freisler, who not long before had sentenced the remaining July plotters to death on Hitler's orders, had himself been killed in an American daylight raid.

The city's population by now was swelling uncontrollably with the constant arrival of new refugees. Many were joining relatives who had been living in Berlin for a generation or more, and an ironic twist was added to the belief, idly cherished in many parts of the city, that the 'best Berliners' were from Silesia anyway. It was a further savage twist that many hundreds of these same refugees, camping in the city streets and courtyards, were to die in the daylight raids that were still to come.

As news came through that the Soviet Army had established a bridgehead at Wriezen, west of the Oder River, and just forty miles from the city outskirts, consternation grew at the startling defencelessness of the city. 'Between Wriezen and Berlin,' said one of Goebbels' lieutenants, 'there is nothing: no anti-tank defences, no obstacles and not a single soldier.' A hurried council of war voted that retired soldiers and Army instructors, some of whom had learned their trade under the Kaiser, should return to the aid of the city. Tanks standing at railway stations, waiting to leave for no longer feasible destinations, were commandeered. So were the city's buses, to transport the men to the front. Women and children were ordered to dig trenches.

Four defensive rings circled the city on paper, with the 'Zitadelle', or heavily guarded fortified government quarter, at its centre. It did not seem to matter that the enemy no longer considered Berlin an important military objective: Lieutenant-General Helmut Reymann, commanding the city area, ordered preparations to defend it 'to the last man and the last shot'. If there had to be house-to-house fighting, then so be it. But at the end, half of the estimated 90,000 often makeshift troops who had been deployed to defend the city in mid-April were without arms, and by Hitler's fifty-sixth birthday, tersely and dramatically celebrated in the underground bunker, the Soviet troops had reached Frohnau and Niederschönhausen, in the north of the city, and Lichtenberg in the east. People queuing for groceries in these areas ran for their lives when the Red Army appeared.

That day, in the half-destroyed Schauspielhaus concert hall— today magnificently restored—stars of the Berlin Opera company came together to perform extracts from Verdi's *Aïda* and from Mozart's *Magic Flute*. A few days earlier, the Berlin Philharmonic Orchestra had given its last concert, consisting of Beethoven's Violin Concerto, a Brückner symphony, and, appropriately enough, the finale from *Götterdämmerung*. For the latter, the audience sat shivering in overcoats. Members of the orchestra, once the concert was over, joined the forces on a tattered, and ever closer, front line.

There was an incongruous luxury about the escapism of listening to music in a city reeling from eighty-five heavy bombing raids in fewer than that number of days. Now, with the Soviet artillery advancing through the suburbs, the exigencies of daily living had become ever more pressing. Berlin had become a city which could only survive by cowering in its cellars. Those who could not get food went hungry and whose who could not get water were often dirty as well. Looting, by troops as well as civilians, was more or less acceptable behaviour. Heating and light, if they were still available, were no longer authorised. What public transport was still in service could only be used by special pass-holders.

And yet still there were isolated pockets of life 'as usual'. In March, a Heroes' Day ceremony was held in Unter den Linden, attended by 120 troops under the Berlin commandant, Lieutenant-General Reymann. A wreath was laid by Göring, but with an uncharacteristic lack of ostentation. One or two cinemas were still open, some even showing comedies. A bank in the Mitte area advertised for a new cleaning woman; the Post Office solemnly announced that parcels delivery might be difficult in some places; and tips for new allotment-holders appeared in the press.

On 22 April bills and posters appeared in the streets announcing that the hour before sunrise is the darkest hour. 'Berliners, take note,' they read, 'anyone who takes steps to weaken our capacity to resist, is a traitor. He will be shot or hanged instantly.' Within hours the bodies of former SS and Party members were hanging from lampposts and trees with pieces of paper or cardboard attached to their clothing, denouncing them as saboteurs or cowards. Those of the living who could afford it bought petrol, and sometimes even motor vehicles, and tried, though it was deemed treachery, to leave the city. Suicides were frequent.

One by one Hitler's aides, who only days before had joined him on his birthday, deserted him. Göring, Himmler and Ribbentrop left the city, and the first two of these, once cornerstones in the building of the 1000-year Reich, were stripped by Hitler in his 'political testament' of party membership. Goebbels, indefatigable to the end, stayed: he was Hitler's own nominee to succeed as Chancellor of the Reich. Another who stayed was Martin Bormann, who had made himself, through a career in the party organisation, indispensable.

On 23 April Goebbels, in his capacity as Defence Commissar, issued a further order to all Berliners. Urging every one of them to fight to the last, he concluded: 'Your *Gauleiter* is with you. With his fellow-workers, he will naturally stay among you. Even his wife and children are here. He, the man who once conquered this city with 200 men, will now do all he can to activate the defence of the Reich capital. The battle for Berlin must set the tone for the nation's last stand; it is for Germany. The capital must not fall into the hands of the Bolsheviks.' Eight days later, Goebbels had murdered his six children in the bunker, and he and his wife committed suicide.

When his words of 23 April appeared, the Soviet troops had already taken large areas of Pankow, Weissensee and Lichtenberg in the east central parts of the city and were moving into Zehlendorf, Tempelhof and Neukölln to the south. Units in the north and west (closing in by way of Charlottenburg and Siemensstadt) were also advancing steadily. German forces, hampered by a lack of weapons as well as essential manpower, could do little. Hitler Youth messengers on bicycles rarely had anything good to report.

Hitler was still the Führer and Supreme Commander of the Nazi forces. For some months, however, he had been seen as walking awkwardly, stooping, with jerky and slow gestures. Captain Gerhard Boldt, a young officer, was introduced to Hitler a few weeks before his suicide. He wrote later: 'His head was slightly wobbling, his left arm hung slackly and his hand trembled a good deal. There was an indescribable flickering glow in his eyes, creating a fearsome and wholly unnatural effect. His face and the parts around his eyes gave the impression of total exhaustion. All his movements were those of a senile man.'

By 28 April, white flags were appearing at the city centre's glassless windows with increasing frequency. The Soviet profusion of red flags continued its advance, in some areas without great difficulties. Spandau, Gatow airport and much of Schöneberg were now taken, and, after some fierce fighting at close quarters, so were the Alexanderplatz and the Halle Gate. Some Berliners had enough ammunition for two days. Others had none. There was almost no food or medicines for the increasing number of wounded lying about the city streets.

On that day, General Nikolai Bersarin issued his first Order as City Commandant of Berlin. He had directed the 5th Shock Army across eastern Germany and the unit which finally captured the Gestapo headquarters in Prinz-Albrecht-Strasse (even as terrified bureaucrats were burning whatever files they could lay their hands on). 'All administrative and political authority,' the Soviet order stated, 'passes into my hands ... the population of the city will maintain complete order and will remain in their own homes.... The Nazi Party and all affiliated organisations are dissolved ...' and so on. One copy was pasted on a wall in the blitzed Alexanderplatz and as a crowd gathered to hear its contents read out in German, the fighting elsewhere in the city continued.

On Sunday 29 April Hitler married his long-standing woman friend, Eva Braun. She was someone he had rarely allowed to be seen in Berlin—preferring to keep her in Munich—but she had turned up a day or two before the Soviet pounding of the Chancellery and bunker began. Soon after this marriage, the Führer called his last war conference. In the words of Berlin's last German commandant, General Helmut Weidling, he looked 'like a man completely resigned to his fate'. Weidling told him the fighting would be over in twenty-four hours, and SS Colonel Wilhelm Mohnke, commanding the forces who were to hold the Zitadelle itself, could only agree. The bunker which at one stage had an HQ staff of more than 600 began to feel eerily empty.

The next day Hitler and his wife committed suicide together. Their bodies, which were never found, are assumed to have been cremated in a trench dug at the bunker entrance. That evening, at 10.50 p.m., a Soviet victory banner was raised high above the Reichstag building. In the basement of the same building, in pitch darkness, some final skirmishes were still being played out. By this time, Walter Ulbricht, one-time Spartacist, Reichstag member and leader of the Communist Party in Berlin, was ready with fellow members of the Communist Action Group, to leave Moscow. He was to dominate political life in Berlin for well over twenty years.

FOUR

1945-1949

Deutschland Deutschland ohne alles
Ohne Butter ohne Speck
Und das bißchen Marmelade
Frißt uns die Besatzung weg[1]

The senses of everyone who was in Berlin on or soon after 1 May 1945 were benumbed by the experience. In the old centre of the city, and in several of the adjoining areas, there was devastation on a scale that no one had ever seen before. In dry weather, the air was filled with dust and dirt and, as the summer wore on, with the insidious stench of human and animal corpses, rotting where they had fallen or been buried beneath countless tons of rubble. 'A no-man's land on the edge of the world,' wrote Willy Brandt, later the city's Governing Mayor, of that scene, 'with every little garden a graveyard.'

The few sounds of the city were odd, too: a paucity of traffic meant that human voices were more audible, as was the constant chip-chipping of the thousands of rubble women who were drafted in to restore to a usable condition the bricks and stonework of ruined buildings. The 'world city' their parents had not so long ago talked and thought about, like the projected Germania, at the centre of the thousand-year-Reich, were mocking irrelevancies now.

'Berlin as a city,' said Air Marshal Arthur Tedder, Deputy Supreme Commander of the Allied Expeditionary Forces, as he looked about him that May, 'has been utterly destroyed. The ruins that were Berlin should be preserved as a modern Babylon or Carthage—a monument to Prussian militarism and the evil Nazi regime. The city is completely dead. One drives for miles

[1] Germany, Germany, ain't got nothing, Got no butter, got no ham. And now the occupying powers, Have gone and pinched our bit of jam.

through desolate and smoking ruins and finds nothing habitable.
It can never be reconstructed. . . .'

In the Kremlin, Stalin, who hitherto had listened to Tedder
with great respect, must have been bemused by these remarks.
His own generals were by now firmly based in the city and were
advising him quite otherwise. Within days of the red flag being
raised over the Reichstag, before the formal signing of the Instru-
ment of Surrender (on 8 May), the machinery had been set in
motion to feed the people in an organised way and to restore the
public utilities—transport, gas and electricity, sewerage, etc.—to
some sort of serviceable degree. Huge portraits of Stalin as much
as twenty times life-size and durably mounted and framed, were
being erected. Certainly they would be removed in due course,
but not in the short term.

The city's population at the war's end was about 2,300,000,
barely more than half what it had been in the summer of 1939. At
least 750,000 had chosen to leave the city in the course of the war,
many in the last three desperate months. Now that hostilities
were over, many were to return. Thousands—sometimes tens of
thousands—came each day into the city, either displaced Berliners
who had evacuated, or pathetic refugees from other parts of
Germany—perhaps in flight from the Soviet Army—who wanted
somehow to start again. Receiving such lost souls was a role Berlin
had played in the past; now, it seemed, it had little choice but to
play it once again.

There are no exact figures for how many Berliners died in the
course of the war. Records of deaths, when they were kept, were
lost in the inferno or, if they were not lost, became a matter of
state security. Police files now indicated, however, that at least
50,000 died as a direct result of Allied air raids. Thousands of
others must have died in the final Soviet offensive. And then the
Jews: of a population of 160,564 in mid-1933, only 5000 now
remained. About 90,000 had been forced to leave the city, and
well over 50,000 had been murdered in the camps.

Almost a quarter of all the city's buildings had been destroyed,
and half of its houses were damaged, many beyond repair. Out of
1,500,000 homes, some 600,000 had been totally destroyed and at
least 100,000 more were badly damaged. Today, there are still
great gaps between some of the older houses, sometimes open
spaces bigger than a parade ground. Here and there one comes
across four- and five-storey buildings reduced to one storey, and

jagged ends of masonry rear up from an undergrowth of weeds. That is where whole streets have not been obliterated. In some districts, where once there was overcrowding and congestion, there is now quite frequently only a disturbing emptiness. Where once there were buildings of 'style' and ornate flamboyance, there are the straighter lines of economy or, where money has been spent lavishly, the more self-indulgent excesses of 'modern architecture'. Berlin has paid for the Second World War in many ways.

In the centre of the city, the war had an untidy end. The fighting, usually between the Soviet troops and remnants of SS units, went on for at least two days after the raising of the Reichstag flag. Often there were frantic one-to-one engagements with fists flying in total blackness, particularly inside some of the bunkers, from which sheltering citizens had been cleared so that ramshackle ad hoc units of troops could make a final stand. Under the Landwehr Canal, SS men planted explosives, flooding the underground railway system, drowning countless hundreds, many of them wounded and helpless, who thought they had found a safe refuge. At the Alexanderplatz station, other SS men carried out 'executions' of German communists in the murky darkness.

At the same time, less repugnant but often strange things were happening. One contingent of Soviet troops spent some of the morning of that May Day—a traditional holiday on the Soviet calendar—sitting down by the Brandenburg Gate, listening to a poetry recital; elsewhere, they brought out accordions and there was, literally, singing and dancing in the streets. Vodka and other hard liquor began to flow. One unit celebrated in the ruins of the Kaiser Wilhelm Gedächtnis Church; another was in the Tiergarten, securely based, for the time being anyway, in what used to be the aquarium.

At 5 a.m. on 2 May, in their new headquarters at No. 2 Schulenburgring, close to Tempelhof Airport, General Vassili Chuikov and General Vassili Sokolovski (both of whom became Marshals of the Soviet Union) received General Weidling. He had been a career soldier for thirty-four years, joining up in 1911, and had seen two German empires come and go. Asked by the Soviet generals whether he now thought the Second World War was over, he replied that in his opinion further sacrifices would be an act of folly and a crime. He then wrote out, and tape-recorded at an old film studio in the south of the city, a military order 'to cease all resistance forthwith'. It was his voice and his message that Berliners heard as loudspeaker vans picked their way to all corners of the shattered city. Forty years on, in 1985, a commemorative plaque was fixed to the wall at No. 2 Schulenburgring.

'It was quiet in Berlin at last,' Chuikov wrote in his memoirs, describing the situation at noon that 1945 day. 'We went out into the street. We could see red flags, the banners of victory flying over government buildings, the Reichstag and the Imperial Chancellery. All was quiet....' The unconditional surrender of all German land, sea, and air forces was signed in a small schoolhouse in northern France five days later.

The 'final act' was signed sixteen minutes after midnight the following day in Berlin, in the canteen of a plain three-storey building which until very recently had been the Wehrmacht's engineering college, at Karlshorst. The building is now a museum, run by the Soviets and visited daily by groups of East German schoolchildren who snake their way through its fourteen sombre rooms to see the proffered evidence of the horrors of Nazism, the tactical brilliance of Marshal Zhukov, who led the final assault of Berlin, and the 'liberation' which was effected by the Soviet Army. There are 15,000 exhibits in all, one of them the replica of a three-ton statue of Lenin, which was wrested from the Nazis who had wanted to melt it down for ammunition. There is, interestingly, little about Generalissimo Stalin.

The dark-panelled room where the signing took place—despite a last-minute show of arrogance by Field Marshal Wilhelm Keitel—is still decorated with the US, Soviet, British and French flags, with furniture arranged as it was on that day. A small separate table, covered in green baize, was used by the Germans. They did not take part in the champagne and caviare banquet organised by Marshal Zhukov immediately after the signing was done.

Eight critical weeks were now to pass before the arrival of the Allied occupation forces in the city. To a request from President Truman that they be allowed to establish themselves in the city somewhat sooner, Stalin replied on 16 June that 'regretfully' this would be difficult. Marshal Zhukov and other military commanders, he said, had been summoned to Moscow for a meeting of the Supreme Soviet and a parade which was to follow. 'Moreover,' Stalin declared, 'some of the districts of Berlin have not yet been cleared of mines, nor can the mine-clearing operations be finished until late June.'

That same day, the first Soviet Commandant of Berlin, General Bersarin, was killed—not by a mine but in a motor accident. His tenure had lasted just over six weeks, but he had gained the reputation of a man more concerned for the people than he was for ideological considerations. However true, or relevant, that may be, much happened during his time as commandant which was to set the seal on Berlin's longer-term future. He authorised seeds to be planted which enabled the city to become, without too much procedural discomfort, the capital of today's East Germany.

His troops knew, as Bersarin himself knew, that Nazi troops in the Soviet Union had massacred, burned, raped and pillaged as they advanced. In Berlin at the same war's end, Soviet soldiers exacted an often unrefined revenge. Where in the 1920s and 1930s Soviets of all sorts of persuasion and Berliners had gravitated towards each other and positively, creatively, had enjoyed each other's company, they now acted out the hostility and the hatred which had been so vigorously encouraged by Hitler and Goebbels, and which, in many parts of the city, has yet to evaporate.

Hitler's campaign against the Soviet Union had been launched four years before and the Soviet urge for revenge had been boiling up throughout that time. Now, in a few weeks in May, thousands of Berlin women, possibly tens of thousands, were raped; tens of thousands of men and women, assumed to have been active Nazis or collaborators, were shipped off—if they were not shot—to requisitioned Nazi concentration camps; factories and offices were plundered repeatedly in the name of reparations; and an administration which the local Soviet authorities deemed appropriate was installed. It was not until 25 May that Bersarin's office announced the setting up of a police force and a public prosecutor's office 'in the interests of a quick return to normal life in the city, to suppress crime and maintain public order'.

Hundreds of thousands of Berliners somehow survived this period in the sort of wretched circumstances that could hardly have been seen since the encampments on the city perimeter in the late nineteenth century. There was overcrowding on a scale that had not been endured since the 1920s. Many continued to live in cellars or in improvised holes in the ground, too frightened to emerge. For weeks, among the dirt and rubble, the litter of the streets included corpses, burnt-out military and civilian vehicles, bicycles, and household belongings, either blasted out of their original settings, or discarded as beyond use. Gas, electricity and water utilities were non-existent where the fighting had been most intense, or the bombing most successful, and in many areas sewage facilities were out of service. Belongings were aimlessly carried about on bicycles, where they had not been commandeered, by wheelbarrow, pram or home-made handcart. A lack of hospital beds and medicines—as well as qualified doctors—meant few sick or wounded people received treatment. The registration of births and, more frequently, deaths was haphazard and burials were often improvised. Bodies were interred in drawers or boxes when coffins were not available, and the burial itself was often in house gardens, or wherever 'suitable' land—not required for growing food—could quickly be found. Sometimes several bodies were buried together. Others, festering in the city's rivers or canals, were not buried at all for some weeks, if then.

Two needs were more pressing than all others: food and fuel. Within days of the end of the fighting, a ration system had been worked out—with food allowances varying strictly according to the recipient's function. It meant, for one thing, that there was no shortage of people, almost all of them women, to clear the city's millions of tons of rubble, because they got extra rations for doing such work. The initial basic daily ration was the equivalent of two biggish potatoes (400 grams) per head; 200 grams of bread; 25 grams of meat; 10 grams each of sugar and salt; and just 2 grams of coffee. One result was that horses, too weak to be of further service, were torn apart in the street or wherever they collapsed, to provide extra meat.

Looting was on such a scale that some department stores had to be blown up, contents and all, as a deterrent. Field kitchens set up by Soviet troop units could be generous when the individual being fed was willing to surrender a watch or a bicycle, or to be raped, in exchange for food. Every available space was sown into allotments, including large areas of the once beloved Tiergarten and, where there was soil, parts even of the Alexanderplatz.

The need for fuel, for warmth as well as cooking, was satisfied to some extent by taking what could be salvaged from ruined buildings and from the several street barricades that had been thrown together, often by children still in their early teens, to deter the Soviet tanks. At least now the barricades had a real usefulness. Trees in the city which had not been torn apart by bombs or by shell-fire were likely to be further plundered with axes and saws so that they could provide some sort of heat. Clearly, the would-be allotment holders in the Tiergarten were delighted, but anyone who had savoured the special delights of walking in the city's parks, from the Kaiser himself to Rosa Luxemburg, would surely have been deeply distressed by such destruction, as well as the reasons why it had come to pass.

Not long ago, some friends spent a rainy Sunday afternoon in the Tiergarten, looking for the 'tree memorial'. This had been erected by the West Berlin Senate in 1951 after the whole park had been 'resurrected' (Baedeker's word) with the planting of more than a million new trees and shrubs. When my friends found the memorial, it was already rather shabby, much of its inscription illegible because of dirt and encroaching weeds. It lists more than forty West German towns, cities and regional authorities who donated trees and plants as the replanting got under way, thereby demonstrating their 'solidarity with Berlin'. And the mention here of 'Berlin' is, incidentally, something of a collector's item, pre-dating as it does the international endorsement later of the title West Berlin for the 'political entity' at whose heart the memorial is situated.

While Stalin's officers in the broken capital set about imple-menting plans that had been hatching on Soviet soil over the preceding two years, the Western Allies sought on a day-to-day basis to extricate themselves from the messy end to the war in other parts of Germany. More than three weeks after the surrender of General Weidling, in charge of the city, on 2 May, there were still pockets of resistance—in northern Germany and Yugoslavia, for instance—that had to be dealt with.

When the US Army sent a reconnaissance group off to Berlin from just west of the Elbe River in mid-June, it was met, according to eye-witnesses, by 'hostile obstruction' from the Soviet troops and officials for most of the way and only a small number got through. 'The road to Berlin,' wrote Colonel Frank Howley, who was to command the first American military detachment in the city, 'was the highroad to Bedlam ... jam-packed with tanks, trucks and other vehicles ... Russian officers, in captured ram-shackle cars and trucks, raced up and down to see we weren't escaping with plunder ... the road was paved with drunks.... A disagreeable summer rain was pelting down when we finally straggled into Berlin late in the afternoon. The Russians had not allowed us to look over our sector before coming in, and none of us knew exactly where to go....'

Those words described the first two or three days of July and say something about the intractable situation that confronted the Western Allies. By that time, the Soviet generals in the city knew precisely what they were doing. Walter Ulbricht and company were willing enough to comply.

Political, economic and structural changes in the running of Berlin in the weeks between the end of hostilities and the installation of the Allied occupation powers were sweeping and usually unambiguous, benefitting both the people of the devastated city and the Soviet policy-makers. Since the Soviet Union had suffered so outrageously from Hitler's war—20 million, or 10 per cent of the population, dead—the price the Germans had to pay was inevitably high. Since the Soviet Union had also been so severely weakened, from the strategic and economic points of view, its determination that such a thing as Barbarossa, and its consequences, should never be allowed to happen again, was total. That determination has governed Soviet attitudes to Europe ever since.

In Moscow, Stalin had set up at the end of 1944 a State Commission to oversee the dismantling of German industry and the payment, as appropriate, of reparations to the Soviet Union. In Berlin, he now had Soviet units deployed in all twenty districts, with approved supervisors (*Obleute*) in almost every street. A few days after the Karlshorst signing, he despatched Anastas Mikoyan, a senior Politburo member, to see how the work was going. Dismantling, he was told, was well in hand at Borsig, AEG, Osram and Siemens, and, in general, the German Communist Party (the KPD) was already ideologically well placed to assist the Soviet political effort. At the centre of this party was the Ulbricht 'Free Germany' Group, which had been formed at a meeting in Krasnogorsk, near Moscow, in 1943, and was now installed in offices in Friedrichsfelde at No. 80 Prinzenallee (now No. 41 Einbeckerstrasse).

This group and its activists had set about their task with energy, seeking out old communists and coaxing new ones into life at all hours of the day and night. When the first Soviet-authorised City Council met on 17 May, it was Karl Maron, an old pre-1933

Communist, who sat as deputy at the elbow of the first post-war Lord Mayor, a known non-communist conservative called Arthur Werner. Maron's closest lieutenant was Arthur Pieck, son of the German Communist Party chairman, Wilhelm Pieck. The council's eighteen members included nine communists.

One of the new council's first measures was to ascertain the political complexion and capabilities of all business and commercial concerns in the city. In a short time it had brought to an end the activities—such as they now were—of all erstwhile business and professional interest groups, and had laid the groundwork for a new and sympathetic trade union organisation. A new judiciary, staffed by approved judges and lawyers, also came into being.

In parallel with these developments, the city's creative artists, including its journalists, were being encouraged along KPD lines. Soon, in addition to the Russians' own daily bulletin (the *Tägliche Rundschau*), where was the *Berliner Zeitung* (which still appears daily in East Berlin). Cultural events were arranged: a chamber evening in the Schöneberg Town Hall, an orchestral concert at the Masurenallee radio centre, a theatrical production at the Renaissance Theatre (an odd choice—*The Rape of the Sabine Women*), and another at the Deutsches Theater. A fine arts school was founded, as was a Cultural Alliance for Germany's Democratic Renewal. This body was headed by the poet Johannes Becher, who had newly returned from Moscow and who was a one-time sparring partner of Bertolt Brecht.

The city began to function in other ways. There was a bus service by 13 May, an underground line by 14 May, and the curfew was lifted on 15 May. Trams started running a few days later, and trains were soon running to suburban stations. The postal service and some telephone links were restored.

On the other hand, more than 400 people were arrested in a single police move against the ubiquitous black market—though it did not manage to restrain its activities elsewhere. Most important, however, was the authorisation given for the new-style SPD to come into being, followed by the Christian Democratic Union (CDU) and the German Democratic Party (DDP), precursors of today's Liberals. These three parties, and the KPD, came together within a short space of time to form an anti-fascist 'Democratic Bloc'.

All these developments, except the last-mentioned 'convergence', took place before the arrival of the US and British occupation forces on 4 July. They came, in other words, a full month after the city had been informed that its destiny henceforth was in the hands of the Inter-Allied Kommandatura, that Berlin was now divided into four sectors, and that in each of these sectors a nationally representative unit of the occupation forces would be in control. The Russians were to take eight of the city's districts; the US six; the British four; and France two.

Under a protocol first agreed by the powers concerned in London, in September 1944, only three months after the D-Day landings but still theoretically valid, the Kommandatura was to be answerable to the Allied Control Council for Germany. The damage to Berlin turned out to be such that some thought was given to locating this Council in another German city—a thought finally abandoned in favour of staying in the capital. The Kommandatura was established at a meeting on 7 July, in the former offices of an insurance company in Kaiserswertherstrasse, in Dahlem. The three remaining Western staffs still meet there from time to time.

The first Order of the Kommandatura was issued on 11 July. Its contents were a matter of surprised debate, not only for Berliners, for it indicated that the Soviet-made 'regulations and ordinances' of the preceding few weeks would remain in force until further notice. It was the Western powers' subsequent efforts to extricate themselves from the commitment and the 'spirit' of this order which was soon enough to divide the Kommandatura and, in due course, Berlin itself.

Such a situation can have done little to cheer those members of the Inter-Allied forces who had somehow to 'occupy' the battered city. 'The entire environment made life profoundly depressing,' two of the US reparations team wrote later. 'Morale was low at all times among Military Government personnel in Berlin.'

Henceforth, when Soviet wishes came into conflict with Western demands, they were to be reinforced with references back to this 11 July order or, if that proved ineffective, with fresh orders decreed at zonal level by Soviet forces responsible for the whole of eastern Germany, of which, as they repeatedly underlined, Berlin was a part. Reparations arguments between East and West were a constant source of friction and tension between the two sides. In fact, the Russians held about 46 per cent of the city's surface area and about one third of its measurable population.

The US, British and French forces occupied the rest. The city boundaries of the 1920 Act and the district boundaries, determined in a law of 1938, remained—and remain today—in force.

By July, the detached Berliner had almost grown used to occupation of one sort or another: it had been a fact of life, he would say, ever since the *Freikorps* consolidated their position after the First War. When the Union Jack and then the French *tricolore* (on 14 July, of course) were hoisted at the Victory Column—originally erected, it will be recalled, to celebrate a German victory over France—the Berliners could hardly rejoice. A knot of them applauded, however, one day in July when Winston Churchill emerged after a brief sight-seeing visit to the remains of Hitler's bunker and the Chancellery. Churchill, by all accounts, was rather thrown by their approbation. More significantly, he had also been thrown by a General Election result that month which removed him from the Prime Ministership of Britain. But he was still given the honour of taking the salute in the Charlottenburg-Chaussee, when the full British victory parade took place, and of opening the forces' so-called Winston Club for servicemen on the Kurfürstendamm a little later.

Nor was much interest shown by Berliners in the progress, and the final verdicts, of the Nuremberg trials. Perhaps they had delivered their own judgments already; certainly many felt they had already paid a sufficient price. And many no doubt were more preoccupied with the availability and the price of bare essentials. Morale was far too battered, and the day-to-day business of living was far too complicated to be bothered with retribution, even on such a scale.

The most active centre for the black market was the Tiergarten, with smaller operations conducted at mainline railway stations. Officially the authorities of all the occupying powers frowned on the market's existence and occasionally did what they could to stamp on its activities. But these were hollow gestures: there is no shortage of photographs in the archives showing British, Soviet or American soldiers present, as uniformed participants rather than law enforcement agencies, at the actual trading.

Bread and butter were among items traded at hugely inflated prices, as were coffee and wine, cigarettes, soap, items of furniture, clothing and fuel. Few penetrating questions were asked about the origins of commodities on offer, but robbery with violence was by now a common offence, committed with relative ease in the many hours of darkness by decree. Questions were superfluous. There were thousands of undetected burglaries in the city every month, and several murders a week.

The majority were characteristically resilient—though the suicide rate leapt alarmingly—but the city seemed to have lost whatever it once had in the way of corporate self-reliance. The post-war dust had settled, and the pictures of Stalin, occasional poster depicting Churchill or President Truman, exhortatory slogans promising a bit of jam tomorrow in return for a lot of effort today, soon had little real meaning. There was a certain different aimlessness in the air, a new sort of cynicism, always tinged with fear. Rumours were given much more credibility than usual.

With the onset of winter, the depression grew deeper as crucial coal supplies became scarce. There were increasing complaints of short measure being given in the legal rations. Children resorted to begging, and their parents would scavenge from the troops' dustbins. Less and less notice was taken of people collapsing in the streets, often from malnutrition or its consequences. Thousands died that winter from the cold, or lack of food or medicine. The hospitals that were still in service—thirty had been destroyed in the war and many more badly damaged—were packed. The infant mortality rate was high and so was the number of deaths from tuberculosis, typhoid and diphtheria. For the susceptible, there was disease in the very air they breathed; the city still had thousands of unburied bodies in its rivers and under its rubble. Rats were present in abundance.

To satisfy the endemic need for a scapegoat, a search was launched for people known to have been active on Hitler's behalf. Ration books were taken away from the worst offenders, and swastikas were painted on the front doors of others. Thousands of ex-Nazis were dismissed from the public service, including the offices of the City Council, and from the professions, and several hundred business enterprises which had been run by Nazi managers were closed down. At the same time newly appointed officials in the public sector—one of them, Dr Andreas Hermes, in overall charge of the city's food distribution—were dismissed for their alleged anti-Sovietism.

One of the worst-off sections of this deprived community was the refugees and others expelled from the east of the country. The flow continued unabated into the winter, though the authorities did seek to slow it down by announcing that incomers, while ostensibly welcome, would be given just one bowl of soup and a piece of bread and would be expected to move on within twenty-four hours. William Peters, 'a soldier' in Berlin at this time, visited Lehrter Bahnhof on 11 October. 'There is a transit camp in a nearby street,' he wrote, 'and here and in the station one can see thousands of people of all ages, wrapped in rags and blankets, carrying all their belongings with them, waiting hours for trains— mothers feeding their babies, hungry, cold children ... human misery. There is sleeping accommodation in the transit camps, but most people have such a fear of not getting into the train that they return to the station at night and stay there on the open platforms. Stations in Berlin have all been bombed and are completely open. There are practically no roofs, often no walls, and people flock together around their meagre belongings on the cold concrete floors....'

A few weeks after these words were written, a debate was held in the British House of Commons on the resources and responsibilities of the United Nations Relief and Rehabilitation Administration. Mr Maurice Edelman, Labour MP and sometime war correspondent, urged that UNRRA activities should be extended to Germany. On a recent visit to Berlin, he announced, he had seen things 'more horrible' than he had seen in any part of Europe or Africa.

'Berlin,' Mr Edelman declared, 'is a corpse of a city—a corpse which is still liable to breed infection, which, unless we control it, will spread throughout Europe and possibly throughout the world ... I went to one of the refugee centres—a refugee transit camp in Kruppstrasse, Spandau, where ... there were 3000 people herded together under conditions which, I am sure, have not existed outside concentration camps—certainly not as bad as concentration camps but almost as bad. I was standing in a very dark corridor where all sorts of shadowy shapes lay crowded together on the floor and I asked the camp commandant to show me a dormitory or a living room. He looked around him and said: "This is a living room."'

The control of Germany, with Berlin the central issue, had been a major talking point at the Potsdam Conference, which ran from mid-July till early August. Of the protagonists from previous summits, Stalin was the only constant. Roosevelt had died twelve weeks before and the hapless Churchill had to step down midway through the talks in favour of Clement Attlee as the defeat in the British elections became clear. The Army's advice to the succeeding British negotiators was that co-operation with the Soviet authorities in the running of Berlin was 'impossible'. The Soviets' ultimate aim, as it was already read by the British representatives at this time, was 'to turn the whole country into a communist satellite'.

This word was later used by General Sir Brian Robertson, soon to become British Commander-in-Chief in Germany and Military Governor. 'Soviet methods at the Berlin conference at Potsdam,' he said in an interview given in 1952, 'were not mere obstruction. They were based on a completely clear idea of what they wanted, and a determination to get it. The British and Americans were not always quite sure *what* their aims were.'

An East German writer, Heinz Heitzer, in his book *The GDR: An Historical Outline*, published in 1981, described 'protracted negotiations, which on the part of the Soviet delegation were being conducted with firmness of principle and patience' and said agreement was reached on 'fundamental measures that would lead to the demilitarisation, de-Nazification and democratisation of Germany.... The great powers pledged support for the German people in establishing a unitary, democratic state.' However, he added, 'the Western powers went about implementing the resolutions of Potsdam in a perfunctory and inconsistent fashion, then disregarded them more and more, and ultimately sabotaged them altogether.' The US and its allies, he argued, were moving towards 'a policy of cold war against socialism'.

Outside the conference room, the Soviet authorities went on working with the KPD, the only German party, as they insisted, which was acting in the 'spirit' of Potsdam. And there was underlying urgency and determination about the Communists' objectives. 'The mistakes of 1918,' they announced, in their very first appeal (on 13 June), 'must not be repeated! We must put an end to divisions among the working people! Nazis and reactionaries must not be treated with leniency! Never again must there be hatred and enmity towards the Soviet Union....' And by the time this appeal was published Walter Ulbricht, a man who had witnessed and suffered personally for the 'mistakes' of 1918, was already heading a Central Committee, representing the Neukölln district of Berlin. Otto Winzer, representing Friedrichshain, who had become active in the party in the 1920s and was to become

East Germany's Foreign Minister in 1965, was also on this Committee.

Throughout a harsh winter, the humourless Ulbricht and his team, efficiently supported by the Soviet authorities, worked to ensure there would be no more 'mistakes'. They knew that KPD support was not as great as they wished—and that it was perceptibly falling away in some rural areas—and pursued with increasing ardour a new relationship with selected members of the SPD. A separate 'German road to socialism' became a theme for debate, and elements of the two parties came together to see if they could embark on that road as soon as possible. Their resolve was doubtless sharpened by General Dwight D. Eisenhower, commanding US forces in Germany, when he wrote in the *Neue Zeitung*, the newspaper of those forces, that this trend in co-operation was not consistent with US ideas of democracy. It was further sharpened when Churchill, in March 1946, announced for all who cared to hear that an 'iron curtain' had descended over Europe, and that the Soviet Union had expansionary ambitions.

In the western sectors of the city, the SPD leader was one Franz Neumann. He had spent a lifetime in Berlin trade union and political activities, despite at one stage being threatened with a sentence for treason by the Nazis. He was to become an SPD member of the Bundestag. In eastern Berlin eyes, he was now seen as leading a 'reformist' group, recruited mainly from the middle classes and from among the intellectuals (as opposed to the working classes). This group, furthermore, was perceived by the Communists as a Trojan horse for the ideas of Kurt Schumacher, leader of the SPD in western Germany and a politician impervious to KPD blandishments. Schumacher's strong views had been reinforced by many years in concentration camps during the Nazi period. But his health suffered and he was to die in 1952. SPD preoccupations at this time were anyway very different in the west: they centred around such issues, for instance, as 'a United States of Europe'—a favoured Schumacher theme—and the activities of Konrad Adenauer. He was the unashamed anti-communist conservative who was on his way to becoming the first Chancellor of West Germany.

In eastern Berlin, the SPD Central Committee leader was Otto Grotewohl, a one-time printer and active trade unionist who is today remembered mainly for pro-KPD activities. In fact he had joined the SPD in 1912, one of its headier periods, and was elected an SPD member of the Reichstag in 1925. Now, twenty years on, he had committed himself to joining up with the KPD, and on 22 February 1946 he was in the Admiralspalast, opposite Friedrichstrasse station, at a meeting intended to mark the birthday of August Bebel. The main speaker was Wilhelm Pieck, the old KPD leader, who was once at the side of Liebknecht and Luxemburg. He denounced Schumacher and his supporters for their reactionary attempts to divide the working class.

At its first post-war congress, other members of the Berlin SPD, meeting the previous November at the Prater cinema, in the Kastanienallee in Charlottenburg's Westend, had spoken out vociferously *against* uniting with the Communists. In March 1946 a poll of SPD members in the western sectors of the city found 19,529 members against the fusion, 2937 in favour, with nearly 9000 abstaining. But, in the same poll, nearly 15,000 voted for closer collaboration with the KPD. This poll was something which confused the Soviet authorities in the east: on the one hand they claimed that they had not had any applications for the holding of such a poll of SPD members in their part of the city, while on the other hand, ballot boxes were deployed in some districts only to be withdrawn because, they said, certain regulations had been ignored.

One year to the day after the first Soviet troops had entered Berlin the conference to cement unity was held. It was also in the flower-bedecked Admiralspalast. However, detailed manifestos had already been drawn up and the presses were ready to roll for production of the first issue of *Neues Deutschland*, the new newspaper of the new party, the Socialist Unity Party of Germany (the SED). So far as this particular gathering was concerned, its business was perhaps historic, but its outcome was very much a foregone conclusion. No amount of protest from the West could undo what was achieved at the moment when Wilhelm Pieck and Otto Grotewohl ceremoniously joined forces by shaking hands with one another.

For Walter Ulbricht, who had campaigned for such unity for the last ten years, it was a pivotal moment. Savouring it to the full, he now deliberately played the role of provocative patriot. 'From the capital city of our German fatherland,' he told delegates, roaring their approval as the conference came to its end, 'the banner of the Socialist Unity Party has been raised for the whole German people. It is the banner of the unity of the

German working class, the banner for the struggle for the unity of all democratic forces, the banner of the unity of Germany.'

An immediate consequence was that the Allies feared there might be a repercussive loosening of their tenuous grip in the western sectors, and military authorities therefore ordered a closer check on the activities of both the SED and the SPD. The possibility of this happening had been discussed some weeks before the Admiralspalast ceremony with Kurt Schumacher, who was now obliged to accept the inevitable, even though he knew there was little prospect of Ulbricht's idea of 'unity' being realised. These were not events over which he had any control, any more than he could influence the prison sentences just given to twelve KPD members who had been arrested and tried for seditious activities in the district of Schöneberg.

On 13 August 1946 the four Commandants, as the Kommandatura, solemnly handed the City Council a draft constitution for Berlin intended to come into force with elections the following October. These elections were duly held and just over two million Berliners—92 per cent of those eligible—voted. Of the votes cast, 48.7 per cent went to the SPD; 22.2 per cent to the CDU; 19.8 per cent—only—to the SED; and 9.3 per cent to the Liberals (LDP). This led to a new council of 130, of whom sixty-three, including a new Lord Mayor, Otto Ostrowski, were SPD; twenty-nine were CDU; twenty-six SED and twelve LDP. The outcome of this election, according to East Berlin historians twenty-odd years later, was a disastrously bad decision (*eine verhängnisvolle Fehlentscheidung*) on the part of most Berliners.

As the various factions within the Kommandatura and the City Council continued with their arguments, the people outside began to grapple with the severity of the 1946–47 winter. It was to be one of the worst recorded in Europe. More than 1100 people were to die of cold in the city, and well over 40,000 had to be treated for hypothermia. An acute shortage of coal and strict limitations on power consumption meant that more than 1000 companies in the city had to close down and that 150,000 workers had to be laid off. In some districts, public transport stopped running altogether and in the city centre, cinemas, theatres and cabaret organisers either had to bring their times of performance forward to a relatively warmer—and strangely unsuitable—hour of the day or to close down until the freeze came to an end. In a typical gesture of corporate concern, public 'warm rooms' were opened to people in need. In all, around 700,000 people were dependent on public funds for survival. There were many more recorded deaths in the city than there were live births.

In April 1947 Ostrowski stepped down as Lord Mayor and Ernst Reuter, recently returned from exile in Turkey to run the city's transport, was nominated to succeed him. This move was immediately vetoed by the new Soviet Commandant, General Alexander Kotikov, who said that Reuter was anti-Soviet in his attitudes.

In a city where literally thousands of people had been arrested in recent times for their political activities, or had just disappeared, the reports of Soviet 'objections' were no longer remarkable. What was remarkable was the choice of Reuter as victim. He had started his political career as a schoolteacher who was also a member of the SPD. In the First War, he was taken prisoner by the Russians and became a communist. Yugoslavia's Tito and Hungary's Bela Kun belonged to the same period. Reuter met Lenin, Stalin and Trotsky while in the Soviet Union and was persuaded by them that he was a man to lead Germany into revolution. He therefore returned to Berlin as a Spartacus organiser, only to leave the Communists after a dispute with the Soviets over the extent to which he should subordinate his activities to those of the Soviet-run Third International. Today's East Germans describe him as a 'cynical demagogue' and an 'obsessive anti-communist'. Not surprisingly, Wilhelm Pieck, with whom he had been working, chose that moment to stay with the Communists. Not for the last time, he and Reuter were to find themselves on opposite sides.

While, in 1947, the Soviet authorities mulled over Reuter's latest position—which was essentially pro-Soviet but anti-Stalin—the US Senate was expressing concern at what it saw as the Soviet Union's increasingly 'aggressive and expansionist' foreign policy. The so-called Truman Doctrine, to defend 'freedom' against alleged Communist encroachments, was formulated, and General George Marshall began work on his plans for an economic aid package for Europe. They were plans in which the Soviet Union and its newly-forged allies in Eastern Europe refused to have any part, and the SED, at its second Party Congress, again in the Admiralspalast, debated the feasibility of its own economic plan for the whole of Germany. It was suddenly clear that Europe was now a divided continent.

General Lucius Clay, who had succeeded Eisenhower as US Military Governor in 1946, found himself moving towards a position where, so he thought, the possibility of a new war in Germany could not be discounted, and it began to be fashionable, as it has remained intermittently fashionable ever since, to talk of Berlin—meaning essentially West Berlin—as a hostage city. Such talk arose as the Soviet military authorities once more expressed public reservations about certain politicians who were active (this time on behalf of the CDU) in the city. They also began to carry out new and protracted bureaucratic checks on road and rail traffic coming into the city from the western zones.

The centenary of the 1848 revolution, which had meant so much in Berlin, brought a distraction which was not a distraction. Celebratory parades were held in both parts of the city. At the Friedrichshain park, Pieck used the opportunity of unveiling the monument to those who had died to harangue those present on the evils, as he saw them, of American monopoly capital as well as of those German politicians who, he claimed, were trying to 'split' Germany.

In the west, a ceremony was held at the City Opera House where Paul Löbe, the last president of the Reichstag before the Göring takeover, also spoke of the similarities between 1848 and 1948. Once again the issue was democratic representation, he said, and once again the unity of the country was in danger. But the biggest crowd of the day gathered outside the Reichstag building where Reuter declared—'in the style of Goebbels', according to East German historians, that 'the flood of communism will break against our iron will.'

Some weeks before, at a meeting of the Control Council for Germany, Marshal Vassili Sokolovski, who had succeeded the redoubtable Marshal Georgi Zhukov as Soviet Military governor, complained angrily about carefully formulated US and British plans to run their two zones as a joint operation, known as Bizonia, in the interests of greater economic efficiency. Inevitably, the plans did nothing to further the cause of Socialism or Communism, and, according to Sokolovski, they went against inter-Allied agreements and amounted to a proposal for a separate government within the city. He would therefore have none of them.

After the public sniping ceremonies to mark 1848, Zhukov

repeated these complaints with more vigour. The US-British agreement, he argued, went against what had been agreed at Yalta and Potsdam. It undermined the efficacy of the Council itself. It was effectively 'tearing up' the agreement on control 'machinery'. With that, Sokolovski, who on this occasion was also the meeting's chairman, called for an adjournment and, with his entourage, left the Kleistpark building, never to return.

For a while, the Kommandatura went on meeting, but its sessions were now fraught and tense. The Soviet team withdrew from a four-power military athletics contest which was to be held in the Olympic stadium in January. General Clay's office reported to Washington that the Soviets were seeking 'to liquidate this remaining "centre of reaction" east of the iron curtain' but also warned that there would be 'severe psychological repercussions' if the Americans decided to withdraw from the city. Winston Churchill, still a single-minded autocrat, even as leader of the political opposition, demanded that Soviet troops be withdrawn to the Polish frontier or face the consequences. In his thinking, these would amount to war.

In Frankfurt, meanwhile, the talk was of the Marshall Plan for the recovery of war-damaged western Europe, and Germany in particular, and arrangements were going ahead for the replacement of every ten almost worthless Reichsmarks with just one new Deutsche Mark. This radical move was more than enough to break the tension in the Kommandatura: late in the evening of 16 June, Colonel A. Yelisarov, acting for the Soviet side, chose a break in a heated discussion about wage levels in the city to rise to his feet and lead his delegation from the room. That moment was historically decisive since it marked the end of four-power control of Berlin, and from that moment the city was, de facto, divided.

During the ponderous and inexorable moves towards the breakdown of inter-Allied control, the city's rubble women, sometimes joined by the old men of the city and many of its children, pressed on with their enormous and thankless task of cleaning and restoring what they could in the way of still viable building materials. In monetary terms, they would earn enough in one week to buy five cigarettes on the black market, even though their wages were supplemented by a higher food allocation. Several thousand of them were engaged at any one time and the groups, large and small, in which they worked often formed the basis for a new community spirit. They also developed grapevines giving news, as well as rumours, as to the whereabouts of their countless missing relatives and friends. Their resolution and continuity, coupled with the evidence that they were restoring order of some sort out of overwhelming chaos, fostered in many Berliners a new sense of self-respect and a fresh will for corporate wholeness. These nuances made nonsense of proposals, implicit in the Morgenthau Plan advanced at that time for the 'pastoralisation' of Germany, that Berlin should be razed to the ground once and for all and re-erected elsewhere, perhaps on the Lüneberg Heath. Statues stand today in honour of these 'rubble women' in many cities in both Germanies.

Destruction provided scope for new plans. Albert Speer must have sighed wistfully in Spandau Prison as he contemplated what-might-have-been in the devastated city centre on which he had had so many designs. In the event, the new city fathers did what they could to keep to the old main thoroughfares and open spaces, but to change, where necessary or appropriate, the use of land in between. With so many million tonnes of rubble to be cleared from so many thousands of acres, it was inevitable that several 'centres' of the old city had gone or had assumed totally different characters. A whole list of household names—of hotels, restaurants, department stores, eating houses, small shops, bars and street kiosks—had been wiped out. The vocabulary, if not the vernacular of the city, had changed. The substance was different.

The non-stop noise and movement of the Potsdamer Platz and Leipziger Platz had been halted; the architectural backcloth to the sleazy street-level 'style' of the Kurfürstendamm had been ripped away; the intersection of Friedrichstrasse and Unter den Linden, where Kranzler's and Café Bauer had facilitated a flourishing business and a continuous social whirl, was gone; so, too, was much of Unter den Linden itself, much of Alexanderplatz, and so on. Only the use of anthrax bombs on the city, earnestly discussed at one point by Churchill with his War Cabinet in early 1945, could have provoked more anguish among Berliners engaged in an unwished-for search for what was now irretrievably lost.

*   *   *

Hans Scharoun, an eminent, academically inclined German architect with a long-standing and Europe-wide reputation, was the city's first post-war planning officer. Somehow, he was able to conjure creative thoughts out of the desolation that surrounded him, hindering whenever he could those who sought to bulldoze out of existence the war-damaged remains of the city's heritage, while at the same time forging ahead with reconstruction elsewhere. The Kommandatura would not allow him to produce his own master-plan, but a 'planning collective' of his contriving was able to come forward with all-embracing proposals for a 'new' city. These were exhibited in the ruins of the City Palace in 1946, and were based on a replacement of the former radial pattern by one based on bands: a business and entertainment area at the centre, surrounded by bands of residential developments. However, the running political arguments between the occupiers and the occupied over who should manage the city, and how, meant none of these proposals was to be implemented. They also meant that Scharoun lost his position as chief planning officer.

In January 1947 a document was produced by a small working party which had been headed by Willi Stoph, a former bricklayer who had studied architecture and who later became East Germany's Prime Minister; Kurt Liebknecht, nephew of the revolutionary, Karl Liebknecht, and now a senior member of the city planning administration; and Hermann Henselmann, an architect of great energy and personality who had been living and working in the city on and off since the 1920s. This document outlined plans for a new Institute of Building Studies, within the framework of the Academy of Sciences, and Scharoun was appointed its first principal.

From 1946 to 1958 Scharoun was also head of the architecture faculty at the Technical University (previously the Technical High School) which opened its doors in April 1946. He died in 1972 in West Berlin, leaving a legacy which included the curvaceous new Philharmonie building (completed in 1963) and the State Library (completed 1978), as well as some of the housing on the Karl-Marx-Allee in East Berlin, and pre-war developments in Siemensstadt and Charlottenburg. Henselmann himself stayed in East Berlin where he was to have overall responsibility for much of the city centre, including the Karl-Marx-Allee (part of the former Frankfurter Allee—for some years also known as the Stalinallee) and the new-style Alexanderplatz.

An acceleration in the process of renaming the city's streets and squares took place. It was not, of course, the first time this had happened. Kaiser Wilhelm's departure had occasioned the introduction of some new names during the Weimar period, as did the arrival of Hitler in 1933. Neither the Weimar nor the Nazi administrations, however, was to sweep out these trappings of the old regime as comprehensively as the Berlin city fathers, and especially the highly motivated East Berlin city fathers, were to do after the end of the war in 1945 and the formal division of Germany in 1949, respectively.

By July 1947 forty streets had been renamed. Adolf-Hitler-Platz, which is today Theodor-Heuss-Platz, was an early casualty, as was Hermann-Göring-Strasse, which reverted to its pre-1933 title of Ebert-Strasse, and the Strasse der SA, which reverted to Kaiserstrasse. Horst-Wessel-Stadt, the working-class district to the east of Alexanderplatz, became—again—Friedrichshain, though Horst-Wessel-Platz itself was to become Rosa-Luxemburg-Platz, rather than Bülow-Platz, which it had been earlier. Comparing today's map with one of 1936, there is just one Kaiser-Wilhelm-Strasse (in a southern suburb of West Berlin) compared with more than twelve in the earlier year, and five Bismarck-Strasses (all in West Berlin) compared with more than twenty before the last war.

Berlin is today, as it has always been, a city of statues and memorials. It has, after all, a great deal to remember, and every other street and open space—those now vanished as well as those still standing—has a story to tell. The innumerable old ladies with their little dogs, I always feel, must surely have more than the usual share of anecdotal evidence of what history was really like. But the statues and the memorials fill only some of the gaps.

The Siegesallee, built across a stretch of the Tiergarten by Wilhelm II to celebrate in statuary the heroes of Germany's great past, was destroyed in the war. It was strangely symbolic that a member of General Weidling's surrender team, Col. Hans-Oscar Wöhlermann, forced to crawl through the mud of the Tiergarten in the last hours of that war, should have been so disturbed by what he saw. 'Every single statue had been smashed,' he later noted, 'and the pieces scattered over the ground. It was a ghostly sight, quite the wrong thing for anyone with weak nerves. We had to crawl over the white marble heads, bodies and legs of the

Hohenzollerns, all of them gleaming weirdly in the reflected glow of the burning sky. . . .'

Today, at the northern end of the Siegesallee, across what until mid-1953 was called the Charlottenburger Chaussee, stands the Soviet war memorial. This was designed and built by Soviet technicians and unveiled, after gangs of workmen had laboured day and night to complete it, on 11 November 1945. It incorporates the tombs of two colonels and bears the names of thousands who died in the last battles, and was constructed mainly with marble from the Reichschancellery. It is floodlit at night (which serves as a precaution against vandals) and guarded by Soviet soldiers, who have billets in the surrounding undergrowth of the Tiergarten.

The avenue, now called the Strasse des 17. Juni (to commemorate the 1953 workers' uprising), had been widened by Speer and re-opened, with great ceremony, on Hitler's fiftieth birthday in April 1939. An exhibition on the other side of the avenue was erected by the Soviets after the war, opposite their own memorial. This brought together some of the trophies of the last weeks of fighting—a German tank, an armoured car, a gun, and the remains of an aeroplane—but it was an exhibition someone quickly decided they could do without and for this reason it was soon dismantled.

The main monument 'to Fallen Soviet War Heroes', which incorporates the mass graves of 5000 war dead, is in Treptow Park, scene in the pre-Nazi past of so many Communist-organised and other public gatherings. The original idea was a more or less conventional war cemetery to the Soviet dead, but in the summer of 1947 work started under Soviet instructions on clearing the main central part of the park, which had first been landscaped in the 1870s. Some 1200 people were involved in an undertaking which lasted all of two years. Two hundred stonemasons and ninety sculptors were engaged.

The end result, inaugurated on 8 May 1949, is monumental even by Berlin standards and is understandably included in the itinerary of any distinguished Soviet, or Warsaw Pact, visitor. Once again red marble—hundreds of tonnes of it—was taken from the old Chancellery. The central figure, rising high above the mausoleum, is a Soviet soldier carrying a child in one arm and resting his unsheathed sword on a broken swastika. This figure, made in bronze, proved too much for a German foundry, and had to be made in Leningrad. In the forecourt, a huge stone statue represents the grieving Motherland while along the Grove of Honour, there is an ornamentally carved stone sarcophagus for each Soviet republic.

A third Soviet war memorial, where 13,000 are buried, lies in Schönholzer Heide park, quite close to the 1961 Wall as it passes between Reinickendorf in the West and Niederschönhausen in the East. The central feature here is a Finnish granite obelisk, nearly a hundred feet high, over a memorial hall. The whole covers an area just as big as Treptow and took six months longer to complete before it was inaugurated in November 1949.

The many thousands of Berliners who died in, and fighting for, their erstwhile capital—an estimated 62,000 if one also includes refugees and bomb victims—have never been properly counted nor, within the city boundaries, have they ever been collectively honoured with any substantial monument. Certainly there are a large number of war graves (from both world wars) in the St John's cemetery in Neukölln, but there is nothing on the scale of Treptow, and the feelings that must be harboured for and on behalf of those who fell are generally kept very private. Most of those who were buried with any ceremony at all lie in separate graves in dozens of cemeteries in all parts of Berlin.

A British war cemetery, meanwhile, commemorating 3000 who died either in air raids over the city or in prisoner-of-war camps in the Berlin area, is situated about five miles west of the city centre. It is just off the Heer-Strasse, in the greener part of Charlottenburg, immaculately kept, on a wooded slope over-looking the Havel River.

By early summer 1948, when the Control Council for Germany and the Kommandatura for Berlin met for the last time in full session, life in Berlin for the ordinary citizen was still a matter of acute discomfort. Many people were still confined to cellars or other makeshift accommodation, such as Army nissen huts, and many were still without minimal comforts like windows, baths or properly functioning lavatories. Most foods remained on ration and the black market, despite sporadic raids by the multifarious forces of law and order, continued to flourish. Health hazards were still a major factor of life, and the vigour of the huge rat population was undiminished.

Then for more than a year, from April 1948 onwards, the Soviet authorities maintained that 'technical difficulties' were preventing the free flow of road, rail and canal traffic into and out of the city. They offered western-sector Berliners a chance to buy their foodstuffs in the eastern part of the city, on production of the usual ration cards, if they so wished, but not more than 20,000 people are believed to have taken up this offer. The rest of the two million people directly concerned endured and mostly survived. The 'haves' had become momentarily indistinguishable from the 'have nots' and suddenly there was a new rapport even with benefactors from countries with which they had so recently been at war. The standing of the Soviet Union in Berlin was clearly not improved as a result of the blockade to come, though the word blockade is not used by Soviet officials. They prefer to speak only of the 'so-called Berlin crisis'.

It became apparent that existence could only be sustained—in the western sector—through the services of an Allied airlift. There were heavy sighs all round, coupled with feelings that while things had been atrociously bad in the not so recent past, if they had to be atrociously bad once again, well, perhaps even that could be endured. Stoicism, even amongst the provident, was tempered with some more of that sense of solidarity which was not so very obvious during the war but which had firmly taken root after it ended.

As a peacetime operational exercise, the airlift was totally without precedent, an exercise which has become a legend for cold war storytellers. It was devised largely by US Army General Albert Wedemeyer and Air Chief Marshal Sir Charles Portal, of the RAF, and over its full period of 462 days—finally ending in September 1949—brought more than 1.8 million tonnes of goods to the beleaguered city on no less than 277,264 flights. A large part of the tonnage carried had to be coal, for domestic heating and for the city's power stations. There was also nearly a quarter of a million tonnes of essential foods.

The thirteen months of the actual blockade are now seen as a time of cold war at its most intense. General Clay continued to talk of hot war, of the feasibility of driving tanks across the Soviet zone to the city, but he was told to cool such talk as it was not helpful. In fact, this period too was one of continued, if strained, dialogue, with the commandants' offices in east and west passing each other terse and unyielding messages throughout. At the end of June, 1948, there was also a long appeal to the United Nations from Louise Schröder and Dr Ferdinand Friedensburg, joint acting Mayors under Ernst Reuter, writing on behalf of the City Government of Greater Berlin.

The imposition of the blockade made life in the whole of Berlin more difficult, since it led the Western powers to instigate a reciprocal but minimally effective blockade of the Soviet zone. However, the real complications were to be created by the introduction, first in the west and then in the east, of new currencies to replace the Reichsmark. For some months, producers, retailers and ordinary individuals were juggling simultaneously with a Deutsche Mark and an Ostmark—the former being worth about four times as much as the latter. Finally, with the split between east and west unbridgeable, the Western Military Governors eventually announced that the Deutsche Mark, which had been circulating in the Western-occupied zone since the previous June, would become the only legal tender in the western sectors of Berlin—with effect from March 1949.

Gas and electricity supplies in the west were severely cut as the blockade began to 'bite' and it was of course in the western sector that the economic impact was most visible. By the end of 1948, more than a quarter of the sector's 62,500 enterprises had been forced either to close or to go over to short-time working. On 31 December, 113,000 people were registered as unemployed and 67,000 had been reduced to working part-time. The amount of new marks allowed to circulate had to be strictly controlled and a complicated system of bridging loans, to prevent the collapse of banks or companies, had to be introduced.

Early calculations showed that about 4500 tonnes of supplies a day would have to be flown into the city to keep it going. In the early days, this was a figure rarely reached; in the later days, when aircraft were often flying in at the rate of one every ninety seconds or less, it was almost doubled. The return flights carried a meagre proportion of exports from west Berlin, meagre because production was limited either by short-time working or the non-availability or raw materials. They also carried people—old people who were not necessarily going to survive indefinite hardship, or sick people, often with tuberculosis, requiring specialist hospital treatment, or young people—more than 15,000 of them—who needed a more assured future. The turn-round time of aircraft, once the operation was in full swing, was brought down to six minutes, including unloading and loading as appropriate, refuelling as necessary, and whatever servicing had to be done.

Flying conditions around the city are not ideal at the best of times. Pilots during the airlift had not only to cope with the rigours of an artificially narrow flight 'corridor' from the British Zone, but also with Berlin's peculiar climate. Fog as well as rain are features of the local weather, even in August, and heavy snow during the winter had to be cleared as quickly as it fell. But in addition there were risks involved in landing an over-heavy aircraft at an airfield situated within the confines of a crowded city.

'As we came in looking for this place,' one American pilot later reported, 'all we could see were bombed-out buildings all around. Then we spied this grass field—it seemed more like a pasture than an airfield—and came over the homing beacon and sure enough it was Tempelhof. . . . We came right on over the top of an apartment building and over a little opening in the barbed wire fence and there we were. It kind of reminded me of the feeling that a crop duster would have in western America, landing on a highroad or in the pasture he's dusting.'

Life inside the western sectors of the city was dominated by the shortages, by long hours of darkness and cold induced by the scarcity of fuel, and by the unceasing noise of low-flying aircraft overhead. It was, according to current East German historians, 'a dead city'—underlining the separateness which had now been all but effected. The daily diet was somehow constructed around powdered potatoes, powdered milk and powdered eggs. Fresh fruit and vegetables, when they could be obtained, were occasions for joy. Fuel needs could still be met by cutting down the city's remaining trees but their falling numbers were to become, in October, a matter for stormy controversy. In the expectation that coal deposits might be found, Mayor Friedensburg (a mining engineer) organised the sinking of 15 boreholes in Reinickendorf (north), Spandau (west) and Marienfelde (south), but nothing viable, even in these straitened times, was found.

The appetite for news was fed by the ten newspapers which continued to appear as a result of newsprint being flown in, and by RIAS, the US sector radio station, which had started operating just before the blockade. It still operates out of premises in Schöneberg, much to the political chagrin of the authorities east of the Wall. An appetite for humour—unquenchable in this city—was met by listening to the cavortings, on the radio and on stage, of the hugely popular and succulently irreverent Günter Neumann, in a serialised entertainment aptly called *Die Insulaner* (*The Islanders*). A rubble 'mountain' named in honour of this serial stands in the southern part of Schöneberg.

Inevitably, the implementation and control of the blockade and the airlift that it engendered, with the accompanying currency dispute, led to a central crisis-within-the-crisis. This related to the City Council, and who should be running Gross-Berlin, and it reached an early crescendo on 26 August 1948. An ostensibly routine meeting was called of the City Council under the chairmanship of Dr Otto Suhr, a long-standing senior member (in non-Nazi times) of the city administration. But the climate of the time led the SED to see the call as a sign that the SPD were preparing a 'putsch' in the City Hall. Suhr, backed by Reuter, responded with an immediate call on SPD members to demonstrate their cohesion and willingness to resist whatever retaliatory move might be made by the SED, by holding a rally in front of the old Reichstag. A smaller SED rally was held at the Potsdamer Platz.

No council meeting was possible that day, nor the next day when a Soviet Army presence, backed by a Soviet-authorised police team, did nothing effective to stop SED supporters from disrupting proceedings. Council employees were on strike.

In the following days, the Soviet authorities stepped up pressure for the new Eastmark to become currency throughout the city. The SPD group, backed by the western Allied authorities, refused to accept this, and the utter confusion in the so-called New City Hall (situated in Parochialstrasse, just behind the refurbished Red City Hall) steadily increased. This confusion erupted into violent chaos on 6 September, when police and stewards brought in by both sides collided head-on. The SPD-led group was forced to withdraw and to meet a few hours later in protest at the students' hostel in the Steinplatz, on Hardenbergstrasse, while the SED stayed behind to approve what it called a 'winter emergency programme'. New elections to new city bodies were discussed, and from that day on, there have been two city administrations in Berlin.

Each side had its man for the hour. Ernst Reuter, the one-time revolutionary who had worked with Lenin and Stalin, now rallied a crowd of 300,000—so it is usually estimated—which filled the open space outside the Reichstag on 9 September. 'We Berliners,' he declared, from in front of the ruined fabric of Germany's one-time democracy, 'we are not a subject for barter, for trading off and for selling.' He called upon the 'peoples of the world' not to abandon the people of the city in their hour of need. The Soviet flag was torn down—not for the last time—from its place on top of the Brandenburg Gate, and in clashes with the police and other demonstrators from the east, at least a dozen individuals were injured and a fifteen-year-old child died.

A second mass rally, also running to hundreds of thousands, was organised towards the end of November in the Soviet sector. This was held under the auspices of the SED and brought together trade unionists and representatives of other mass groups to demonstrate support for a newly proclaimed, SED-controlled city council with Friedrich Ebert, son of the first president of the Weimar Republic, as Lord Mayor. Ebert had been active in the SPD until the 1946 fusion, editing *Vorwärts* and sitting as an SPD member in the Reichstag until 1933. The name of his father was anathema to the Nazis, and is today to some East German Communists, and he himself was for a while in a Nazi concentration camp. He was to remain East Berlin's Mayor until 1967 (when he was seventy-three) and from 1950 to 1958 was president of the German-Soviet Friendship Society, formed in October 1947.

The enthusiasm shown at these two mass rallies, though several weeks apart, emphasised the irreconcilability of the two sides. With some difficulty, the Hitler inheritance had been expunged. The complications involved in doing this were symbolised in one sense by the inordinate time spent exploding and demolishing the great concrete bunkers that he had built. But, more important, the immediate post-war shaking-down had come to an end. There were many more teething pains to be endured and there was going to be much more friction between the two sides, but in the history of Berlin, a traumatic phase was coming to its end. From now on, this history would be, in so many significant respects, a tale not of one, but of two cities.

⋆　　⋆　　⋆

The secretary of the SPD Berlin executive during the time of the blockade was Willy Brandt, a sometime ship-broker and journalist who had emigrated to Norway when Hitler came to power but had returned intermittently during the war to do what he could in the resistance. He was to become, in 1949, one of the first SPD members of the new Federal Parliament (the Bundestag); in 1957, the Governing Mayor of West Berlin; and, in 1969, Chancellor of West Germany. Twenty-five years after the end of the 1948–49 blockade he was back in Berlin for a special ceremony at Tempelhof's Hangar One. Germans had shown, he said on that occasion, that in spite of total defeat, they could still fight, freeze and go hungry for a cause.

He was of course referring, in a language which became increasing current after the blockade ended—at one minute past midnight on 12 May—to what he called 'the cause of freedom'. This was in spite of the fact that freedom, at the end of the blockade, meant different things to different people. In the same way, the reverberations and consequences of the airlift which had been necessitated by the blockade varied according to perspective.

The personal consequence for Christa Wichmann, a Berliner now living in London, was doubtless shared by countless others. She says that every time she hears an aeroplane overhead nowadays she experiences almost no irritation, only undiluted happiness.

For Clement Attlee, who visited West Berlin as Britain's Prime Minister in early March 1949, the consequence was one with endless international ramifications. 'It wasn't until the Berlin airlift,' he told an interviewer some years after his visit, 'that American public opinion really wakened up to the facts of life. Their own troops were involved in that. Before that, there'd been a lot of wishful thinking. I don't think they really appreciated communist tactics until Berlin.'

For the city of Berlin, a major consequence was the construction of Tegel Airport. This took place in just ninety days in the French sector between 5 August and 5 November 1948. Until that time, the city's main airport had been the Tempelhof field, which was originally used as a parade ground by the royal regiments, who had to march in formation the entire length of Friedrichstrasse to get there. More recently, Tempelhof had been used by the Wright brothers (in 1908) to demonstrate powered flight and (in 1923) by entrepreneurs as a starting point for German civil air transport.

The new German airline, Lufthansa, took it over in 1927, and ten years later it was converted by Hitler's architect, Ernst Sagebiel—ironic, perhaps, that Hitler provided such fine facilities for the post-war emergency. (Sagebiel was also responsible for the Air Ministry building erected at that time for Göring, as head of the Reich Air Force, and now used to accommodate the offices of nine East German ministries.) Gatow Airport, now used by British forces, had been built in 1935–6 as a training centre for the Nazi Air Force.

Tegel's pedigree was totally different. It was called for during the emergency of the airlift because Tempelhof could not cope with such an unplanned rush of traffic, and was constructed by teams of labourers—19,000 in all—working round the clock, assisted by just four bulldozers. The Soviet military authorities did nothing to help in the construction project, even refusing to remove two radio transmission masts, 370 feet and 250 feet high, which were seen as a danger to incoming aircraft. To this refusal, the French commandant General Ganeval responded with nicely Gallic lack of equivocation by blowing them up. When an angry Soviet general asked him how he could possibly do such a thing, Ganeval is reported to have replied: 'With dynamite, of course.'

On completion, Tegel had the longest runway ($1\frac{1}{2}$ miles) in Europe. It is situated close to the old training ground used before and during the First War by pilots of the Berlin airship battalion, and to the site where, in the early 1930s, Wernher von Braun, later to emigrate to the US, conducted his first experiments with high-powered rockets. On 2 January 1960, it was formally inaugurated as West Berlin's second airport.

The students and intellectuals of the city had their own roles to play in the post-war years. For the former it was a time, in every conceivable sense, to start again, while for the latter, it was—perhaps—a time to resume activities which had been so ruthlessly interrupted so long before.

The first university in the city, founded in 1810 by Wilhelm von Humboldt (brother of the naturalist, Alexander), was—and still is—housed mainly in the former palace on Unter den Linden. Despite incurring its share of war damage, it opened its doors for lectures again in November 1945, with around 4000 students enrolled. A formal re-opening ceremony was held in the Admiralspalast the following January at which the rector, the philologist Johannes Stroux, pledged that the traditions of Wilhelm Humboldt would be continued. Previously known as the Friedrich-Wilhelm-University it was henceforth to be known as the Humboldt University.

However, it became apparent almost as soon as this institution resumed teaching that a number of would-be students did not wish to learn as much about the thinking of Karl Marx as the then authorities were demanding. A movement was initiated, with the students themselves to the fore, for a new university. This movement gathered pace in the uncertain weeks of April 1948, and soon afterwards appeals for support were launched, one of them addressed to the responsive General Clay. The result was that the Free University, as it is now known, was launched in December 1948, in the heart of Dahlem, with the historian Friedrich Meinecke as its first rector. It started in two rooms, and in its first twelve months depended heavily on US support. It now has 30,000 students, about the same number as attend the Humboldt in East Berlin.

Finally, there is the Technical University. This adjoins the Ernst-Reuter-Platz and became fully fledged in what used to be the Technical High School, in 1946. This institution had first become noticeably pre-eminent in the technologically revolutionary *Gründerjahre* of the 1870s, and its main building, a quaintly preserved palatial structure, unlike anything else in Berlin, dates from that period. Though it too suffered bomb damage in the air raids and though much was stolen from within its walls immediately afterwards, it still contains many trophies and relics from the city's early years as an industrial centre.

As post-war Berlin sought to pick up the pieces, what, it may be asked, had become of those men and women whose creative energies had been so evident in the exploding 'golden era' and beyond? One answer is that many of them were Jewish and, if they were not taken by the SS, they had fled. Most of the rest also fled, sometimes to convey still urgent signals to the wider world, sometimes to withdraw into that strange no-man's-land of introspection which draws so many exiles. If, as Brecht wrote on the eve of his own departure, 'there is no greater crime than leaving', these were the ones—with Berlin itself—who paid the price.

Those few who came back were occasionally politically motivated, but more often culturally disoriented. Some were looking for a landfall between the two. The city to which they returned was patently not the one they had been obliged to leave. In most cases the city's need for them outweighed their own need, in the new order of things, for the city. It was not until the autumn of 1947 that the violinist Yehudi Menuhin, could return to play there. He is a person who loves the city, and first played there, with Bruno Walter and the Berlin Philharmonic Orchestra, as a boy of thirteen. The reception which he received in 1947 was overwhelming. Tears that grown men and women shed that evening had been twelve years and more in the coming. The world had moved on.

By this time many of the artists most closely and vividly associated with Berlin in the 1920s and early 1930s had left, most of them never to return, and many of them to get short shrift even now from regimes to which they might once upon a time have given service or, at the very least, lip-service.

Max Beckmann, for instance, turned down invitations to teach in Berlin and died in New York. Otto Dix, though today he is formally respected in both Germanies, lived a sort of half-existence in Berlin through most of the war but was to die in Bavaria. George Grosz, looking for one knows not what through the bottom of an empty glass, died in 1959 just six weeks after returning to (West) Berlin for a second time, from a life he had tried to make in the US. John Heartfield, ever an exceptional man, returned from exile in Britain and the US to East Berlin in 1950, working closely with Brecht and teaching art. He died in East Berlin in 1968. Käthe Kollwitz, who lost immediate relatives in both wars, died just outside Dresden a few days before the war ended. Christian Schad, an artist as penetrating in his time as Grosz and Dix, died in virtual obscurity in a small town near Aschaffenburg in 1982.

One painter, deeply immersed in the city in a very different way before and after the war, was Werner Heldt. He was born in a strictly religious household in Berlin and educated in the city. Before the war he had concentrated on Berlin cityscapes, influenced in part by a lively friendship with the satirical artist Heinrich Zille. After fifteen years which involved a course of psychoanalysis, a lengthy period of war service and a spell as prisoner-of-war, he returned to the city once more. His pictures now took on the same mute, almost lifeless, quality of the British artist,

171

Paul Nash, but he stayed with the city, increasingly melancholy and abstracted, until his death in 1954.

The appearance of two city councils with some measure of autonomy gave new scope to architects. These were people belonging to a profession which since the war has been much attracted by the magnetic pull of, and the opportunities presented by, the pulverised city. Some of those architects who had emerged before, and others during, the 1920s 'golden era' survived and returned to be of service to the city. Others died in obscurity elsewhere. Peter Behrens, who had continued to practice under the Nazis, earning some praise for his work from Hitler and designing a substantial AEG contribution to the proposed North-South Axis, died in Berlin in 1940. Bruno Taut, who had gone to work in the Soviet Union, died in Istanbul in 1938.

Mies van der Rohe and Walter Gropius both settled in the US after their enforced emigration and both influenced strongly the changing shape of America's big cities, especially Chicago. Mies, however, returned to give Berlin a new National Gallery, situated by the Potsdamer Bridge over the Landwehrkanal and opened in 1968. Gropius, too, involved himself heavily in working for the city he once knew so well, and took responsibility for the design of a large housing area in the southern part of West Berlin and close to the city's boundary in Buckow: the area, comprising more than 18,000 dwellings and housing 43,000 people, is now called Gropiusstadt. He also designed, but did not live to see completed, a new building erected to commemorate the work of the Bauhaus. It was to have been built in the city of Darmstadt, but adaptations were made to the design and the completed work now stands in West Berlin, just south of the Tiergarten. Mies was to die in Chicago in 1969, and Gropius in Massachusetts in the same year.

Alfred Döblin, whose novel, *Berlin Alexanderplatz* had appeared in 1929, came back to see the city in late 1947. He was shattered by what he saw. Describing events in which he had once participated, he reflected: 'Nothing remains of that any more, none of the people, none of the buildings, the whole place is now brought to ground level. Historically, the past has been totally expunged.'

The writers, Stephen Spender and Christopher Isherwood, whose work had once so vividly synthesised the pre-Nazi city, returned briefly after the war. Both wrote on this experience, but this time, as with Döblin, the essence had gone.

Despite several pressing invitations from both parts of Germany, neither Thomas nor Heinrich Mann seems to have been back to linger in post-war Berlin. As the war had come to an end, in early 1945, Heinrich wrote an open letter 'to the people of Berlin', urging them to see through the revolution which had failed after 1918. A dozen years before, the works of both brothers had been used to fuel the 1933 book-burning. But Thomas was to die in 1955 in Switzerland, where he was also buried, while Heinrich had died in California in 1950. Some months before, he had been offered a villa and office premises in eastern Berlin—an offer he declined. Even so, his posthumous ashes were to be re-interred in the Dorotheen Cemetery, off the Chaussee-Strasse, East Berlin, and the stone which has been erected there describes him as 'a co-founder of our socialist German state'.

In the world of the theatre, the dominant pre-Nazi forces had been Max Reinhardt, Erwin Piscator and Bertolt Brecht. All had left with the coming of Hitler, and Reinhardt died in the US, an American citizen, in 1943. Piscator, who was twenty years younger, returned from exile in 1962 to live in Bingerstrasse, Friedenau. In his last years he was a director of the West Berlin Freie Volksbühne, and died in Berlin in March 1966.

Brecht, who had foretold in one of his many city poems that one day 'only the wind passing through' would remain, returned to a political hero's welcome in the eastern sector in October 1948. His play, *Fear and Misery in the Third Reich,* written in exile in 1938, had been produced earlier that year in the Deutsches Theater in Schumannstrasse. A banquet was given in his honour by the newly formed Cultural Alliance, with Wilhelm Pieck, the SED leader, his old friend and enemy, the poet Johannes Becher, and a colonel from the Soviet commandant's office as his main hosts.

For a short while he stayed in emergency accommodation in what remained of the Adlon Hotel, before moving into a villa presented to him in the Weissensee district of the city, just out of the city centre. The address was No. 190 Berliner Allee, now known as the Klement-Gottwald-Allee. Brecht, very pointedly, hung a picture of 'the Doubter' on his wall.

In a poem of the time, he noted that every time he drove through the ruins of the city, he was reminded of the privileges to which he owed such a house. He kept a suitcase ready, close to his manuscripts, and was uneasy with himself and the regime, off and on, for the rest of his days. They put on *Mother Courage* in the Eastern sector, with Helene Weigel, whom he later married, in the title role, and it was received as a great success. But not many years were to pass before he was disagreeing violently with those in charge of the Berlin in which he now lived. For the time being, he summarised his feelings in another highly political poem, which he called *Wahrnehmung*. The word translates as 'Observation' but in the sense which also carries a hint of warning.

> When I returned
> My hair was not yet grey
> And I was glad.
> The travails of the mountains lay behind us.
> Before us lie the travails of the plains.

These few words distilled the thoughts, spoken or unspoken, of every Berliner of that time.

Above: 1901: Bismarck's statue was erected in front of the Reichstag. In 1938, Hitler had it removed to the Tiergarten, where it remains.

Left: 1902: In Wedding district, rooms to let but apparently not much work. Hints, down the road, of once opulent architecture.

1905: Depression, and a queue for offal and normally unsaleable meat.

1913: Palace Bridge, now Marx-Engels-Bridge. The statues were reinstated in 1984; the Royal Palace (background) has gone.

1918: December, and Karl Liebknecht harangues a crowd in the Tiergarten, honouring revolutionaries already dead.

1932: Hitler, in one hotel, prepares for power; in another, shown here, a yo-yo competition is held.

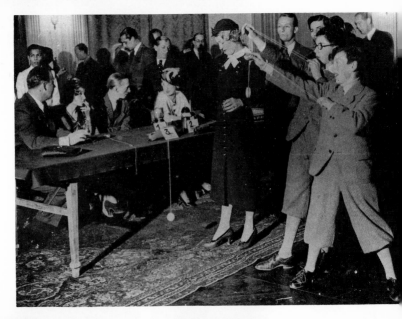

1933, April and the anti-Jew boycott ('Germans beware—Do not buy in Jewish shops'). It is not the success that Goebbels wanted.

1941: The Compiègne 'armistice' railway carriage is made a trophy of war. It was subsequently 'lost'.

Above: 1943: Heavy bombing, and gas masks on the Kurfürstendamm. The Gloria cinema shows 'Journey into the Past'.
Right: 1947: Schinkel's great architecture of 1830, latterly Gestapo headquarters. Now gone.

Above: 1945: Romanisches Café, one-time cradle of Dada Movement and haunt of artists. The Europa Centre now occupies the site.

Left: 1949: 'Rubble women' on both sides restored millions of bricks.

Friedrichstrasse crosses Unter den Linden in 1946 (above) and in 1898 (below).

Tauentzienstrasse, looking towards the Kaiser Wilhelm Church, from near to where Christopher Isherwood once stayed. In 1897 . . .

1946 . . .

1985.

1953: Reception centre in Charlottenburg for refugees coming west.

1963: Gen. Lucius Clay thanks West Berliners for their gratitude! President Kennedy on his left.

1961: November, and the Wall of August is reinforced.

Kreuzberg, seen in 1945 (above) and in 1980, from almost identical viewpoints.

FIVE

1949-1961

Auf der schwäbschen Eisebahne
Kommt der Chruschtschow angefahre
Mit zwei Bomben unterm Arm
Das bedeutet Kriegsalarm
Alle rennen in den Keller
Adenauer noch viel schneller
Und der kleine Willy Brandt
Kommt durch ganz Berlin gerannt[1]

In the late 1940s, Berlin began to witness scenes which, for those with long enough memories, bore a distressing resemblance to those last witnessed in late 1918 and early 1919. Then, at least, the city was intact. Now people were swirling about in a totally shattered environment, looking for a new leader who could take them out of the quagmire of misery, deprivation and utter political confusion in which they now found themselves. Their partiality, or lack of it, for one or other of the four occupation powers, meant that this process was not entirely aimless, but the overwhelming scale of the destruction in so many parts of the city induced a sense of hopelessness that can only be imagined by outsiders. More than any other Germans, one SPD political strategist declared in late 1948, Berliners were the ones who had learned that 'he who wants to earn his freedom has to sacrifice for it'.

While the airlift was a visible manifestation of what the East–West battle for the heart of the city was all about, it was also, while it lasted, a sort of distraction, a continuing high drama which gave people on all sides something new to talk about every day. Once it was over, political tension remained high, but the

[1] On the train from Swabia, old Khrushchev trundles in—with a bomb under each arm. That means war is in the air, so everyone's running to their cellars. Adenauer runs like mad, but little Willy Brandt—he runs through Berlin like merry hell.

changed realities of everyday life again took precedence. As the dismantling of around 500 of the city's factories (with no fewer than 50,000 machines being taken from twenty of them in the name of reparations) came to an end, the city's own output, and eventually its own exports, began at last to creep upwards. But so, for many, did the level of wretchedness at which they were obliged to exist.

By 1949, according to a later East German account, only a small part, perhaps a quarter, of the great piles of rubble had been cleared from the streets, and many urban road and railway bridges remained out of commission. The shortage of glass meant that 'home' was a place where most windows were still boarded up or stuffed with paper. Work was a place where supplies of raw materials or semi-finished products were non-existent or erratic. Factories which had not been blitzed or dismantled, and where the machinery was not obsolete, were forced at unpredictable moments to stop producing. The Soviet sector claimed it had no measurable unemployment; the western sectors admitted to over 300,000 without work at the beginning of 1950, a situation made more complicated with the influx, virtually every day, of hundreds of new refugees from the east.

What, therefore, the blockade had achieved for Soviet strategists, apart from an unquantifiable sharpening of their political resolve, was not entirely clear. In its way, it had strengthened corporate morale in the western sectors of the city and had turned many waverers away from what they now perceived as Communism. It had also strengthened Allied determination to hold on to what it had. The Soviet Union, Stalin had declared in 1945, did not intend to dismember Germany or to destroy it; four-and-a-half years later his words had a less certain ring.

The Soviet authorities and those Germans working closely with them conducted many of their deliberations behind firmly closed doors. The growing food crisis was a matter of acute public concern, but there was no heated public debate about decisions to nationalise the land or what remained of eastern Germany's industry, or to subsume the SPD into the SED. Nor, in the eastern sector, was there any vociferous opposition to the assumption that Berlin should be the capital of the new East German state, perhaps—still—of a unified Germany. Those who opposed such decisions and assumptions tended, when they were able, to do so with their feet—by going west.

There was no such collective single-mindedness in the western sector, or in western Germany. One reason was that while Stalin remained, as it were, a constant, his ideological adversaries were changing. Another reason was that the US, British and French occupation forces did not always see eye to eye among themselves. A third reason was that SPD-dominated Berlin, and Ernst Reuter in particular, did not see eye to eye with the so-called Parliamentary Council which had started meeting in Bonn, at the height of the blockade, under the chairmanship of the CDU's Konrad Adenauer. The comparatively warm and open Reuter who was to remind Willy Brandt of 'an old tree which had braved many storms', was not infrequently at odds with the more austere Kurt Schumacher, leader of the SPD at quasi-national level. It was not the first time the SPD had been split in a crisis.

Arguments were inevitable over the choice of a 'seat of government' for the now proposed federal republic. The case was considered by the Parliamentary Council for Bonn, Frankfurt, Kassel and Stuttgart. Adenauer, seventy-three years old and living in the vicinity, carried the CDU with him in support of Bonn, while the SPD had argued strongly for Frankfurt. On 10 May, the day before the blockade ended, the vote went thirty-three to twenty-nine in favour of Bonn, with the two Communists abstaining. It was conceded, however, that Bonn was unsuitable as a capital. It would be a 'provisional' choice.

Two days earlier, and five weeks after the founding of NATO, a brief series of moves was initiated which would change the face of Europe. The Parliamentary Council had approved, despite opposition from the recalcitrant Schumacher, the Basic Law (*Grundgesetz*) to form the Federal Republic of Germany. A fortnight after that Reuter, as Lord Mayor in West Berlin, joined Council members in signing the legal document, and the new country formally came into existence. West Berlin remained occupied territory under the aegis of the Kommandatura, but Federal legislation was also to be enforceable in the city, so long as it was passed by the city's own assembly.

During all these deliberations, the main preoccupation in the city itself was a strike by railwaymen. They were employed by the East Berlin-based Deutsche Reichsbahn, an imperial title the same railway bears to this day, and the strike, which lasted nearly six weeks, was over money. The workers wanted Western rather than Eastern marks, and there were some violent skirmishes between the workers themselves, the railway police and members of the occupying forces, including the British. One person died and several were hurt in shooting incidents, but in the end it was agreed that 60 per cent of the workers' wages would henceforth be in Western marks. It was also agreed that nearly 400 of the strikers should either be dismissed or, if it suited their politics, be redeployed to take up new posts with the railway in the Soviet sector.

Between mid-August and mid-September, the new Federal Republic held its first general election, elected Theodor Heuss, an academic who had been highly critical of the Nazi regime, as president, and approved Konrad Adenauer, former Mayor of Cologne and an apparently contented federalist by persuasion, as Chancellor. Six weeks after the oath-taking ceremonies of the new Government, President Heuss came to West Berlin, but it was more than seven months before there was a visit from the new Chancellor. More than 200,000 people gathered in front of the Schöneberg Town Hall to hear Heuss underline the links which he said were so close between the city and the new Republic. According to Willy Brandt, the later Chancellor, Berliners had become the 'stepchildren' of the Basic Law.

In the Soviet sector, they had their own so-called People's Council, set up in May in response to the alarming developments in Bonn. This body met at midday on 7 October in Göring's scarred old Air Ministry building in Leipzigerstrasse, not far from where the first Imperial Reichstag had once met under Bismarck. The building is today the House of Ministries of the East German Government. The Council voted to reform itself as a 'provisional' People's Assembly and, by the evening, had proclaimed the birth of the German Democratic Republic. It gave Otto Grotewohl the responsibility of forming its first government. In his earlier days, the same Grotewohl had been a less than conspicuous SPD member of the Reichstag.

Three days later, General Vassili Chuikov, who had played such a key role in the taking of the city in 1945, ceremonially handed over those constitutional functions which for the last four and a half years had been exercised by Soviet military forces. From this moment on, decisions concerning East Germans were made—albeit with Soviet endorsements when necessary—by East Germans.

Wilhelm Pieck, aged seventy-seven, an old communist with

anti-Nazi credentials at least as imposing as those of Theodor Heuss, was named President and became the focal point of a big rally organised on 11 October outside the university in Unter den Linden. Its climax was a torchlight procession of several thousand young people from the Brandenburg Gate. Speeches were given by Friedrich Ebert, the Lord Mayor of the 'new' capital, and by Erich Honecker, then still in his thirties and responsible for disseminating Communist thinking amongst the country's young people, through the Free German Youth organisation. Honecker became East Germany's president and leader of the SED from 1971.

Both Chancellor Adenauer and Lord Mayor Reuter expressed public reservations about what they saw, and what the now departed General Clay would have seen, as the aggressively expansionist flavour of these speeches, but the reservations were rejected in East Berlin as the last straw if there was to be any 'serious' debate about reunification. For the East Germans now demanded 'a unified (*einheitlich*), democratic, peaceful Germany' with a similarly unified Berlin as that country's capital. Ebert, more specifically, called for the tearing down of zonal and sectoral frontiers. The GDR's capital, he declared, was 'constitutionally the capital of all Germany'.

The former manor house, now the castle, at Niederschönhausen, which at one time had been refurbished by Frederick the Great as a present for his wife, was now handed over to Pieck, the former joiner, as his residence. The Prime Minister, Grotewohl, moved into the old city administration offices in Klosterstrasse, while the People's Assembly convened in premises on the Luisenstrasse, now Hermann-Matern-Strasse. Bigger meetings of the SED were held in a hall newly erected on the site of an old city slaughterhouse.

The two hundredth anniversary of Goethe's birthday was a distraction ostentatiously celebrated on both sides. His was a heritage for all Germans to draw upon at will. Not so in the case of German art. When the Soviet sector administration had opened the National Gallery on their side in mid-1949, there were just 150 paintings on show. Hundreds of others had been sequestered by the Nazis as 'degenerate art'. Others, until recently stored for safety in western Germany, were displayed in the orangery of Charlottenburg Palace—later to be re-housed in the purpose-built creation of Mies van der Rohe.

At the end of 1949, a long stretch of the Frankfurter Allee, the main route of entry for Soviet tanks nearly five years earlier, was renamed Stalin-Allee. It had been pounded almost into non-existence but was still navigable for traffic. When the main ceremony of speech-making and poem-reading—it was Stalin's seventieth birthday—took place in the early December evening, there was a certain eeriness about the proceedings. It was dark, for one thing, and there were heaps of rubble as far as the eye could see. Soviet generals and staff officers were almost as numerous as German dignitaries, though Lord Mayor Ebert was absent. He was in Moscow. Signed papers on the significance of the renaming were laid in the foundations of the building project for the Allee which was on the drawing board. Now this thoroughfare has been renamed (in 1961) the Karl-Marx-Allee. It would seem that the founder of Communism is to be haunted by Stalin for the rest of his days—unless the name is changed once again or the foundations are re-dug.

Konrad Adenauer's city, Cologne, was largely devastated in the war and he cannot have been unduly surprised by the desolation that confronted him in Berlin. The old capital was a city he never particularly cared for, though he had spent time in 'exile' in the city during the Nazi era. Now, he arrived at a time of heightened political tension, amid talk of reinstating the airlift, and of undeniable need. Shortly before his arrival, his government had declared West Berlin a disaster area. Paul Hertz, an SPD man of the Weimar period, was brought in by Reuter from exile in New York, and appointed to take over planning of the western sector's economy. Liaising closely with industrialists who had stayed in the city—Borsig had just resumed production—and with US and other aid-givers, he launched a four-year investment programme to get West Berlin back onto its feet.

In the eastern sector of the city, the priority was 'to construct Berlin as a socialist capital', with special emphases on electrical and mechanical engineering industries. These had been the pre-eminent sectors in the city's industrial scene for a hundred years and now had to revive as best they could. An SED conference to galvanise the city economically was held in January 1950, but some companies which had been taken over completely by the Soviet authorities were not handed back until 1954.

May Day 1950 was celebrated on both sides of the 'red' city with an élan which had not been seen since before Hitler. East Berliners gathered in the Lustgarten, which for a while had been called Stalin-Platz, but had now reverted to being the Lustgarten once again. West Berliners, more than half a million of them, met outside the shell of the Reichstag building. Both sides set out unashamedly to score political points. West Berlin's theme, chalked up in slogan form for all to see, was 'No to Unity in Chains; Yes to Peace and Freedom'. For all the élan, there were grey moments: some among the crowds carried hand-made posters demanding, or offering, work for the war-wounded and the handicapped.

Sport provided some escape from politics, though the work brigades of young people who were drafted in to demolish the old barracks in Chaussee-Strasse and build a new stadium for 70,000 spectators—completing roughly two years' work in four months—may have had different notions of escape. On 27 May 1950, the Walter-Ulbricht-Stadium was opened.

Less than a month after, the West Berliners were authorised to throw open the Olympic Stadium for a championship football match. The game was watched by 100,000 spectators. A new rivalry between the two parts of the city, extending even to the staging of sporting events, was emerging, a way as decisive as any of ensuring their very separate development from now on.

Between the autumn of 1950 and the late spring of 1951 two important Berlin institutions were finally blown up by city authorities who said they were no longer serviceable and the sites occupied by them cleared. The first of these was the City Palace, which no Hohenzollern had lived in since 1918 but which was still seen by many Berliners as the 'soul' of their city.

It dated, after all, from at least the fifteenth century. The city's history, including its renovations, was bound up with it, and the sight that it presented in 1950 was a source of seemingly inextinguishable sadness. It has been gutted, yes, but it had already been serviceable enough for the holding of a couple of exhibitions. Self-evidently, there were large and very solid parts that could be saved and perhaps rebuilt.

The city fathers of the new administration, however, saw that it presented a unique opportunity. The removal of such a potent symbol from an ideologically unlamented past would be an emphatic gesture to confirm their resolve as socialists and—though they did not say it out loud—an act of atonement for the revolution which failed in 1919. Berlin, they had determined, would rise again as a German capital, the *Hauptstadt* of the German Democratic Republic, and it would have a memorial to Marx and Engels, the founding fathers of communism, at its centre rather than an edifice which had previously served a rejected ruling class. In fact, this memorial to the two men, unveiled in early 1986, was not seen as impressive, but as an anti-climax.

These city fathers had reckoned without popular resistance to their plans. One of the new republic's senior and distinguished citizens, Richard Hamann, was the newly installed professor of art history of Berlin University. He had been respected in art circles since the early 1900s, when he published a treatise on the Impressionists. He was now a member of the new state's Academy of Sciences, a recipient already of its National Prize. His views could only be heard with respect.

In August 1950 he wrote a letter to the GDR's first Prime Minister, Otto Grotewohl, and to the new city's Mayor, Friedrich Ebert. 'Berlin,' he said, 'is poor in monuments from the past. But it possesses one work which bears comparison with the greatest and is discussed in all art histories: the City Palace. It was created by North Germany's greatest sculptor and architect: Andreas Schlüter....'

Hamann declared that he was presenting his case as a staunch Berliner and, in the event that his political judgment might be questioned, as '*ein Sohn des Ostens*'—a 'son of the East'. Berliners, he argued, wanted to keep their Palace as they wanted to keep Unter den Linden. Like the Linden, it was a thing of quality from the past, comparable with the Louvre in Paris or the Kremlin in Moscow. Supporting him were Dr Johannes Stroux, head of the pro-establishment Academy of Sciences, and Hermann Henselmann, one of the new capital's leading architects.

Ebert, however, would not be moved. He had lost two brothers in the Kaiser's war; his father had been Republican Germany's first president—the man who, according to GDR historians, had 'betrayed' the 1919 revolution. On both counts, he had to recover lost ground, and his reply, while it pleased the new broom socialists, shocked and saddened many others, including pathological nationalists who still lived in a foggy past. Berlin, he declared, was not a city of ruins, like Rome; the Palace had been 80 per cent destroyed, and no one in the City Council had argued for conservation, which would have been too expensive anyway. 'We now have the most thankless task,' he wrote, 'to clear up the mess which others have made for us . . .'

In fact, irreversible decisions had already been made by the Council, some weeks before. Shortly after noon on 7 September, the first explosives were ignited under the Palace's east wing. In wretched conditions—a dull day and raining steadily—about a hundred workmen embarked on one of Europe's most disputed demolition jobs. Over the preceding twenty-five years there had been much thieving from the palace, but now they were guided by experts and art historians who salvaged what they could, and there were armed police at the site perimeter. The noisy, dirty and hugely symbolic work was to go on all through the winter, prolonging, it seemed, a gesture which stunned Berliners on all sides with its impact and which still arouses in many of them a deep sense of personal loss.

Around the Palace it is another story altogether. Other buildings of comparable quality, though not the same historical interest, have been retained. Some have been tampered with—such as the Neue Wache, built to a design by Karl Friedrich Schinkel in 1816—and a number have changed use, but the unity and the harmony of Frederick the Great's original baroque grouping, the Forum Fredericianum, can still, just, be felt. The great Cathedral of a later date, which some wanted to demolish with the Palace, has been altered a number of times in ways which do not please the purists, and the great Schinkel, one of its first contributing designers, would grimace at what would confront him today. But the early leaders of the Socialist Unity Party have had their way. Now, the evidence of their ambivalence and doubts, masquerading as political selectivity, is there for all to see.

One price paid for their early planning, heightened by the building of the 1961 Wall, is that Unter den Linden, once one of the very busiest through roads in the city, where everyone of note in Germany must have set foot at one time or another, is now one of the quietest. Until the war's end it was joined to the Charlottenburg-Chaussee (now the Strasse of 17 June) to form the main East–West axis. Today destinations in East Berlin which lie to the west of the Palace site are reached by other routes.

Around 300 new lime trees were planted along its length soon after the war ended and the Brandenburg Gate has been grandly restored, but it is no longer a gate. The adjoining Pariser Platz, where used to be the British Embassy (itself a former palace) and the world-famous Adlon Hotel, is motionless and flat. Occasionally Army guards move about around the foot of the Gate's columns. Undisturbed, they pursue their rituals and routines where endless streams of traffic, and almost every procession of any consequence, would once come and go, and where once the fashionable promenaded.

Halfway down Unter den Linden, on what used to be its classy side, the Soviet Embassy is also quiet. The present building has replaced a comparatively modest Russian Embassy which was there before. That embassy was fashioned out of yet another royal palace which had been purchased by Tsar Nicholas I in 1837. The current one was planned and constructed by a Soviet-German team in the early 1950s, an example of stark Stalinist architecture compromising minimally to meet the demands of such a German context. For geo-political reasons it is now one of the city's most important buildings, consisting of more than 300 rooms. It runs for about a hundred yards along the Linden and reaches back about the same distance to Behren-Strasse behind. Inside, one assumes, diplomats and bureaucrats conduct business of far-reaching significance—perhaps between endless glasses of Russian tea—though in the late evening the faintly audible sounds of roistering from a distant room suggests something other than glasses of tea.

Occasionally there is movement at the main entrance as a visitor of substance calls on the ambassador, but the overwhelming impression from the street is of order and things in their place. Along the Linden itself there is activity certainly—buildings which were once the homes of a would-be assassin or people of Prussian substance are now offices or shops (or possibly empty spaces), but there is almost no bustle. The Prussians might have appreciated the orderliness, but this is emphatically a silence which belongs uniquely to the late twentieth century, to people who wait between tension and détente. Here the most intrusive sound is likely to be that of a patrolling helicopter overhead.

★　　★　　★

Some East Berlin architects will today willingly concede that the building erected on the site of the City Palace has nothing of the grandeur to be expected, particularly in a German context, of its title—the Palace of the Republic. And, they add, the car park alternating as a parade ground which stands in front of it, on land which once also supported the royal Palace, is surely an inappropriate use for such a place in the city's consciousness.

The second building to go at this time was the Kroll Theatre, where the Reichstag had been obliged to meet after the organised fire in the main building in 1933. Its last meeting, under Hitler, was in April 1942, and it was badly bombed in November, 1943.

The Kroll was situated across what is now called the Platz der Republik, directly opposite the old Reichstag. Nothing of it stands today—there are only young birch trees—and it is not even mentioned in the guide books. It had been a theatre, however, in the Berlin tradition, introducing opera and concert-goers to much that was new and innovative. Otto Klemperer conducted there many times, and Ernst Legal, director of the first play to be put on in Berlin after the war in 1945, was a director there in the 1920s. A consolation was provided for the enthusiast on the western side when President Heuss returned to the city in September 1951 to open the Schiller Theatre, not far from what was then called the Platz am Knie (Knee Square), now Ernst-Reuter-Platz. In 1987, plans were announced for the re-building of the Kroll.

Six months after it formally came into being, the GDR Ministry for Construction went to Moscow for a six-week visit. In a sense, it was a wheel come full circle. The Russians had much to pass on relating to the economies of building in a frugal environment. But they, in their own learning process during the period before the recent war, had listened with attention to one of Berlin's foremost architects, Bruno Taut. He had come to the Soviet Union to escape the Nazis; now the people he had taught were passing on whatever seemed appropriate to fellow Germans.

Hermann Henselmann had become, with the departure westwards of Hans Scharoun, one of East Berlin's leading architects, and from 1953 to 1959 was the appointed chief architect for Greater Berlin. After much argument, designs were finally approved under him for 'the first socialist street in Berlin', the Stalin-Allee. More than two years after the 'consecration' ceremony just described, the foundation stone was laid in February 1952. It was to be two miles long, consisting of more or less symmetrical blocks, largely residential but with department stores, restaurants and other public facilities incorporated at ground and first floor levels. At the Frankfurter Tor, site of the old gateway into the city, Henselmann had two distinctive tower blocks built, each topped by circular, glass-covered turrets. In one of these turrets he lived while the building process went on around him, giving orders in his pugnacious way and vehemently arguing his case as he saw fit. These tower blocks, he told me during a richly amusing evening in early 1984 (when he was nearly eighty) were the buildings which gave him most pleasure out of all those with which he had been so closely associated in so many parts of the new city.

In the five years or so between 1945 and 1950, some 80 street names were changed in East Berlin. But in the weeks between 12 April and the end of May 1951, the number changed was 159. Names adopted were not always explicitly pro-Soviet, nor even unambiguously pro-KPD in orientation. But the ones rejected were almost invariably associated with the royal household, or with the now abolished Kingdom of Prussia. Out went names like Wilhelm (several times over), Heinrich, Augusta-Viktoria and Bismarck; in came the names of men and women revered for what they had done, in this century or the one before, for the socialist cause, as well as the sprinkling of others regarded as fittingly 'progressive'—such as Marie Curie, Garibaldi, and even Abraham Lincoln.

Two important memorials were unveiled in highly political ceremonies in the summer of 1951. On 10 July, in front of the main Tempelhof Airport administration buildings, Ernst Reuter dedicated the seventy-foot-high concrete memorial to seventy-seven airmen and ground staff who died during the 1948–49 airlift. The three ribs of this memorial point west, representing the air 'lanes' to Hamburg, Hannover and Frankfurt, along which supplies had been brought. Since Reuter had done so much to rally the city in its latest hour of extreme need, it was in a sense a monument to himself.

A month later, Walter Ulbricht, who the year before had become SED party leader, unveiled the bronze statue of Stalin on the Stalin-Allee. Similar statues were to be erected on prominent sites in other East European capitals, but for Ulbricht this one had a particular meaning. It was to Stalin that he owed his present position, and it was Stalin's thinking—rather than undiluted Marx or Lenin—which was so clearly to influence his own, both in policy-making in the new GDR and in dealing summarily with opposition to his policies. The statue was to stand for a little over ten years—longer, at least, than its counterpart in Budapest—but the thoughts of Ulbricht at its removal have yet to be recorded. He, after all, had unveiled a monument, if not to himself, then to his closest mentor.

'Berlin at the beginning of our century,' wrote Goerd Peschken, one of Germany's more outstanding thinkers in urban planning, in a dissertation published in the early 1980s, 'it was still standing when one studied architecture there in 1953. Even the Berlin of the "Gründerzeit" was still visible as a shell: in the city, one could see façade after façade prickly with decoration and elaborate gables with wrought-iron flag-poles bizarrely silhouetted against the sky.... All these skeleton buildings might still be standing had there been no need to make room for the compulsively oversize buildings of the East–West competition: buildings neither side is particularly proud of now.'

The city has always been a magnet for aspiring architects. There has been space and opportunity for them, however physically limited, and the nature of 'the East–West competition' has been such that for almost forty years the greater the impact a new building makes on the hearts and the minds of the citizens, the stronger their sense of belonging. West Berlin, in throwing open its doors to the architects of the wider world for the International Building Exhibitions of 1957 and then in 1987, ensured at the same time a new durability in the stake that the wider world had in the city.

On the other hand, 'making room' during the 1950s did immeasurable damage to the fabric of the old inner city. It is going much too far to suggest, as some architects have done, that the city has as consequence become faceless, or even anonymous. But it has made it more than ever a city where visual gems have often to be sought out and found, where those buildings most worth lingering over seem frequently to stand in splendid isolation. Happily, however, almost no one goes to Berlin for its buildings alone.

This said, it should be noted that there was intense debate in the early 1950s over whether or not to preserve, for instance, the Charlottenburg Palace, over whether to keep the stump and bits and pieces that remained of the Kaiser Wilhelm Gedächt- nis Church, or the eminently salvageable works of seminal 1920s architects such as Erich Mendelsohn and Bruno Taut. In the event, the first two were saved and the second two trans- mogrified into something barely recognisable. The Prinz Albrecht Palace, designed by Schinkel and used during the Second War as a headquarters building for the Gestapo, was pulled down— partly, one suspects, for understandable emotional reasons. The site became a vehicle testing track. Less understandable were the reasons for demolishing what remained of the great Anhalter and Lehrter railway stations. Of the Anhalter only a small, evocative portion of the front portico remains; the site is to become, ironi- cally, a transport museum.

East Berlin's planners gave early priority in their 'making room' and rebuilding to the East–West axis. This entailed drawing a line from the Stalin-Allee through the unrecognisable Alexanderplatz into Unter den Linden and down to the Brandenburg Gate. The first tenants in the Stalin-Allee, arriving by horse-drawn cart, took up residence in 1953, but not before thousands of volunteers were drafted in to where the great bronze figure of Stalin looked down as they cleared load after back-breaking load of rubble to produce small mountains of bricks and other materials for re- cycling. Further afield, they created bigger mountains in the city's open spaces. One of these is in the Friedrichshain park, where two massive concrete air-raid shelters, also incorporating anti- aircraft defences, have been covered over to produce Mount Klamott. Klamott is a slang word for rubbish; this heap is over 250 feet high.

In West Berlin, almost a quarter of the city's rubble total (estimated as at least 90m. cubic metres) was piled up in the north- east corner of the Grunewald to create the Teufelsberg. This is nearly 400 feet high and was a dozen years in the making. The result is a popular leisure area, including two ski jumps, where Berliners, making a very oblique symbolic gesture on the ruins of Nazism, like to take their leisure.

Activities associated with East–West 'competition' could not be, and never really have been, openly acknowledged as such, but for anyone familiar with both sides of the city they remain an inescapable, almost tangible, fact of life. In the early 1950s, as the global cold war intensified, competition was the main influence on the utterances of local politicians and also on the nature of the interest shown in them by their respective international patrons. This was the time when the very word 'Berlin' began to catch popular imagination in the outside world, when infiltration began of Germans among Germans (spying is not really the apposite word), and when the onlookers' clichés started their seemingly unstoppable flow. For West Berlin, the favourite terms were 'bastion', 'front line', 'showpiece of the free world', or 'island of freedom'. Such terms are today readily deployed by West Berliners in the business of commerce or tourism but are resented by ideological speech-makers east of the Wall. The irony is that the same competition imbues many East Berliners; they also feel that they are living in some sort of front-line showpiece of a city.

Political argument during the cold war kept 'the Berlin question' high on the international agenda. Stalin's less than rational behaviour in his final months rippled out from Moscow to his generals in their Berlin outpost, and thence to Allied generals on the western side. So, too, did the reverberations coming out of the US where assorted senators were increasingly obsessed by what they saw as the threat of communism. International perceptions of the city, and projected scenarios for its future, began to change.

Within their geographic limits, Ulbricht and Reuter remained dominant. Ulbricht decided to approve a tightening of frontier formalities, rigorously restricting access for West Berliners to the eastern part of the city, either by halting altogether or interrupting the flow of intra-sector public transport, by sealing off completely streets which were cut across by the frontier, by instituting new pass requirements, and by cutting telephone links. Characteristically undeterred by the death of Stalin (March 1953) he moved on from what he called 'the last phase of Sovietisation' to the 'new course' for socialism in the GDR, entailing much more discipline in the economy and increased militarisation. The word 'discipline' has been a hallmark of the economy ever since.

Reuter meanwhile had the title of Governing Mayor. He anticipated Stalin's death with his own ideas about vacillation in the Kremlin and uncertainties in the Ulbricht camp. It is now believed that he would like to have seen a new deal for the city in the spring of 1953, based perhaps on a meeting in Berlin between Georgi Malenkov, who had taken over from Stalin, and the new US President, Dwight Eisenhower. There was talk in the air of occupation troops being withdrawn on both sides. But the meeting Reuter envisaged did not take place.

Speculation about possible scenarios and/or developments provided endless raw material for broadcasters in both East and West Berlin. From East Berlin came calls on the SPD and the trade unions in the western zones to rise up against the conservative policies of Adenauer; from West Berlin came the voice of Reuter himself and a range of debate on Ulbricht's policies which, by their critical tone, can only have strengthened his hold.

The movement of refugees had increased dramatically, and the effect on morale in the eastern zone, and especially in East Berlin, was marked. By March 1953, well over 1000 people a day were crossing over to the west. East Germany, it was argued now, was losing its life-blood. Industrial output was suffering. Conditions in the transit camps which these people filled at Marienfelde and the city's southern outskirts gave increased cause for concern. Members of the US Administration, flown in from Washington, were photographed visiting them. The opening of the multi-star Kempinski Hotel on the Kurfürstendamm, at such a fraught period as this, was somehow very *berlinisch* in its timing and appropriateness; so was the conspicuous ceremony organised by the Russians at their war memorial to the west of the Brandenburg Gate.

The increasing tension was bound to lead to an explosion of some sort. It finally came in the middle of June, and East German historians today insist on seeing it as a 'long prepared counter-revolutionary putsch'. On the fifteenth, Grotewohl had refused to receive a workers' delegation seeking to discuss increased output quotas. On the sixteenth, a group of not more than about 200 construction workers at site No. 40 on the Stalin-Allee, angry at this refusal, downed tools and announced they were exercising their constitutional right to strike. They started to march to the House of Ministries and were soon joined by hundreds of fellow workers who had decided at street-corner meetings that they would show their support.

Some time between that evening and the morning of 17 June, the call went up for a rescinding of the new quotas—a call which then blurred into demands for the Government to resign, for fresh elections, and for a general strike. The Government had itself admitted 'failings' some days before; now its response to a situation which Lord Mayor Ebert's father would have quickly recognised, was one of blatant unpreparedness and hesitant uncertainty.

A relatively junior minister appeared, tried to reason with the crowds, but was shouted down. The strike which had become a full-throated protest now became a full-scale demonstration. SED members distanced themselves, when they could, from what was going on, but general support increased. There was some ill-disguised pleasure in the West at the thought of workers protesting against a workers' regime.

Ulbricht, despite demands that he should come forward to state his case, had declined to appear. After a night of unceasing agitation, demonstrators swarmed about the city centre. Diplomats and others in and around the new Soviet Embassy on Unter den Linden must have been astonished at what they saw. Berliners in the Friedrichstrasse, another area of intense activity, must have sighed heavily. They had seen such things before.

A meeting to clarify demands was held at the old Friedrichstadtpalast (the now gone Grosses Schauspielhaus). It achieved nothing and did nothing to dampen the ardour of the demonstrators. Party propaganda kiosks in the streets were soon set on fire, security men were beaten up, police vehicles were overturned, the Soviet flag was hauled down from the top of the Brandenburg Gate, where it had flown for more than eight years, and set on fire. (This, say today's East Germans, was done by fascist elements.) The shouted slogans were directed at Ulbricht (or 'Spitzbart' as he was contemptuously called, on account of his pointed beard) and at the SED in general.

The People's Police resorted to methods which in the preceding generation had been employed by the *Freikorps*. One handful went over to the demonstrators and another handful, according to eye-witnesses, ran off through the Brandenburg Gate to seek a new start in life. But the majority waded in with truncheons flying as soon as the stoning of government windows began. Then, when frontier notices—'You Are Leaving The Democratic Sector'—were torn down, they opened fire. By evening, the central office of the SED was under siege, and several buildings were blazing. In the current East German account, looting was getting out of hand.

The Soviet Military Commandant, Major-General Pawel

Dibrov, waited until well into the evening before declaring a state of emergency. That was hours after units of armoured cars and tanks had been brought in to play. The tanks surged up and down Unter den Linden, the Friedrichstrasse and the Lustgarten. Some had their tracks sabotaged, some had their aerials broken by the demonstrators. Others roared towards defiant crowds who were then machine-gunned down in front of them.

Nobody knows today how many were killed and injured during these confrontations. Nobody knows how many of the several thousand individuals freed when the prisons were stormed actually remained free. What is known is that at least 4000 men and women were arrested in East Berlin, and at least four times as many during parallel demonstrations up and down the country. It is also known that the Soviet authorities held their own courts martial where at least sixteen death sentences, and probably very many more, were pronounced.

A reading of the several accounts of these events that have since appeared, in East and West, makes plain that whether or not they can be regarded as 'a long-prepared counter-revolutionary putsch', most of those who participated in them had little liking for the regime, increased quotas and all, that they were working under. They must in some measure have been influenced by what they had heard incessantly on radio broadcasts from outside the Soviet-run zone, and clearly there were groups of West Berliners who did participate at their side, sometimes spontaneously. With hindsight, however, it seems very probable that western 'de-stabilising' agencies played an influential part in what had happened.

Ulbricht, by remaining out of sight, had survived an astonishing vote of no-confidence. He had suffered the indignity of seeing his party flags torn down and his own portrait trampled underfoot. The sort of Germany that he had endorsed had been rejected out of hand. Publicly he said nothing, and a book of his speeches and essays 'on the national question', published some years later by the East German Government, has no offering at all from him between May 1952 and April 1954. Even so, these two years saw the summary dismissal of the Berlin head of the SED (Hans Jendretsky), the Minister of State Security (Wilhelm Zaisser) and the chief editor of the Party newspaper (Rudolf Herrnstadt). The main highlight in Ulbricht's life for June, 1953, according to the authorised biographical data, was the award of the title 'Hero of

Labour' on the occasion of his sixtieth birthday. Perhaps, in a way, he earned it.

Robert Havemann had been a respected member of the SED and of the East German academic establishment. He witnessed and thought deeply about the June events. 'At the decisive moment,' he later concluded, 'the Party was virtually without leadership. But the uprising also lacked political leadership at the decisive moment. It lost sight of its original aim and objectively assumed counter-revolutionary aspects. Thus it was destined to collapse.'

Ernst Reuter saw what he imagined was a remarkable opportunity slip from his grasp. At the height of the events, his own party had issued an appeal to the Allied powers to initiate talks with the new Soviet leadership to end what it described as 'the intolerable conditions' in the Soviet zone. There was no response and, as in Hungary three years later and in Czechoslovakia twelve years after that, the West, disunited and uneven in the strength of its feelings, did nothing.

A fortnight afterwards, when some of the dust had settled, the Federal Parliament in Bonn declared that henceforth 17 June would be called 'German Unity Day'. 'Unfortunately,' Willy Brandt wrote some years afterwards, 'to many in West Germany it has become nothing more than an additional holiday.'

The bodies of seven of those who died in the uprising were brought before the Schöneberg Town Hall on 23 June, when Chancellor Adenauer, Governing Mayor Reuter and others addressed a crowd of around 125,000 who had come to pay their last respects. The addresses were not without their inflammatory moments. A few days later it was agreed in the same town hall that the two-and-a-half mile stretch of the east–west axis to the west of the Brandenburg Gate should be renamed the Street of 17 June. In mid-July, the Soviet authorities lifted the state of emergency they had imposed the month before. Ten weeks later, Reuter himself was felled by a heart attack; hundreds of thousands watched his funeral procession.

Bertolt Brecht was one of many in East Berlin who were sorely disenchanted by the outcome of the uprising. He had expressed support for the demonstrators' cause but felt sure they were being exploited by forces 'outside'. The way in which it was snuffed out added to his own gnawing feeling of alienation (his word) from the East German authorities, and in a brief poem he was scathing about the gall of a government that could now call on 'the people' to redouble its efforts as a way of winning back the confidence of the Government. 'Would it not be easier,' he asked, 'for the government/To dissolve the people/And elect another?'

Brecht felt compelled to seek a new modus vivendi with the single-minded Ulbricht and wrote to him with his proposals. The attempt misfired when Brecht referred to 'mistakes on all sides', not a phrase to win support from a man in Ulbricht's mould.

In April 1954 the Berliner Ensemble, now a little over four years old but already well into its stride as a national and international institution, moved into its own theatre. This was on the Schiffbauerdamm, just off the Friedrichstrasse, overlooking the Spree and almost next door to the old and historic Grosses Schauspielhaus. Brecht was given a more modest home to share with Helene Weigel, at No. 125 Chaussee-Strasse, near to the site of the former Oranienburg Gate. Today, this house is a slightly lugubrious museum, with an attached archive, bookshop and small restaurant.

In his last years, Brecht was perpetually a square peg in a round hole. He was, at various times, in dispute with the Writers' Union, the Ministry of Culture, the Academy of Arts, as well as artists who were working closely with him. One particular quarrel was with government bureaucrats and functionaries who obstructed the work of creative artists, and one result of his protests was a restructuring of the Ministry. Then he was seriously at odds with officials who wanted to block the publishing of some of his best anti-war poems. There was a minor victory when the book finally appeared, in a limited edition, in 1955. Still further tangles ended with Brecht refusing to accept some of the public honours which the Ulbricht regime wanted to bestow upon him.

Finally, and most piquantly, he drafted a memorandum just before he died, asking that he should not be given a state funeral and that there should be no declamatory orations after his death. His wishes were granted. He died in 1956 and his grave, with the one word—'Brecht'—on the stone, is in the Dorotheen Cemetery, just behind his last home. Helene Weigel lies nearby, and so does the political philosopher whom Brecht so much admired, Hegel.

★　　★　　★

The acrimony between East and West which had found voice during the 1953 uprising was not quickly dissipated. Nothing was achieved when the Foreign Ministers of the four occupying powers convened in early 1954 'to reduce world tension'. They held their sessions alternately in East Berlin and West Berlin, looking out on prospects which showed both sides in graphic terms how far apart they really were. No surprise, then, that the terms of a Western proposal, spelled out by the British Foreign Secretary, Anthony Eden, that Germany should be reunited—on the basis of 'free' elections—were rejected by the Soviet team.

And no surprise either, given the climate of the times, that the three Western powers should issue a prepared guarantee that they would now do 'everything in their power' to improve (West) Berlin's situation and promote its economic welfare. Five weeks later, the Soviet Union announced diplomatic recognition of the German Democratic Republic.

Acceptance of new realities did not reduce tension. Rather, to the extent that that acceptance became commitment, it increased it. In quick succession West Germany became a sovereign state; West Germany and its new army (the Bundeswehr) joined the NATO Alliance; East Germany became a signatory-founder member of the Warsaw Pact. Reunification, Khrushchev declared (in July, 1955) could only be achieved if there was 'collective security' in Europe.

Berlin remained an occupied city. In theory, troops from the West German forces and from the East German forces could not be stationed there.

East and West, in other words, were now as far apart as, say, Ulbricht and Adenauer. If one accepts the notion that living in Berlin today—East or West—has come to be like living without an arm or a leg that was lost in infancy, then this was the period when it became plain to both sides that amputation was inescapable and the limb would have to go. The acrimony stemmed, in other words, from vulnerability.

Willy Brandt now emerged as a major force in the city's politics. He had resumed responsibilities for Berlin with the SPD in 1946, soon after returning from war-time exile in Norway. In a sense he was a traditionalist: the August Bebel influence had been strong on his early mentors, and he had listened to and learned from Julius Leber (who died after the 1944 plot) and, more recently, Schumacher and Reuter. He identified closely with the city—one of the city's first leaders to do so—and he turned down an offer to stand for the SPD in Schleswig-Holstein. He became recognised in Bonn as a Berlin spokesman, and argued there for more of the new government's departments to be established in the old capital rather than the temporary one by the Rhein.

By 1956 he was clearly interested in becoming Governing Mayor in succession to Otto Suhr, an incumbent who was seriously ill throughout most of his tenure. In that year the Federal Parliament met in Berlin—at the Physics Institute of the Technical University. Brandt came to the fore at precisely a moment when both East and West Berliners—and their backers—showed how nakedly susceptible they were to wider world politics. This happened when Soviet tanks moved into Budapest to quell the Hungarian uprising just as they had moved into Berlin three and a half years before. A highly charged protest demonstration, with possibly 100,000 participating, was once again held outside the Schöneberg Town Hall, and a breakaway group set off for the Brandenburg Gate, its sights set uncertainly on the Soviet Embassy two or three hundred yards beyond, along the Linden. Soviet tanks were reportedly ready if they also decided to encroach on East Berlin soil. At the western side of the Gate, however, the group was met and harangued from the top of a car by Brandt who warned them of the implausibility and the potential enormity of what they were doing. His message underlined the incompatibility of the two confronting sides, an incompatibility to be reinforced by his own ascendancy as a politician.

Brandt saw the amputation was on the cards, even if he did not publicly say so. An unquantifiable number now realised that the Soviet authorities and the Western Allies had at some point decided separately (presumably separately) to cut their losses and make do with what they had. That point may have been reached when the New Town Hall session of the City Council for Grossberlin was broken up on 6 September 1948. More probably it was on the cards long before that—perhaps at the London Conference of September 1944.

Stalin the imperialist may have preferred to have had the whole of defeated post-war Germany in his new empire, but Stalin the strategist—wanting a tangible security on his western flank— was quite happy to see Germany on its knees, and divided. His successors in the Kremlin were to share this view. The iron curtain, as Churchill, the ideological adversary, had called it, had to be drawn somewhere—so why not across the broken capital of the defeated enemy? The deployment of Soviet tanks in 1953 and again in 1956, reinforced and defined the geographical limitations on the zone inherited by Stalin's heirs.

Throughout the 1950s, and increasingly, the fate of Berlin was discussed in places far removed from the city itself. As the decade progressed, Ulbricht asserted himself at the head of the administration of the new GDR, with (East) Berlin its proclaimed capital. Manœuvrings in the Kremlin following the death of Stalin—an occasion which provoked tears among German communists as it did among their Soviet counterparts—led to the irrepressible and calculating Ukrainian, Nikita Khrushchev, becoming Ulbricht's new guide.

Emboldened perhaps by the Hungarian experience, when the West could only react with heavy protest, Khrushchev threw himself into a campaign to have West Berlin declared a free and demilitarised city. Britain and France made occasional proposals, and Brandt and Ulbricht offered pointed contributions, but the decisive moves relating to the city's fate came from Khrushchev and Eisenhower, to be followed by John F. Kennedy.

Inside the city, meanwhile, life was much more about building, rebuilding—and living. Berliners who grew up in the city in the early 1950s recollect today a life which seems to belong, as indeed it did, to another world. The streets, they say, were uncannily quiet, especially where public transport had not been restored. Often there were great piles of unmoved rubble on both sides, and progress was a matter of picking one's way through them, sometimes over long distances. In a family where there was still no recognised bread-winner, money could be scarce and going to the cinema, a traditional Berlin activity, was a major event.

Many houses and villas were still under the control of the respective city authorities and rented out on a multi-occupancy basis. Larger rooms might have a curtain drawn across the middle to separate the lives of one family from another. Food, though usually no longer on ration, was a problem area. Farm produce would be brought in by horse and cart and sold at negotiable prices on the street; pig-breeders, ever ready to take away peelings and unwanted leftovers, did well. So, as a consequence, did the pork butchers.

Refugees, and particularly those with a Polish flavour from 'the east', were treated with, at least, reserve. Sometimes, they were 'like foreigners in their own country'. Fights would break out between the different children, and not only the children, of residents and of the incomers. Schooling would often be organised in shifts to keep the groups apart. Growing up in such an environment, it seems, it was 'very difficult not to get involved in politics' by the 1960s.

In the summer of 1957, there were celebrations at No. 52 Kommandantenstrasse, in Kreuzberg, not far from today's Checkpoint Charlie, as the 100,000th municipally funded post-war dwelling was handed over to its first tenants. Siting it so close to the east–west frontier, according to the Governing Mayor, meant there could be no no-man's-land here. It was on the western side, but a couple of minutes walk from Leipziger Strasse.

In the same summer, just north of the Tiergarten, the 'pregnant oyster' Congress Hall, a gift to the western sector from the Americans, was ceremonially opened. As so often with monuments conceived and/or favoured by the authorities (for instance, the late Kaiser's Siegesallee) there was a measure of mockery at the end product: the bizarre nickname was on account of the shaping of the building's bizarre roof, a 600-tonne structure stretched between specially reinforced concrete arches. It was a poignant if not symbolic moment when this roof fell in twenty-three years later—several years after a plenary meeting held there by the Federal Parliament from Bonn. The hall was rebuilt

The international building exhibition, of which the Congress Hall was a part, took place in 1957. The exhibition was a vehicle which enabled substantial building programmes for the city to proceed, often involving some of the Western world's most distinguished architects and builders. Thus, half a century almost after his first experiences in Berlin, Le Corbusier was back. A 1000-room, seventeen-storey complex of his creation stands by the Olympic Stadium. On a massive site, north and west of the Tiergarten, more than forty architects joined forces to produce a new Hanseatic residential area—replacing one which had become highly fashionable at the end of the nineteenth century.

In East Berlin, a great deal of rebuilding was going on—often in the old and historic Mitte area. Otherwise, it was a time of acute economic stringency, when much of the work was being done on drawing boards rather than on the ground. The Palace of the Republic, the Foreign Ministry, the new Leipziger Strasse, were all yet to be. But the Marx-Engels-Platz, laid out on the site of the old City Palace, was already a recognised space for demonstrations—and in the summer of 1957 Khrushchev was presented with one big enough to deliver a harangue on the subject of Chancellor Adenauer's 'German policy'. (One wonders how many among the thousands present understood a word of what he said. ...)

As these separately conceived, funded and executed building and rebuilding projects went ahead, so the real possibilities for the reunification of Germany, with an entity called Grossberlin at its centre, began to crumble. In early 1958 US military trains making for Berlin were stopped by the Soviet authorities and passengers were cross-examined. Then an American Army major's wife was stopped and questioned while on a shopping expedition in East Berlin. More vigorous customs controls were introduced. West Berlin, Khrushchev declared, had become 'a bone in our throat'.

As the noise of the arguments increased—the clash, it transpired, of sabres being violently rattled on both sides—the people of West Berlin prepared for the worst. Ten years before, the blockade had taught them an improbable lesson—that, in the event of the cold war turning hot, one had to be ready. The city authorities had enough food set by in 1958 to weather a year's blockade, should the need arise. A fraught situation in the city was not eased when a right-wing Parliamentarian in the 'so-called capital' ventured to suggest that the communist administration in East Berlin should be 'liquidated'.

In late November, six weeks before Willy Brandt became West Berlin's Governing Mayor, Khrushchev delivered an ultimatum. It took the form of a 'note', delivered simultaneously to the US, British, French and West German embassies, and started from the premise (one of many) that, although western Berlin was a 'detached' part of the GDR, it had also developed politically and economically 'in a different direction' from eastern Berlin. He therefore proposed that West Berlin should be 'demilitarised' and converted into 'an independent political unit', in whose affairs neither East nor West Germany, nor any of the present occupying forces, would interfere. Agreement, he suggested, should be reached 'without haste and unnecessary friction', but within six months. If agreement were not reached, the note concluded, then the Soviet Union would carry out 'the planned measures' through an agreement with the GDR.

'Berlin,' the Khrushchev ultimatum said in a passage of some colour, 'instead of being a hotbed of unrest and tension could become a centre for contacts and co-operation between both parts of Germany in the interests of its peaceful future and the unity of the German nation.'

On cue, Willy Brandt strode into the role which was to give him a global reputation. The people of Berlin turned at a moment like this, he declared, to their friends throughout the world. 'In the coming weeks,' he added, 'it is a matter not only of the fate of our city, but of the German people.' The initial Western reaction was one of some firmness, but when Ulbricht said that another airlift would be construed by him as 'a military threat', West Berliners reacted with a panic buying of coffee, sugar and other foods that had been so hard to get in the crisis of ten years before.

When Chancellor Adenauer joined Brandt at the hustings for the West Berlin city elections that December, he was heard with an enthusiasm which was heavily laced with scepticism. His message that 'although the clouds had darkened over Berlin, we shall not be frightened' was not enough to stop the SPD from taking more than half the votes cast, while the CDU (Adenauer's party) had to make do with just over a third.

The formal Western response to the ultimatum was enunciated on 31 December. 'If Berlin has become a focus of international tension,' the Allies noted, 'it is because the Soviet government has deliberately threatened to disturb the existing arrangements at present in force there, arrangements to which the Soviet government is itself a party.' Then, advancing a piece of the post-election evidence which had just been so sweetly placed on their plate, they added: 'The inhabitants of West Berlin have recently reaffirmed in a free vote their overwhelming approval and support for the existing status of that city.' This was a way of pointing out that the SED had taken just 1.9 per cent of the poll—31,529 votes out of more than 1,600,000 that were cast.

If West Berlin's election results dismayed the East Berlin administration, they emboldened their opposite numbers in Bonn. In its own long reply to the Soviet note, delivered on 5 January, Bonn referred to 'the aggressive attitude' of the 'so-called GDR', described the division of the city as anomalous and claimed that the creation of a 'free' unit, as proposed by the Russians, 'would deprive Berlin of any effective protection'. The Berlin question, it postulated, could only be solved in the context of the German problem as a whole.

The Soviet authorities and their Communist allies could not credibly reply to the eloquence of the West Berlin electorate. They chose therefore to participate in the exchange of proposals and counter-proposals which was now to take place, as it were, over the heads of the Berliners. But by the time Khrushchev reached the city in early March, he had to warn the over-eager Ulbricht to slow down. The time, Khrushchev argued, was not yet ripe for 'the new order of things'. Eisenhower announced that 'responsibilities' would not be shirked, and that the two million 'free' people in Berlin would not be forsaken.

If there was a feeling of helplessness in the streets of the re-building city, which sometimes bordered on panic, it also ebbed and flowed with disturbing unpredictability. While the uneventful passing of Khrushchev's six months deadline (at the end of May) brought some relief, Western proposals some weeks later to limit their garrisons, to grant the East Germans new powers over access, and to reduce intelligence activities in both parts of the city, were read as concessions and a cause for consternation. In fact these proposals were to point the Khrushchev team towards a way out they had to find.

Certainly there was a change in the Soviet tune. When, some weeks later, Khrushchev reached the US, he felt able to announce that 'since there is no united Germany we think that peace should be signed with the two German states'. Such a move, he suggested, would 'extinguish the sparks smouldering in West Berlin'. His description of the situation in the city as 'abnormal' was quickly echoed by the President.

Ulbricht seized with alacrity every opportunity he could to exercise his powers as leader of the East German state. In October 1959, on the tenth birthday of this state, he did it with flags— GDR flags, which he ordered to be raised over every one of the city's S-bahn railway stations. In vain, Brandt demanded riot police assistance to have them removed. But a month later, when it was proposed the same flags be raised once again to mark the 1917 revolution, officials of the US occupation forces waded in with a warning that they would take 'whatever action was neces-sary' to remove them. It was Ulbricht's turn to climb down.

Then, early in 1960, it suddenly seemed in Berlin that the smouldering referred to by Khrushchev would turn to flames, possibly even an explosion of unimaginable proportions. In February, the Warsaw Pact members called in Moscow for separate peace treaties with the GDR. In March, Eisenhower reaffirmed to Adenauer that the US were staying in Berlin. In April, Khrushchev declared that the US and their allies would have to leave the city; in May, a U-2 spy plane was shot down over Soviet territory and a climactic Paris 'summit', bringing Khrushchev and Eisenhower together, collapsed. In June, a session of the Federal Parliament, scheduled to take place in West Berlin, was cancelled at GDR insistence.

As Khrushchev had conceded in his note of 1958, the way of life in the two parts of the city was 'entirely different' one from the other. By mid-1960, fifteen years after the war was over, two distinct economies were taking shape. In both, the service industries were an inevitable growth area, but so too were the (long-established) engineering and electrical equipment manufacturing. These were in due course joined by such comparatively 'light' areas as pharmaceuticals, electronics, printing, and so on.

As in previous eras, small builders and jobbers emerged and, for the most part, flourished. Heavy subsidies were available for new projects on both sides. Sometimes, workmanship and 'finish' were of questionable quality, but these 'small' men were constantly in demand to work by floodlight through the night. The elegant external walls of older buildings were retained in many, still visible, instances, but in others they were deemed dispensable in the name of progress. The demolition companies were also in demand.

Possibly 100,000 East Berliners worked in West Berlin. They crossed each day under their own steam or by public transport from one side to the other to earn 'hard' currency which was worth notionally three or four times as much as the currency in the East. Shopping, particularly for consumer durables, was better in the Western part of the city, and the quality of life, as measured in material terms, was higher. Pressures on East Berliners and uprooted people from other parts of East Germany intensified. Sometimes these were direct, in the form of totally unsubtle Western propaganda; sometimes they were indirect, in the form of new travel restrictions announced by the GDR authorities. The harder it became for *Grenzgänger* (as frontier-crossing commuters were called) to cross, the more inclined many of them became to settle on one side or the other for good.

Employment was by no means the only reason for cross-frontier mobility. Relatives, naturally enough, liked to visit each other. In addition, churchgoers wanted to worship on the 'other' side; cinema, theatre or concert-goers sought out their entertainment regardless of geography; hairdressers and barbers drew an a-political clientèle, and so on. One account of this period published by the GDR Foreign Ministry (in 1966) says that 'in 1960 and the first half of 1961 tension in Germany became even more acute and provocations against the GDR were more and more frequent. Psychological warfare against the GDR went hand in hand with economic plundering, sabotage, terrorism and open appeals to overthrow the government of the GDR.'

Understandably, East German accounts do not dwell for long on the question of refugees—the hundreds of thousands who, ever since 1945, had been steadily moving from East to West in search of an elusive, but preferred, life-style. A very substantial number had no political motives for making the change, but did so in the knowledge that the right to live and work in any part of the country—and the city of Berlin—had been in fact underwritten by the four occupying powers from the start. For many, the nearest they had got to political protest had been to declare that they had had enough of shortages of even the most unexceptional items, and that they had had enough of requests, sometimes demands, that they should attend political meetings. For such people, the seven-year economic plan announced in October 1959, the required collectivisation of farming, and even the declaration that East Germany might somehow 'overtake' West Germany by 1961, had little appeal.

In the first four years after the war, an estimated one million Germans had moved from East to West. The number is uncertain because by no means all chose to register their move. By the same token, an estimated two and a half to three millions moved over between 1949 and the building of the 1961 Wall. The migrants were from all social classes and age groups. Skilled came with unskilled, civil servants and professionals with labourers and road menders, university teachers with students. Some 2000 under-graduates from the Humboldt University had been ready to enrol when the new Free University of West Berlin opened its doors in

1948. In all parts of the GDR, colleges and institutions, factories, farms and workshops, were having to survive in a perpetual and unpredictable state of confusion through loss of staff. A large proportion of these were going through Berlin to be processed at the barrack-like centre of Marienfelde.

In 1959 alone, a total of 143,917 East Germans crossed to live in West Germany, the smallest total and the 'best' year for the GDR since 1950. But in 1960, as international exchanges grew more heated, the total climbed to almost 200,000—of whom at least 4000 were card-carrying members of the SED. Ulbricht's decision to institute legal proceedings against people fleeing the country, with the threat of a two-year prison term for the 'crime', was no deterrent. More than half of those crossing were under the age of twenty-five, and East Germany's future was the loser. There was no way round the fact that this was another humiliation, whatever the cause, for Ulbricht and the Soviet leadership. Great damage, as the East Germans later acknowledged, was being done to East Berlin, and the GDR, economically, politically, and—at least as important—in terms of morale.

In such a climate, the erection of the Berlin Wall of 1961 was inevitable: there was no longer a proper agenda for negotiation. It became a reality on the hot night of Saturday–Sunday, 12 to 13 August when, at about 1 a.m., border guards started unrolling barbed wire across the Potsdamer Platz. Although this square was bleak and empty, it had become a central meeting place. Whatever the emotions of the onlookers—fury, frustration, anger, sadness—it took the form, from the Western side, of jeering and catcalls. The men detailed to perform the task took no pleasure in what they were doing, and they were backed with all the panoply of a sophisticated military operation. Tanks and troop-carrying vehicles were deployed close to Unter den Linden and at other by now recognisable potential trouble spots. Field kitchens had been set up, and were constantly busy, in many side streets. Armed guards moved about amongst the men engaged in the actual building operation, or stood squarely and inscrutably facing the knots of Westerners who were mocking and seeking to humiliate them. By noon on Sunday, more than 5000 West Berliners had congregated at the Brandenburg Gate. By noon twenty-four hours later, the Gate was closed—a gesture which in itself constituted an historical act.

It was a noisy operation. Pneumatic drills and other mechanical digging equipment were needed to put in place the concrete posts which were to retain the several miles of barbed wire. Unsightly piles of rubble once again formed along a jagged line through the city which had been moving heaven and earth to get rid of just such piles over the last sixteen years. With unsettling suddenness, it was now confirmed that the trams which had once circled Potsdamer Platz—for instance—would never do so again; that four-storey houses along the divide would never, after all, be serviceable as houses again; that a church burial ground would now be separated from the church which was its raison d'être; that the number of crossing points had been dramatically reduced; and that the separation was total.

The first barrier—the barbed wire precursor to the now familiar Wall—was for the most part completed in a matter of hours. The precision of the military operation, and its success in these terms, could not be questioned. Military-style parades past the leadership to celebrate the achievement were held in the ensuing days, and the new frontier's existence has been proclaimed with questionable pride by the East German authorities ever since.

Albert Norden, who had joined the SED policy-making Politburo three years before, wrote afterwards that it provided 'an example of how Socialism can deal a fatal blow to bellicose aggressors'. NATO, he argued in the same polemic, had had thirty-two different plans for Berlin, all with annexation in mind and at their most extreme involving the use of nuclear weapons. That, he said, was why the Wall went up.

A generation and more later, the deep pain caused by its existence, separating—still—hundreds of thousands of closely related people on both sides, remains undiminished, though for some it has dissipated with the passage of time. A semi-helpless and wordless shrug of the shoulders, possibly accompanied by an epithet of pointed contempt, is what Berliners now offer when questioned about its significance for them today.

Clearly, it is a different thing to each side—conceptually, and in its socio-political ramifications.

Some years ago, when I sought an interview with a GDR trade unionist, the taxi took me on a circuitous-seeming route through the streets of East Berlin until we came to a quiet cul de sac in, I think, the north-western corner of Treptow. Our destination was a union branch office, a room in a tenement block immediately adjacent to the Wall, and my taxi was the only vehicle in sight.

Children played and shouted about the tidy cobbled street, a small idyll of innocent happiness. The Wall, painted an aseptic white and unmarked on this side, cut across the street and was an integral part of their play area. Their curiosity about what might lie on the other side had yet to take root.

In West Berlin, innocence is not protected for so long, and curiosity comes earlier. Anyone can climb to the top of the several viewing platforms, roughly twenty feet high, and look over, as if into a strangely diseased area or a compound of dangerous animals. Anyone, it seems, can also contribute to the writing on the Wall. This started as truculent graffiti and is now a snaking riot of colour, the most elongated cartoon in the world. The designs are often extraordinarily elaborate, works of art in themselves. They have generally ceased to be products of bitter unhappiness about the cut which the Wall represents and have become gestures of rivalrous complexity. Defiance, which is what the exercise has always been about, has softened; angry explicitness has given way to mocking, sometimes puerile, humour.

In East Berlin, the Wall is reflected upon rather than talked about. At the western end of Unter den Linden, where the old Pariser Platz has been partly paved over and planted with flowers, visitors photograph each other with the Brandenburg Gate—no longer a gate—as background. Others, in ones and twos, stand quietly to one side, keeping their thoughts to themselves. Some seem to be praying. Others, on the Western side, looking East, go through similar private rituals.

Ironically, for West Berlin the Wall represents a substantial source of income. Coachload after coachload of visitors winds its way alongside—sometimes, as I have experienced, with inane political platitudes from the guide. Chattering children of all (Western) nationalities queue to climb the steps to have a look, followed perhaps by a polite posse of Japanese businessmen, a group of provincial politicians, or newly arrived diplomats doing their basic homework. Few seem to know the details of the historic buildings, or ruins, or empty sites which stretch out before them, and the rabbits which have proliferated on the grassy swathe of no-man's-land are what catch many eyes. The garishly printed panorama of folding paper, obtainable from the kiosks below, helps a little, despite misprints and omissions. Coca-Cola, posters of popular singers and all manner of kitsch, sell well.

It is easy to conclude that the moral affront of the Wall remains.

206

But how many today deeply care? Adenauer, Ulbricht and Khrushchev are all dead and the world has other issues and flashpoints with which to concern itself. People who were middle-aged when it was built are now pensioners, and people who are thirty or younger have not known life without it. The great old 'Heimatstadt' (the city as home) which Berlin once represented ceased to exist long before 1961, its spirit destroyed even in the early 1930s. Perhaps for those with long memories it is a consolation that the city's humour, its vinegary toughness of character, its obdurate survival instinct, exist still—in two communities.

A commemorative postage stamp was issued by the East Germans to mark the Wall's 25th anniversary in 1986. It showed smiling militiamen who had helped to build it, standing in front of the Brandenburg Gate as they are presented with flowers from members of the Free German Youth organisation. The inscription says the stamp marks '25 years of the anti-Fascist Defence Wall'. On the East side, an anniversary parade was held and speeches made on how it has 'saved' peace in Europe. A rally on the Western side heard a speech from Willy Brandt; the message was rather different.

The bald statistics of the Wall, being security matters, are State secrets and not openly discussed in East Germany. In West Berlin, they have become indispensable propaganda material. Thus, from the West Berlin Information Centre, we learn that its overall length is just over 100 miles, of which seventy are the now familiar concrete structure—usually about nine feet high—and the rest, when not the co-opted remains of house fronts and the like, impenetrable wire fencing. There are ditches deep enough to swallow a tank and patrol paths as far as the eye can see, and literally hundreds of watchtowers and guard-dog runs.

Firearms, it is reported, have been used by the frontier police on nearly 2000 occasions since 1961, and tear gas more than 500 times. Nevertheless, more than 40,000 known refugees—and registered as such—have crossed to the West in the same period, often employing mind-boggling ingenuity to deceive these same border guards. More than fifty have been shot dead trying to make the crossing and at least twice that number have been injured. Well over 3000 people are said to have been arrested while making the attempt.

The north–south cut across the city is a zig-zag which starts in the almost rural environment of Tegel. A stream runs along the northern perimeter and there is a bird sanctuary nearby. It is, intriguingly, the coldest part of the city in winter. Coming south, the Wall runs through parks, past back gardens and allotments and then follows the Frohnau-Lichtenrade S-bahn line, before turning right to follow, for over a mile, the course of Bernauerstrasse. Here the houses on one side became West Berlin, while those opposite became East.

Thereafter, the Wall goes north, then back south-east, past churches, cemeteries, disused sports grounds and an East German police hospital. From here, it courses more or less due south past the old city centre—then close to the West German mission, the largely eighteenth-century Charité hospital, Lehrter station, the Reichstag, the Brandenburg Gate, and across the Tiergarten to the Potsdamer Platz. Next, the line runs east for several miles, taking in Checkpoint Charlie, rubbing against the Axel Springer publishing house, and the Heinrich Heine crossing point. Here, on Wednesdays, both sides show an almost surreal respect for each other's dead: coffins are exchanged, though only after the necessary formalities have been gone through. Then, the Wall passes through one of the city's most congested areas, taking in another hospital, dock developments (including the main port of East Berlin) along the River Spree, a short stretch of the Landwehr Canal and a much longer stretch of the Teltow Canal. After that it runs approximately south, towards Schönefeld Airport through about four miles of relatively recent housing.

SIX

1961 to the Present

Allah ist mächtig
Allah ist groß
Fünfmetersechzig
Und arbeitslos[1]

The building of the Berlin Wall gave no-one any visible pleasure. It was rationalised by speech-makers and justified by policy-makers, but never rejoiced over. 'No-one can say,' Walter Ulbricht declared only a few days after the first barriers went up, 'that we enjoy having barbed wire.' And though Nikita Khrushchev was reported later to have said he 'liked' the Wall, he also described it as 'ugly' and 'a defect'. Both men, one committed to an administration based at the front line, the other vociferously arguing from the rear, were engaged in ideological warfare, but warfare none the less. The Warsaw Pact had solemnly agreed to the Wall going up, but going through with that agreement was an uncomfortable but calculated and necessary risk. A failure to take it, on the very soil where bids for revolution had failed just over forty years before, would have set back indefinitely the cause of Communism in Europe.

By the end of the 1970s, the Wall had become a very solid structure and the process of rationalisation had begun. East German chroniclers were saying that 'securing the borders' was in fact 'a decisive precondition for continuing with the construction of socialism without the direct economic and political intrusion of imperialism'. In later years, Erich Honecker, the East German party leader who had a major hand in organising the actual building of the Wall, preferred to measure his country's achievements from the year—1971—that he took office. SED

[1] Allah is mighty and Allah is great. He's twenty feet tall, but he's still on the dole.

209

party historians, writing in 1978, argued that 1961 was the moment when economic foundations and social relationships were 'secured'. Up to the Wall, they added, there had been no fewer than 25,000 'provocations' directed from West Berlin against 'the State frontier of the GDR'.

But the immediate aftermath was consternation and no little distress in the streets. For Berliners on both sides, something dramatic had long been predicted though nobody knew quite what was coming. Once the more or less expected had taken place, there was stunned incredulity that a city which was still home for nearly three million people, should be cut in two, and that Germans, even in uniform, should shoot to kill other Germans who were merely wanting to move from one part of their own city to another.

Hours after the first barbed wire had been rolled into place, Willy Brandt left the train he was taking to an election meeting in Kiel, caught an early flight to Tempelhof and was driven by way of Potsdamerplatz straight to the Brandenburg Gate. This was the scene, as he well knew, of previous confrontations. There, he later recorded, he looked into 'the vacant eyes of uniformed compatriots doing their duty on the other side'. Then, after an emergency session of the Senate—as the West Berlin council called itself—he went, for the first and only time during his Mayorship, to the Allied Kommandatura building in Kaiserswertherstrasse. Here, to his surprise, he found there was still a picture of the long-absent Soviet Commandant, General Alexander Kotikov, hanging on the wall. He also learned that the Allied Commandants were 'just as disconcerted and disoriented' as the Berliners themselves. Grave problems, the Governing Mayor reported, confronted them. They needed no telling.

The gravity of the situation was articulated in the response of West Berliners. Western leaders, who in their way had done so much to bring the drama about, were on holiday—in yachts at sea, watching baseball, or, in the British case, shooting grouse. In open spaces and streets by the city's new barriers, loudspeakers were erected to broadcast angry protests and posters were stuck up comparing Berlin in 1961 with the betrayal at Munich in 1938. Crowds gathered and wept, or taunted and abused the vacant-eyed men who were 'doing their duty'. Contingents of Allied troops moved forward to strategic points for eyeball-to-eyeball confrontation, and squads of West Berlin riot police were placed on the alert. Railings had to be erected round the Soviet memorial in West Berlin to protect Red Army troops on guard.

Distraction took different forms in the different parts of the city. In East Berlin, Communists were relieved that the haemorrhaging of the country's life-blood might now be staunched, though in fact more time was still needed for that. But there was also a realisation that a move had been made which was disturbingly final in character. While many wept in the privacy of their own homes, others in the workers' state talked and debated in factories and offices, and at unevenly effective Party briefings. How could they be wholly effective, when Ulbricht himself admitted that erecting the Wall had brought him the deepest humiliation of his career? There was also a perplexed apprehension at various levels: what would become now of contacts with one's nearest and dearest, and what would be the ramifications beyond Berlin's, and Germany's, frontiers?

In West Berlin, expressions of collective anger and frustration were more overt. If there were observers then, as there are today, who saw the new barriers as 'the basis for stabilising relations between the two sectors of the city as well as between the two Germanies', they kept such thoughts to themselves. Work was out of the question and protest, urged on by the will of the majority, was the pressing order of the day. There were strident calls for retaliatory measures and, somewhat oddly, for reunification.

As the week beginning 13 August progressed, railways running from East into West Berlin were torn up, and houses along the newly defined frontier were evacuated, bricked up and boarded over. By the weekend, the process of converting the barbed wire into a more durable concrete wall was under way. Orders were that the twenty-eight mile line through the city's heart should be completed during the weekend.

On Saturday, in steadily pouring rain, the US Vice-President, Lyndon Johnson, arrived and was greeted by Willy Brandt. He immediately plunged into stirring words about 'the high and holy cause of human freedom'. His presence probably meant more than his words and crowds mobbed him on his way from Tempelhof, by way of the Wall, to the Schöneberg Town Hall, finally forcing him to abandon his motorcade. Many were overcome and crying openly. Johnson himself, when he addressed them from the City Hall, was also close to tears.

General Clay, the belligerent no-nonsense 'hero' of the airlift, was then photographed clambering up—like a small child—to peep over to the other side. He too was deeply moved when he declared: 'What we started twelve years ago, we will finish together and Berlin will still be free.' What this meant exactly was not all that clear, and the imprecision of the occasion was compounded as the police band struck with the 'Star Spangled Banner' and with faint incongruity, 'Deutschland, Deutschland über alles'. Then came a rendering of the old music-hall favourite about the Berliner Luft. The freedom bell was rung.

Next day, Johnson greeted incoming US troop reinforcements. He stood on the same platform to take the salute which had been used by General Omar Bradley in 1945. To cheers and flowers, the parade of 1500 men of a tank unit proceeded the length of the Clay-Allee, up into the Kurfürstendamm and along Tauent-zienstrasse. In terms of mileage alone, it was one of the city's longest processions. Few in the West missed seeing it; few in the East failed to understand its meaning.

At the same time, the international ritual continued. A some-what restrained Western protest to the Soviet Union, which had taken four days to formulate, was delivered by messenger. It stressed the 'illegal' nature of what the GDR had done. A reply from the Soviet Commandant the following day suggested it was 'quite natural' for the GDR to take action against 'intolerable international provocations' being mounted from West Berlin. Neither communist 'tricks' nor communist 'threats', Lyndon Johnson countered, would separate the Allies from the cause of West Berlin.

Invisible, during these fraught times, were the subterranean differences between Walter Ulbricht and his Soviet patron on the one hand, and between Willy Brandt and an unsympathetic Chancellor Adenauer on the other. Differences between the two Communists were of temperament, experience and short-term expectations. The calculating Ulbricht had been active in or on behalf of the city for close to forty years; Khrushchev was a sometimes clumsy innovator who preferred quick results. In the West, Brandt from the Left of the political spectrum faced a Chancellor of the Right, a much older man, who did not care too much for Berlin (which matters in Germany) and was a separatist by inclination. He was also a Catholic where Berliners have been traditionally anti-Catholic by inclination.

Such differences as these, and the nuances that came from them, account for the fundamental variations in flavour between the pronouncements of supra-national statesmen on the role and fate of the city, when compared with those of the Berliners themselves, whose temperament, immediate needs and idiosyncratic lifestyles often concerned them just as much. In what other city in the world would a police band strike up with a music-hall favourite to mark that city being cut in half?

The evolution of two Berlins continued in spite of the Wall. In East Berlin, planners persisted in their endeavours to have a capital worthy of 'the socialist fatherland'. The accent was on control, and peace and order prevailed. In West Berlin, account had to be taken of edicts from a new 'capital' 300 miles away. The accent here was on accommodation, tempered by what might be called subsidised freedom.

The East was still losing people to the West. In the twenty weeks from mid-August until the end of 1961, a total of 51,624 people made their decisive move—more than 360 each day. Was the Wall in fact the biggest mistake that communism had yet made? Ulbricht spoke of the losses in people to the West as representing losses of about 30,000 million marks. Western economists claimed the figure was perhaps four times higher than that—equivalent, as East German officials balefully acknowledged, to the sum invested in East German industry during the 1950s.

Above Berliners' heads, the Soviet Union and the US exchanged views about the use of air corridors into the city, but then, as 'incidents' along the Wall began to horrify everyone who became aware of them, also about developments on the ground. General Clay abandoned retirement to become President Kennedy's 'personal representative' in West Berlin. Alexei Adzhubei, editor of *Izvestia* and son-in-law of Khrushchev, was told by the President that an 'understanding' was needed between East and West over the city's future. (A defeated Soviet people, Kennedy noted to his interviewers, would surely have objected to 'a line' through Moscow and their country, just as the Americans would have disliked a line down the Mississippi River.)

The US, in 'notes' to the Soviet Union, referred specifically to 'the cold-blooded killing of many Germans' by East German authorities operating in areas of the city for which the Soviet Government was responsible. The most stark of these was the shooting by East German guards of Peter Fechter, an eighteen-year-old who was trying to cross to the West. He was seriously wounded but lay against the bottom of the Wall, without help, for an hour before he died—close to where the building of the Springer publishing house now stands—and was unceremoniously carried away.

Today, along the Western side of the Wall, are the graves marked with simple crosses of others who had died in similar circumstances. In East Berlin, there are memorials, too, for frontier guards who have died in skirmishes with the West.

The Soviet 'Notes' declined to discuss 'incidents', choosing instead to concentrate on the more abstract theoretical issue of the troops stationed in West Berlin. Khrushchev proposed units from Denmark and Norway, or 'even' Belgium and Holland, to join others from Czechoslovakia and Poland, as a UN replacement force. Speaking to East German Communists at their Congress in East Berlin in January 1963, he declared that the socialist countries did not 'need' West Berlin—'they get along fine without it', he said—and nor, in his view, did the West.

This remark lowered temperatures by a degree or two. It also indicated a small tentative step in a different direction, along the road to what was repeatedly to be called 'peaceful co-existence'.

Both Kennedy and Khrushchev came to Berlin in mid-1963. With Brandt and Adenauer together at his side, Kennedy addressed, according to some estimates, more than 450,000 Berliners who had packed the square outside the Schönberg Town Hall, their highly-charged emotions ranging from anxiety to ecstasy. It was a speech which, especially for West Berliners, proved to be the most resounding declaration yet in favour of their rights to exist and against the iniquities, as they saw them, of the sort of communism which erected walls. It was also a speech which ignored, for understandable reasons, the iniquities of Hitler. 'I know of no town, no city, which has been besieged for eighteen years that still lives with the vitality and force, and the hope and the determination of the city of West Berlin. While the Wall is the most obvious and vivid demonstration of the failures of the communist system, for all the world to see, we take no satisfaction in it.... All free men, wherever they may live, are citizens of Berlin, and therefore as a free man, I take pride in the words "*Ich bin ein Berliner*".'

Just six days later, Khrushchev, accompanied by Ulbricht,

told East Berliners that Kennedy's contribution had only 'added poison to the international atmosphere'. He referred explicitly and facetiously to 'the so-called Berlin Wall', but stated that it was a legitimate border of East Germany and that it helped the cause of 'normalising' relations between states and 'the cause of peace'. It was a natural and legitimate desire of Germans to see their country united, he went on, and 'the best way to solve the question of reunification is to abolish capitalism in Western Germany and create a single German state on a socialist foundation. . . . But when and how this will happen is the business of the German people themselves. . . .'

Six months after these speeches were made, Kennedy had been assassinated; a year later, Khrushchev had been summarily removed from his own Politburo.

History changed course for a second time in East Berlin in 1961— just three months after the erection of the Wall. One wet and blustery night in mid-November, the Stalin-Allee was sealed off by police and traffic was diverted away from it. Once again gangs of workers were called into action with penumatic drills, this time to remove all signs bearing Stalin's name and, most dramatic of all, to remove the great bronze statue of the Soviet leader himself. By morning there was no sign of the man who had orchestrated the 'liberation' of Berlin. The street, which had been named in his honour in 1949, had become part Karl-Marx-Allee and, once again, part Frankfurter Allee. The statue which Ulbricht had dedicated with such ceremony in 1951 was broken into pieces and removed, without any ceremony whatsoever, on the backs of lorries. Only a few paragraphs announcing this fundamental change appeared in *Neues Deutschland*.

What Ulbricht made of it has yet to be disclosed. After Khrushchev's great de-Stalinisation speech of 1956 he had been a reluctant de-Staliniser; but he survived in power for ten years beyond the removal of the statue. These years, according to some East Germans, saw some growth in the cult of Ulbricht's own personality. The death of President Pieck, at the age of eighty-four and after several years of non-productive activity, assisted in this process.

The Wall gave both sides—not just Ulbricht—a sorely needed

opportunity for consolidation. On both sides, after all, the process of recovery was continuing and resources had to be measurable rather than merely possible—in men as well as materials. Plant and office managers, if they were to attain stipulated targets, had to know the size of their workforce from one day to the next. In East Berlin, the losses—especially of the under-twenty-five age group—had gone on long enough; in West Berlin, there was a feeling that enough incomers had been absorbed already. New arrivals from the East were not always getting the traditional Berlin welcome.

Once the movement of people began to stabilise, development became easier. Ulbricht pushed for what he billed as a new phase in 'the building of socialism', intended to carry the populace into an environment of 'true humanity, equality and fraternity, peace and freedom'. Compulsory military service, it was decided, would be a means of achieving this. This was a decision severely condemned by the Allied occupiers. West Berliners were, and remain, exempt from military service. One result is that the city's population now includes several thousand draft 'dodgers'. These are a group whose often iconoclastic ways have over the years had a profound and disturbing impact on the thoughts and actions of West Berlin's own younger elements.

The Wall momentarily halted the free and open 'market' in West German marks and Western goods. At least 60,000 East Berliners had had jobs in the West, earning 'hard' marks as a proportion of their wages. They would either spend these marks in the attractively stocked shops of the West before returning home, or exchange them at inflated rates once they got home. It was a natural enough, *berlinisch* way of doing things. Now, a new black market was started in money as well as goods, and the authorities turned a blind eye. Ever so discreetly, the same market persists today.

International pressures, and more readily understandable pressures nearer home, led to the Wall being opened for Christmas 1963. Probably every other citizen had a close relative on the 'other' side, and in the sixteen days from 20 December, a total of 730,000 West Berliners made 1.2 million crossings to the Eastern side. For many, this was in spite of angry exchanges with slow-moving officials at the crossing point. The 'concession' was negotiated by bureaucrats from both sides, and implied formal recognition of the authority of GDR state officials. It was to be

216

repeated a number of times until the institutionalisation of crossing procedures was clarified in the four-power agreement of 1971.
'Urgent family reasons' were invoked with some success by individual West Berliners during non-concessionary periods.

The early 1960s were a strangely heady time in the old capital.
On both sides there was by now a sizeable group which had grown
up knowing only a city divided, which had little or nothing to do
with the war, and was now determined in one way or another to
assert itself.

In East Berlin, determination was expressed through experimentation. Many words were expended and some tentative steps
taken in the realm of economic management, giving factories and
other production units slightly more independence. Writers and
artists and others who were engaged in expressing themselves—
for the socialist ideal whenever possible—became more daring.
Satire returned to the East Berlin stage: not the wild and gaudy
irreverence of the pre-Hitler days, but gibes and prods for discerning audiences. Smiles rather than guffaws became the rule—
and the leadership was never a target. There is still satire, strictly
rationed, today and the *Distel* (Thistle) cabaret show which
opened opposite the Friedrichstrasse station soon after Stalin's
death plays to packed houses. Down the road, at a glittering new
Friedrichstadtpalast, light musical entertainment, with unsubtly
deployed sequins, is on offer, while, up the road nearer to Unter
den Linden, there is an open space where the old Wintergarten is
somehow to be recreated.

In West Berlin, a decision was taken at municipal level to
create a new city 'centre' around the Kaiser Wilhelm Gedächtnis
Church. The truncated spire has since become the postcard
symbol of the truncated city; it is being carefully preserved, as a
stump, with a new place of worship, completed in the year of the
Wall, next door. A stone's throw away is the Europa Centre,
opened in 1965, the multi-storey mélange of eating and drinking
houses, places of entertainment and shops, where West Berliners
and curious visitors circulate and let their hair down in all sorts
of ways. It went up on the site of the Romanisches Café where
Berlin Dada started, though not a sign of this café survives. Exotic
flavours of old Bohemia have been displaced by a staple take-it-
or-leave-it diet of rock music, and nostalgists, if any now stray at
all into this vicinity, have to shout through the noisy brashness to
make themselves heard. (The Rolling Stones pop group started a

riot in the streets when they came to Berlin in 1965; another group, Genesis, started a totally different, cross-Wall riot when they played in the city in 1987.)

In October 1963 the irascible Konrad Adenauer finally resigned as Chancellor. He had served Berliners and Germans well by breaking through to a formal relationship with Moscow when one was badly needed. Berliners, out of gratitude, were obliged to swallow their personal reservations about the old man and made him an honorary citizen of the half-city. Ludwig Erhard, another Christian Democrat whom Brandt was later to see as 'an a-political politician', succeeded him and West Germany's political relations with the communists went into the doldrums. It was the time of enforcement of the Hallstein Doctrine—refusing diplomatic relations with countries that recognised the GDR—and of the growth, stunted but significant, of the National Democratic (neo-Nazi) Party.

There was a deep sense of shock in Berlin when President Kennedy was assassinated in Texas. Today's very perceptible American flavour in West Berlin (and indeed throughout West Germany), emanated in part from influences of the last fifty years, but in part from the actions of, and interest taken in the city by, this man. He did more even than Adenauer to rally West Berliners' spirits when the Wall went up. The square in front of Schöneberg Town Hall now bears his name, and a plaque with his likeness and some of his words is embedded in the Town Hall wall.

Then, less than a year after Kennedy's death, Khrushchev was sacked—removed from office by those who had apparently been closest to him, while he was holidaying in the Crimea. The manner of his going indicated that his policies as well as his personality were wrong. Today, he is barely mentioned in East Berlin; there are no streets or avenues bearing his name, no statues or plaques in his honour. His aggression vis-à-vis the West over Berlin had been effective in the first post-Stalin years, but after the Wall went up he became, so far as the city was concerned, more or less deprived of a role. Ulbricht and Brandt were the antagonists now.

Leonid Brezhnev, the Communist Party apparatchik who became the new Soviet leader, was more stable but less colourful than Khrushchev. His ideologically assertive but superficially accommodating 'style', such as it was, suited the ambitious Erich Honecker, who was increasingly ready to take over from the outdated and expendable Ulbricht. The latter, like Khrushchev, had served his purpose and could now go. Willy Brandt, however, now faced a Soviet leadership which was to respond in kind to his evolving *Ostpolitik* of reaching out to the countries of the Warsaw Pact.

Actual and incipient changes in Moscow's and East Berlin's leadership coincided with a winding down of the phase of experimentation in East Berlin. Individuals quietly persisted with whatever was possible in the creative arts, sometimes running into trouble—as the eccentrically talented and highly popular poet and singer, Wolf Biermann, was to learn. His work was (and is) liked on both sides of the Wall, but conservatism and conformity—so foreign in many ways to the ordinary Berliner's temperament—took over in the East. Biermann, his back to the Wall, was restricted in his movements, and natural tendencies of young people towards long-haired intractability, of the media towards sex and violence, of writers or artists or satirists to tinker with ways of expressing an outrageous honesty, were all repressed. The creative things which Berliners had done so vigorously and so well in the past were, in the eastern part of the city, deemed to be no longer acceptable. Even today, there seem to be hidden tensions about the way in which some East Berliners enjoy themselves.

In the Western part of the city, young people—and some of their elders—fell prey to the fashion for fashions which was taking root in Western consciousness elsewhere. The Wall may have made tactical sense but, outside the economy, it did nothing to end the ambivalence caused among the Left by geo-political uncertainties. Tension now was between those who wanted to reinstate the 'old order' or to establish a new West European 'order' and those who were devising new sets of values, philosophies and ideas—however phoney. One 'philosophy' said: 'We are an island surrounded by a Communist sea, let us eat, drink and be merry, for tomorrow we may be swept to oblivion.' A second philosophy set out to find all sorts of 'alternative' ways of living.

When these 'alternatives' took to the streets to express themselves, and then to 'demonstrate', the authorities panicked. Water cannon were used to sweep them, almost literally, out of sight, and squatters were ejected, but it was difficult for the authorities to ask questions. The more things changed, the more something or other which was very *berlinisch* remained the same. Important new ways of thinking and expression were found in the arts, but the fashion for 'dropping out', promiscuity, for flower power, for drugs, for the 'way out' and the 'off beat', also found there was still fertile soil in West Berlin. With multifarious other plants, they all rather quirkishly and self-consciously continue to flourish today.

One elemental 'colour' which had virtually drained away from the fabric of the city in Hitler's time, and which is barely noticeable today, was that provided by the city's Jews. On 10 January 1958, the skeletal ruins of the great Fasanenstrasse synagogue, off the Kurfürstendamm, were blown up. It had opened its doors in 1912, when Jews, despite some anti-Semitic sniping, were prospering; now there were not even enough Jews left in Berlin to exploit a campaign for the building's restoration. However, in September the following year, the new Jewish community house did open on the same site.

The architects (Dieter Knoblauch and Hans Heise) incorporated ornamental stonework retrieved from the old synagogue to make an arched porchway into the new house. The fragments used look oddly fragile and contrast with the assured firmness of the modern structure. An opening ceremony was attended by Willy Brandt and by the elected head of the community, Heinz Galinski. It was an event overlaid with poignancy, an over-modest tribute to hundreds, if not thousands, of personalities who had contributed so much to the city.

Richard von Weizsäcker, son of Hitler's senior foreign policy adviser and later to become Governing Mayor of West Berlin from 1981 to 1984, did much to renew confidence in the relationship between Berliners and their wary Jewish community. He was to become, as he put it, 'a normal and frequent guest' at the community's houses in Fasanenstrasse, and in 1982 was to attend (as Governing Mayor) a conference convened at the Am Grossen Wannsee villa to mark the fortieth anniversary of the meeting which formulated the 'final solution' to the Jewish question. He thanked the Israeli Government representative for attending. Later the same year he was at an event to remember the Warsaw Ghetto uprising, and on that occasion said: 'I have the feeling that the human bridge between Jews and Germans is still sensitive and fragile. . . . But it is holding. We want to see that it never collapses again.'

When, in 1971, Berlin's Jews celebrated the 300th anniversary of their community, there were just 5000 of them left in the city.

Probably there were not more than 600 left in East Berlin—only a third of whom were thought to be practising. The anniversary was marked formally with an exhibition at the Berlin Museum, a converted former court house, in Lindenstrasse, Kreuzberg. But many of the city's Jews choose to do their remembering quietly.

A guide-book for 1936 lists twenty-four synagogues in the whole city. Today, they can be counted on the fingers of one hand. One, refurbished, was reopened in Pestalozzistrasse, just north of Savignyplatz, in 1953; a second, frequented by less affluent members of the community, was opened—also in 1959—on the Fraenkelufer, by the Landwehr Canal. The first new purpose-built synagogue since the 1920s was dedicated at Herbartstrasse, by the Lietzensee, in 1981. It is named after Leo Baeck, the community's leader throughout most of the Nazi peiod, who had died in London in 1956. Carl von Ossietzky, the Jews' leading pre-war intellectual, is remembered in West Berlin with a plaque on the wall at 152 Kantstrasse, the address of the east Jewish Centre during the war. In East Berlin, there is a street and a square with his name.

The Jewish 'parent' organisation in East Berlin is based in rather mean-looking premises in Oranienburgerstrasse, which once housed the city's Jewish school. It is the Association of Jewish Communities in the GDR. It adjoins the haunted shell of the Byzantine showpiece style of Jewish architecture—the Oranienburgerstrasse synagogue—wrecked in the Reichskristallnacht. According to an East German government pronouncement of 1986, this is now scheduled to be restored.

The Association organises its own events and runs a library. Like so many religious bodies in the communist countries, it has responsibility for welfare work among the elderly, the handicapped, and other social casualties. There is a Jewish old people's home in Niederschönhausen, but the Auguststrasse hospital, erected in 1861 and from which old people were forcibly taken to Nazi concentration camps, has become a school. Worship for East Berlin's Jews is conducted at a synagogue in Rykestrasse, not far from Senefelder-Platz and near the old city centre. (It is situated close to where the artist Käthe Kollwitz used to live and where the Nazis' martyr Horst Wessel was buried. There is a monument to her, but nothing at all to him.)

The biggest Jewish cemetery in Europe, with well over 100,000 graves and established in the time of Kaiser Wilhelm I, is also in the East Berlin Association's care. It occupies an extensive site opposite East Berlin's newest leisure centre between Prenzlauer Berg and Weissensee. Ancestors of Jews who have been prominent in East German public life are buried there.

Since the mid-1970s colour and sounds of a totally different sort have been provided in West Berlin by the city's Turkish immigrants. There are now between 100,000 and 200,000 of them—many more than belong to the next biggest immigrant group, the Yugoslavs—and they represent easily the fastest growing ethnic community in the city. Despite occasional expressions of resentment and racial harassment from non-Turks, they tend to keep to quickly recognisable and well-defined areas. Their homes, their shops, and their very active places of entertainment are often in the poorer and more overcrowded parts of Kreuzberg, close to the Wall, where the crumbling tenement blocks have been only minimally refurbished. But Turkish community life, and Turkish-run businesses, flourish.

At the centre of one of the main Turkish areas is the old Bethany Hospital, built in the mid-nineteenth century and one of the biggest in Berlin. It was closed as a hospital in early 1970 and after much fierce debate over the building's fate—it is considered an historic specimen by architects—was reopened, after a spell of being occupied by 300 assorted squatters, as a community arts centre. Now, it has been designated by the Senate as a cultural centre and it is used by Turks and Germans together for all sorts of celebrations, study and worship. Turks living in this immediate area seem to co-exist harmoniously with the local, mainly younger-generation Berliners—many of them now legal squatters—working together and sharing welfare facilities, with their children playing noisily in the streets. But in considering the city's Turkish population, it is hard to avoid the thought that ill-intended Berliners could quickly find a scapegoat on their doorstep if ever the need arose.

By definition and by age, most Berliners in the 1960s had been chastened by the 1939–45 war and by post-war uncertainties. But the inborn buoyancy of others, coupled with a general need for all sorts of escapism meant that a range of cultural and entertainment facilities, from the racy to the respectable, were quickly and successfully grafted onto the two city landscapes. East–West competition has taken many forms.

Both sides cultivated their own prestige theatres, opera houses and concert halls; both were able to assemble museums of national history, 'national' galleries, several libraries, to foster their own fully-fledged universities, institutes of higher learning and research, academies of arts and sciences, to nurture artists in all disciplines, actors and directors, orchestras and conductors, writers and performers, all of international stature.

The over-riding irony now is that most of the two populations cannot spontaneously cross to the other side to see the performers they would like to see. But even so, the tradition of making waves, and making history, in the arts, which gave the city an unequalled reputation from, say, the turn of the century, has been continued. Sometimes, this has been achieved with a restrained sort of energy and a strange precision, and often with financial backing which, when all is said and done, is politically motivated. But it has worked. Berlin's old glitter may have gone, but a certain magnetism, for the aficionado and the enthusiast as well as the truly talented, has been retrieved.

It is no novelty that there are more 'active' theatres than there are 'active' churches—that was the case before the war. But patterns of patronage have changed: dotted all over the city there are church buildings, in many cases gaunt and in poor repair, underused, and, some of them, totally unused. They are falling into wistful decay. The Klosterkirche ruins (dating from the thirteenth century) are used for exhibitions, while others, in East and West, are used for concerts. No matter how many church-goers or believers, or simply avid, agnostic debaters, there may be in both Berlins, the pervasive impression remains that these are mainly secular communities.

The polarisation of attitudes which became so clear in the 1960s was roughly determined by the generation differences. The younger, anti-authority generation could not, and would not, accept responsibility for whatever havoc may have been wrought in Europe by their parents. They were disturbed by the coming of the Wall not just because it was a harsh affront to humanitarian principles but because it had led (in the West) to a rejection of Communism and all it stood for, and (in the East) to fundamental differences over the nature of socialism and how it should be put into practice. It was by no means only a Berlin phenomenon, but it was heavily accentuated in this city.

In the West, there was only notional sympathy—outside the purlieus of a very small SED-backed Communist Party—for the political measures which were being enforced beyond the Wall. It was after all the older generation who were the chief enforcers— Ulbricht was seventy in 1963 and still had nearly eight years to go; Khrushchev was only a year younger. When the Wall was finally opened, and the queues formed, for visits to the East during Christmas and New Year, 1963–64, it was usually the older generation that went through. They went burdened with flowers and Christmas presents, often the simple necessities of life, and returned with their emotions in turmoil and with highly vocal accounts of what they automatically considered to be politically unacceptable. When, a year later, the first pensioners from East Berlin were allowed westwards, they were hardly enthusiastic for a regime which had kept them separated for so long from their own kith and kin.

In the summer of 1965, about 10,000 students marched through the centre of West Berlin, to protest at inadequate grants and funding. It was the first of a series of gestures of impatience, all made with great noise and éclat, and contrasted palpably with the stoical bearing of their parents and grandparents who queued, sometimes for hours at a time, to pass through inhospitable check-points in their own city.

The students' demonstration this time was symptomatic of something the city had never before experienced, as strange to its corporate nature and history as the water cannon was strange to the thinking of those at whom it was directed. A composite profile of the city, regardless of the Wall, would still include ingredients of Prussians and Prussianness, of a disoriented aristocracy, of those who worked and lived according to order and routine on the one hand, but on the other hand, also those who rejected utterly all order and routine, and a vast and gregariously earthy 'working class'. These were ingredients which had, one way or another, always been present. Those who now embarked on the demonstration as a way of life, whether privately within four walls or openly along the Kurfürstendamm, were something new. They could afford the luxury of rejecting, justifiably, all their parents had fought for under Hitler as well as the values on which they based their beliefs. They were turning to Allan Ginsberg, Jack

Kerouac, Jean-Paul Sartre, and even Jack London, who were light years away from Thomas Mann and other exponents of the intellectualised respectability. *Guerilla Warfare* by Che Guevara, or the *Thoughts* of Mao Tse-tung, were more easily digested than Karl Marx's *Kapital*.

In Berlin, the thoughts of Berlin-born Herbert Marcuse took root with extraordinary ease. The successors of Ernst Reuter and Willy Brandt suddenly had to contend with almost an entire generation which applauded when Marcuse questioned what he called 'ritualised concepts' of freedom, democracy or equality. He also questioned the role of Marxism in the Soviet Union, and implicitly in East Germany, and, more important, he preached that self-determination should not be obstructed by compliance or restrictions of the state, that sexual freedom went way beyond anything Berliners may have tried in the 'golden' 1920s, and that students were an important group in 'the new revolution'.

A 'movement' evolved, with the sort of animus and energy that had characterised Dada nearly fifty years before. But this movement of the 1960s was formed in the context of cold war, lingering Stalinism, and conservative governments in Bonn and elsewhere.

The students were often living in US-funded accommodation and attending lectures in US-funded university premises and they focused their anger and their violence particularly on the Vietnam war, being fought by the US against a communist enemy elsewhere. They were a strange crowd, wearing odd clothes, sometimes bearing flowers. In early 1966, the centre of West Berlin was brought to a standstill as one group of them sat down in the main thoroughfares, while a second pelted Amerika-Haus, next to the Zoo Station, with eggs and other missiles (what would Isherwood have thought now?...), and a third ostentatiously lowered the American flag to half-mast.

When the Free University authorities decided to rule against political demonstrations, thousands of students decided to stage another sit-down protest. The ruling was lifted. Six weeks after that, there were scuffles in the Kurfürstendamm at the showing of what young people declared was a racist film. Beyond Berlin, it was the US who became the targets; inside Berlin, it was the police. At the end of the year came 'Vietnam Week' and a whole series of events designed to discredit US involvement in the war. These events, said the city authorities, were 'a shock' to West

Berliners, a shock no doubt compounded when the younger elements' leader, a brilliant sociology student (originally from East
Germany) called Rudi Dutschke, won massive support when he
declared in favour of setting up an Extra-Parliamentary Opposition Group. Factions from this group, and smaller splinter
groups, were to disrupt the Berlin—and the West German—
political scene for several years. Violence was only one of their
methods; 'flower power' was another.

Hubert Humphrey, vice-president now to the US leader who
had shared tears with Berliners just a few years before, had stones
and empty bottles hurled at his car when he paid a visit in April
1967. In subsequent protests at the university, police moved in
to make arrests. When the Shah of Iran came to the city a few
weeks after Humphrey, eggs, tomatoes and cartons of milk were
thrown outside the Opera House, but shots were also fired and a
student called Benno Ohnesorg was killed. Mass demonstrations
accompanied the removal of his body for burial a few days later,
and he himself became a martyr to the Left's cause.

In these confused times, Willy Brandt chose to leave Berlin,
having entered Federal politics in Bonn in December 1966.
Though the anti-SPD tide was gradually rising in West Berlin,
many West Berliners were sorry—and some disillusioned—to see
him go. His successor as Governing Mayor was a protestant
minister named Heinrich Albertz, but he did not last long. He
had been appointed only a few days after the Vietnam Week;
within a year, following the outcry at Ohnesorg's death, he was
forced to resign. He was followed by the Senator responsible for
liaising with the Bonn government, Klaus Schütz.

But peace did not return to Berlin. In defiance of further Senate
orders, an International Vietnam Congress, organised by the students, went ahead at the Charlottenburg Technical University.
At its climax about 10,000 of them marched through the centre
of the city. Schütz demanded an end to 'spitting on American
boots', but once again there were anti-Vietnam organised protests,
and further violence. Slogans were shouted for 'Ho-Ho, Ho Chi
Minh', the North Vietnam leader, and Lyndon Johnson, the
erstwhile crowd-puller, was mocked. This time round, Berliners
who had been students thirty years before must have had a dis-
concerting sense of *déjà vu*.

It was an ugly time, and something clearly had to give. This
happened on 11 April 1968, when Dutschke, by now a figure with

an international following, was shot and severely wounded as he walked down the Kurfürstendamm. Two bullets were removed from his head in a five-hour operation which followed. He was to die of these wounds some years later.

Protests which had earlier grown into demonstrations now escalated alarmingly to become mass riots, at times occurring on a daily pitched-battle basis. What was happening was destabilising and, though it originated among the hard-core political Left, now took in a much wider following.

The developments must have been intriguing to those Soviet and East German functionaries—and occasionally ordinary citizens—who looked on from beyond the Wall. It had become a grisly routine that hundreds would be arrested or that scores would be wounded in the mêlées that now ensued. One of the most dramatic occurred at the newly completed twenty-storey headquarters of the Axel Springer newspaper publishing group, a few hundred yards or so away from Checkpoint Charlie. The building had been sited, as a deliberate provocation by the proprietor, right up against the Wall. As the riots had gained in intensity, Springer had had his main block surrounded by barbed wire. The rioters therefore headed for the company's transport department, and several vehicles were set on fire. More than 1000 arrests, sometimes including innocent bystanders, were made.

Mayhem in the city streets, and power-keg tension when there was no mayhem, exceeded anything that had been experienced since the late Weimar period. It was not long before the demonstrators erected makeshift barricades in the streets. These would then be charged by detachments of mounted police, or others in riot gear who would lead indiscriminate baton charges into chanting, mocking crowds hurling cans of paint at them. Peaceful anti-nuclear protestors, who liked to congregate at the Wittenberg Platz on Tauentzienstrasse, were occasionally drawn into the general ruck. If some carried flowers, they were of little use.

The ultimately fatal blow to Dutschke was a blow to the whole. Notwithstanding the fact that some of the protestors had managed to formulate a sort of working relationship with some sympathetic senior members of the Church, the university authorities and the Senate were able to take much of the wind out of their sails by finally agreeing to give the students more say in the running of their affairs, including the appointment of teaching staff. By late 1969, there was a lull in the violence.

In fact, the real violence was yet to come, in a different form—of 'direct action'. As the Vietnam war edged towards its inexorable end and the US towards humiliating defeat by the Viet-Cong, so the dramatic effects of the street demonstrations began to diminish. The attempt at a coup—revolution is too strong a word—by the young Left in West Berlin and the consternation to which that attempt had given rise, slowed down. But like previous bids for fundamental change that had been made by such different people in the same city, it left many of the participants nursing their bruises with determined but unclear notions of how and when to resume the struggle. Maybe it was not Noske all over again, but it was the forces of law and order—armed police with riot gear and water cannon—who were in control.

Simultaneously, East-West antagonists were concentrating less and less on Berlin—at superpower level anyway. The confrontation became once more between East Germans and West Germans, at its oddly comical sharpest when frontier guard faced frontier guard, fixing each other with binoculars from their respective checkpoints.

The hard-core Left seemed to be blurring into something softer, known in West Berlin as the Alternative List, elsewhere as the Green Party. The List was not without its anarchist elements and embraced a sort of belligerent liberalism, placing heavy emphasis on human rights, disarmament, the Third World, co-operative effort and an improved environment. The commune became an accepted way of living together. When, some years after Vietnam, the West Berlin authorities had empty houses on their hands, especially in run-down districts of Kreuzberg and Wedding, they were to find—sometimes to their astonishment—that the former students of the 1960s were the squatters whom they had to contend with. Even more astonishing for some in the bureaucracy was the fact that these supposed adversaries were quite often conciliatory and constructive in their social attitudes.

The second half of the 1960s represented the last phase of Ulbricht and the first of Leonid Brezhnev in Moscow. Twenty years on, it can be seen as a time when East-West cross-currents, as they affected Berlin, became somewhat clearer. Among Eastern Europe's leaderships, there was new apprehension about Brandt's growing stature as a politician and the SPD's growing strength as a political force in West Berlin. Communists in the West were vocal but were getting only a derisory share of the popular vote.

In June 1964 there came—in Khrushchev's final months—a Soviet-led campaign to have West Berlin defined as 'an independent political entity'. This was rejected by Brandt and his supporters and was eloquently and, literally, undermined by fifty-seven East Berliners who forced through a tunnel underneath the Wall to realise their preference for living in the West. However, the phrase 'independent entity', with and without the 'political' adjective, has stuck: Soviet officials made a point of repeating it when discussing the anniversary celebrations of 1987.

The late 1960s were a time for each side to test the other's will, and for tit-for-tat. When the Federal Parliament met—for the eighth time since 1955—in the converted teachers' training college in the Bundesallee in Schöneberg in April 1965, East Germans and Russians retaliated by halting traffic at entry points into West Berlin and flying helicopters noisily overhead. The following year, however, Brandt became West Germany's Foreign Minister and almost straightaway got down to implementing his Ostpolitik of conciliation with Eastern Europe. This initially excluded the East Germans, and the first diplomatic 'bridge' was built between Bonn and Bucharest.

But if détente was in the air, it was clouded severely by the Soviet-led intervention in Czechoslovakia in 1968. An antidote to these clouds was the appointment of Brandt to become West Germany's first SPD Chancellor in 1969. Earlier that year, the new US President, Richard Nixon, went to West Berlin and, choosing the Siemens electronics factory for his main political surge, said the situation in Berlin should be regarded by everyone as 'a call for action and a challenge to end the tensions of a past age'.

Moves for a new, four-power deal on the future of the city had been given fresh impetus, and Brandt, in his inaugural speech as Chancellor, urged the four powers to negotiate. Suddenly there were flurries of activity around the Control Council building in Elssholzstrasse, from which the Soviet delegation had walked out almost twenty-two years before. Suddenly, too, there was a fresh meaning to the ceremony—still conducted every day—of raising the flags of all four occupying powers. At 9 a.m. on Thursday 26 March 1970, the ambassadors of these powers held their first formal meeting. It lasted three hours, was totally confidential, and the US Ambassador, Kenneth Rush, took the chair.

Protocol demanded that all meetings—there were to be ten more at ambassadorial level that year—should be confidential. If ordinary Berliners held their breath as these negotiations proceeded, they did so noisily. It was a time also when the Red Army Fraction, an anarchist group aiming at the violent over-throw of capitalism, came to the fore. On the very day that the four Ambassadors held their third meeting in Elssholzstrasse, for instance, the Fraction also managed to free their leader, Andreas Baader, from a remand centre where he was being held in Dahlem.

The four-power talks were held in the same room where officers who participated in the July 1944 plot against Hitler had been tried and sentenced to death. They progressed with astonishing speed and were paralleled by remarkable developments elsewhere. Brandt made his historic trip to Erfurt in East Germany for an encounter with Prime Minister Stoph. This visit was returned by Stoph a few weeks later when he met Brandt again in the West German town of Kassel. Brandt made the point that in economic, financial, legal and cultural respects, there was no distinction between West Berlin and the Federal Republic. 'Berlin,' he argued, 'is fully part of us'. Stoph was not mobbed and acclaimed in Kassel as Brandt had been in Erfurt—indeed there were tele-phoned threats on his life—but the meetings were solemnly adjudged 'successful'.

A treaty 'between two German States' was agreed, and small but significant steps were taken towards 'normalising' life between the two Berlins. Telephone links, for instance, were re-estab-lished. Brandt then made a fruitful trip to Moscow to discuss a non-aggression treaty with the country which had become Ger-many's prime adversary during the 1939–45 war and which sub-sequently endorsed and presided over the division of Germany itself and its former capital.

The on-going four-power talks had the impetus they needed to move towards a satisfying outcome, but during their deliberations there was a quirkish reaction from the voters of West Berlin. In elections for a new city council in the spring of 1971, the SPD received only just over half the votes cast. The party managed to retain control but had its poorest showing in six municipal elec-

tions. By 1975, when the Brandt diplomatic circus had trau-
matically collapsed (because of the East German spy uncovered
in his entourage), the SPD was receiving only 42 per cent of the
city's votes. The tradition of SPD dominance, sustained even in
the fractured city, was broken; the Berliner Luft would not be the
same again.

In May 1971 Walter Ulbricht was finally discarded. East
Germany grew out of its ultra-defensive posturing and came of
age as diplomatic recognition was increasingly accorded by the
international community. Erich Honecker, almost twenty years
younger, eagerly and belatedly took Ulbricht's place. He had been
born on what is now West German soil and was to have a more
amenable way with the outside world.

The intractability of Ulbricht was apparent even after his death,
in 1973: it was followed by six weeks of argument about where
and precisely how he should be buried. This argument showed
how fundamentally different was the nature of socialism now from
the socialism/communism which had been so vigorously espoused
by men, however fallible, like Karl Liebknecht. In the end,
Ulbricht who bore so much responsibility for the inception of 'the
first socialist state on German soil', was granted a state funeral,
but there were almost no official foreign mourners present, and as
the cortege made its way to the Friedrichsfelde Socialist Memorial
Cemetery, there was no spontaneous filling of the city streets
by thousands who wanted to participate as there had been for
Liebknecht.

The Allied Control Council building, where the four-power
agreement was approved on 3 September 1971, has today reverted
again to being a ghost of its once-busy self. Only thirty of its
486 rooms and conference chambers are in regular use, and its
refreshment bar and recreation rooms (for chess and table-tennis)
are nowadays patronised mainly by handfuls from three of the
four powers. The chief activity is in an upstairs room where,
behind bullet-proof glass, all flights of aircraft into the 'control
zone' of Berlin are meticulously monitored. A Soviet officer
present, if he has reason to object, has orders to use a red stamp
which marks the flight report in Russian with the message that
'the security of the flight is not guaranteed'.

By way of politically orchestrated prelude to the new agreement, a Warsaw Pact summit was held in East Berlin. The Communist Party leaders of the member countries addressed themselves to 'strengthening security and developing peaceful co-operation' in Europe. It created an appropriate climate for the four-power agreement that was to follow.

The agreement itself, as Berliners on both sides concede, did not solve 'the Berlin question', but it did resolve difficult questions and remove causes of unpredictable tension, and it did offer an apparently less cluttered way forward. The four concerned governments agreed, for a start, 'to strive to promote the elimination of tension and the prevention of complications in the relevant area'. They left open the definition of 'the relevant area' and the muffled debate continues to this day over whether the agreement applies to the whole of Berlin or only to West Berlin. Western arguments that the latter is the case are refuted by the Russians and their allies who say that East Berlin is a constituent part of the GDR. Speeches that were made by Western leaders during the 1987 celebrations to the effect that that the Wall should come down made no measurable impact on this point of view.

The 1971 accord also stated that force would not be used to resolve disputes in the city, and that there would be no unilateral changes without four-power authorisation. It also said there should be no impediment to road and rail traffic between West Germany and West Berlin. This, clearly, was a way of saying there would be no physical 'impediment' from the Soviet authorities or the East Germans to such traffic. The more psychological pressures suffered by impressionable motorists along the autobahn corridors to and from their old capital (for instance) were not taken into account. The occupying powers, meanwhile, ensure that there is 'no impediment' by running their own trains every day between West Berlin and the Federal Republic. No Berliners may travel as passengers on these trains.

A further clause stated that West Berliners wanting to make the long-short trek to see friends or relatives in the East, 'for compassionate, family, religious, cultural or commercial reasons'—or indeed going as tourists—would be given a much easier time. This has by no means ended the long, frustrating queues through the East German control points, such as Friedrichstrasse railway station, but it has removed much of the high drama from their situation. It has not removed the resentment that people in these queues invariably feel at being obliged to exchange an exorbitant number of West German marks, per stay, for their 'soft' East German equivalent.

The agreement itself was finally signed in the Control Council building on 3 June 1972 by the four governments' Foreign Ministers (William Rogers, for the US; Sir Alec Douglas-Home, for Britain; Andrei Gromyko, for the Soviet Union; and Maurice Schumann, for France). It came into force with immediate effect, and though inevitably there have been disputes over defining terms, it has remained in force ever since.

It followed by three weeks the ratification of Willy Brandt's treaties with the Soviet Union and with Poland, and preceded by a matter of months the signing of the historic basic treaty governing relations between the two Germanies. Eleven years after the building of the Wall, twenty-seven years after the ending of the war, and (still) less than forty years after Hitler had taken power, a new European milestone had been reached. It was no longer apposite to speak of Berlin as a 'hostage' city; other 'flashpoints' were to replace Berlin in the global consciousness, but Berliners, and particularly West Berliners, were the ones who were most relieved by the consequences of reaching that milestone.

For the US, William Rogers described the four-power agreement as a 'step forward'. The Soviet Communist Party newspaper, *Pravda*, conceded that it was 'an important landmark'. Given the impediments which had obstructed progress on so many fronts in the immediate past, the abuse which had been exchanged, and the uncertainties which had prevailed, these were glowing accolades for the documents now being signed. By May 1974 the West Germans had opened their 'permanent mission' in Invalidenstrasse, East Berlin, and the East Germans had opened theirs in Bonn.

One result of the agreements has been a substantial increase in the contacts between officials of the two Berlins. The West Berlin representatives come nominally from the City Senate and those from East Berlin are of the East German Foreign Ministry, but their prime concern has been what might be called 'domestic arrangements'. They meet about a dozen times a year and have clarified thinking, and reached accord, on such matters as the rescue of children falling into the Spree, on missing persons, aspects of transport and on supplies of (Soviet) gas from East to West. Agreement has also been reached—rather piquantly, say some West Berliners—on the East Germans being responsible for disposing of hundreds of lorry-loads daily of West Berlin rubbish and millions of tonnes of West Berlin sewage.

None of these developments did anything to restrain the 'East-West competition' in the planning and erection of the two new urban centres, which had in fact been gaining in intensity throughout the 1960s. Rather, it could be argued, the agreements of the early 1970s infused new life into this process.

Already, with competing degrees of flamboyance, a series of public amenity buildings had been opened—sometimes as part of an overall conception, but sometimes, it seemed, because they were the accoutrements that no self-respecting city could afford to be without. There were spasms of pain, from those who had known and loved the old city, at the reckless way in which some semi-derelict remnants were removed, but these were dispelled in moments of engineered civic pride as yet another expensive project was unveiled. Pain and pride mingled uneasily when a magnificent concert hall appeared next to a busy freeway, or when a four or five-star hotel of conspicuously twentieth-century design, probably built by an outside contractor, was thrust among some of the city's most treasured baroque creations.

East Berlin developed more or less according to a superimposed master-plan for the whole *Hauptstadt*; West Berlin gave more play to market forces of supply and demand. In both cases, there has been unevenness in the overall end result. Strolling about the two Berlins the visitor quickly notices finished individual structures which are manifestly elegant in themselves, perhaps the creation of an internationally recognised architect or team, but which stand in splendid isolation, somehow unrelated to their immediate surroundings. Mistakes made in the *Gründerjahre* have been repeated—the result, it seems, of trying to do too much too quickly.

Thirty years on from the Interbau exhibition in West Berlin of 1957, a similar exhibition—to coincide with the city's 750th anniversary—afforded opportunities to look at the sort of city which, on both sides, was emerging. In West Berlin, according to Wolfgang Schäche, a prolific writer on the city's architecture, the late 1980s had become a time for sober reassessment, when it became clear that utopia-minded 'modernists' had failed to take account of more tangible problems. What Schäche called the 'exemplary' concepts of the Weimar period, meaning the 'green, peaceful housing estates' built by trade union syndicates—and much trumpeted at the time—had, he said, 'simply ignored the existing densely populated districts and were ultimately instrumental in precipitating their decay'.

By the late 1980s, the aim in West Berlin had become more than ever what the planners called 'urban rehabilitation' for those areas said still to be in jeopardy from 'years of speculative neglect and threatened with demolition'. There had to be 'reconstruction', they declared, in areas which had suffered devastation in the 1939–45 war, or which had been casualties of over-zealous 'technocratic' planners or 'impersonal' post-war redevelopment schemes. In East Berlin, the decision was taken to 'fill in' wherever possible the unsightly gaps between buildings that had been rehabilitated or erected since the war. Many of these gaps, however, will never be filled.

More than forty years after the war's end, sheer necessity dictated that housing in both Berlins was still a major priority. Honecker announced (in 1986) that all East Berlin's housing problems would be solved by 1990—by the end, that is, of the newly started five-year plan. But such was the priority given by the East German leaders to their proclaimed capital that other parts of the country, deprived of urgently needed men, money and resources being poured into Berlin, were increasingly resentful. Spending directed to the 750th anniversary celebrations added fuel to the heat of their feelings.

In West Berlin, with almost twice the population, complications arose from the free-market way of doing things. As well as another corruption scandal—in the building department of the Senate—there were other cracks in the façade of the city's showcase building programmes.

The 250,000th dwelling to be completed in West Berlin since the war had been handed over in June 1964. Before the Wall went up, the strangely tidy Hansa Viertel housing estate was erected, north-west of the Tiergarten and adjoining the eighteenth-century Schloss Bellevue.

The success of this project encouraged the city authorities to press ahead with the Märkisches Viertel, to accommodate 50,000 people, in the district of Reinickendorf. In the south of the city, the Gropiusstadt, masterminded by Walter Gropius, took shape between Buckow and Rudow. In Spandau, approval was given for a new settlement for 25,000. In East Berlin plans were laid for the development of the Marzahn housing project on a 2000-acre green field site eventually to house 100,000 people in the east of the city. All were, in effect, fresh satellite towns within the city.

Finished products in these housing areas often looked good. But the quality of the workmanship, even in the prestige places, was not always of the same standard as it was in other regions of West Germany. Perhaps these regions were deemed to have a more certain political future than Berlin. The recession which hit the Western world in the 1970s—and the communist world just a little later—also cut deeply into the city's housing programmes.

Today's Berlin can of course be read in its entirety as a monument to the victims of Nazism and militarism. It became the imperial capital immediately after the Army's defeat of France in the war of 1870–71, and ceased to be such after the military defeats in the wars which ended in 1918 and 1945. But in both Berlins, specific locations have been dedicated to the memory of the victims. There are ironies in both cases.

In East Berlin, the Neue Wache (New Guardhouse) on Unter den Linden is a small Greek temple-like structure with a Doric-columned entrance, originally created by Schinkel and erected soon after Napoleon's departure from the city in 1816. Ornamentation was by Gottfried Schadow, the designer of the chariot-borne goddess of Peace who faces Moscow from above the Brandenburg Gate. In 1931 President Hindenburg decreed the Neue Wache should remember those who died in 1914–18, and inside a great carved wreath of remembrance was placed before an illuminated cross. After the Second World War, wreath and cross were removed and in 1960, the communists declared the whole to be a memorial 'to the victims of fascism and militarism'. (The word Nazism, because of its 'socialist' ingredient, is barely used.) Today, there is an eternal flame to an unknown warrior and in an hourly ritual that is highly militaristic and faintly menacing, soldiers change guard. Small East Germans in short trousers like to imitate these soldiers' version of the goose-step.

In West Berlin, there is also a flame. It is five times higher than a man and made of bronze, and was installed at Ernst-Reuter-Platz in 1963 in memory of the man who led the resistance to the 1948 blockade. There are specific but unostentatious memorials to the victims of Nazism—and Stalinism—some 500 yards away, tucked in the corners of the gardens of the Steinplatz, near the Technical University. No soldiers change guard here—many Berliners do not even know it is a hallowed place—but occasionally the employees of Hoechst chemical company, which overlooks the garden, come to sunbathe in the summer, or to sit and talk. Hoechst, it will be recalled, was one of the offshoots of IG Farben, the group which manufactured the gas which killed so many in the concentration camps.

Between the re-dedication of the Neue Wache in 1960 and the re-opening for public use of the Reichstag building ten years later, the face of the city changed dramatically. West Berliners acquired new wholesale markets for flowers and food, a bus station (for links to West Germany), an observatory (built on a hill of rubble), and two new hospitals. They also got a clutch of museums (for radio, the Brücke group of artists, and for Berlin itself), as well as the National Gallery and, of course, the restored, and topless, Reichstag.

East Berliners were presented with similarly utilitarian buildings, usually in re-furbished form, a new Ministry of Foreign Affairs by the Spree and, in a welter of nostalgia, a transformed Alexanderplatz. But this is now an 'Alex' almost devoid of traffic, a pedestrianised precinct without the clutter and noise of pre-war days. Nearby, it acquired a television tower, 1200 feet high and in many ways the symbol of the 'new Berlin'. It took four years to construct (with Swedish help) and from its viewing platform there are panoramic vistas of old and new, East and West, which can be achieved nowhere else. It makes a popular Sunday afternoon excursion for East Berlin families to take the lift to the top. A West Berlin television tower, almost as high and decidedly not open to the public, came into operation in the Frohnau district in 1980. The public has been content to make do with its predecessor, less than half as high (at 453 feet), opened in 1926—with a restaurant—as part of the exhibition grounds in Charlottenburg.

Not all Berlin's public buildings have stood the test of time, and not only the Second World War, as these pages have shown, was responsible for their removal. In November 1973, for instance, after years of debate, work began on the dismantling and obliteration of the Sportpalast in the Potsdamerstrasse. It was a decision almost as far-reaching in its significance for many Berliners as the one nearly twenty years before to demolish the Kaiser's

Palace. The Sportpalast had not only echoed with the fulminations of Hitler and Goebbels, so witnessing many pivotal historic moments in Germany's history, but had also been an important part of the pre-Hitler city's landscape and 'colour'. Sports events of all sorts had been held there, including the closely followed six-day bicycle races, championship boxing matches, in addition to all sorts of light entertainment. It was also, in its way, a symbol of continuity, because it had first opened for business in the year 1910.

Other landmarks proved even less durable. One of the first and biggest show-pieces of East Berlin, erected for the people was a massive Youth and Sports Centre on what is now Karl-Marx-Allee. This was completed even before work proper was begun on the Allee itself, and incorporated, as a sign of its latent importance, replicas of those figures which had once graced the main courtyard of the Palace. Like the Sportpalast, this Centre was used for holding of significant sports events and festivals, its main hall holding up to 5000 people at a time. However, after not many years its roof collapsed, the building was found to be unsafe and it was taken down and replaced with more housing. The roof collapse was to be echoed in the fate that befell West Berlin's Congress Hall with the 'pregnant oyster' roof that collapsed in 1980. A new West Berlin congress centre, with high-tech facilities throughout, opened in April 1979, but for several years its precursor looked forlorn, a relic already of a time which was passed. It was re-opened, with minimal fanfare, in 1986.

The charisma of Unter den Linden had been dented badly enough already in the late 1930s when Hitler decided to uproot the celebrated lime-trees which gave it its name. War damage was extensive to buildings along both sides and the debate was intense between those who favoured expensive renewal of the old and those who wanted to start again. The trees have been replanted, but the result, overall, has been a compromise. The happiest parts seem to be the visually impressive rehabilitation of, most notably, the old Zeughaus (Armoury) dating from the 1690s (only fifty years after the Linden was first mapped out) and now housing the Museum of German History. The State Opera House opposite entered the latest of many refurbishments in its long life at the end of 1986. Then there are palaces, restored for use by the university, the city authorities, and ordinary people. The latter, usually students, converge for coffee at what is now called the

Operncafe, or Opera Coffee House. It was previously the palace of a princess. The great Cathedral is undergoing repairs, at West German expense, which are due for completion in the 1990s.

The least happy achievements have been the plain-faced Education Ministry, by the site of the old Adlon Hotel, and opposite, the 1960s Hungarian and Polish Embassies and the Ministry of Foreign Trade. Max Liebermann, the artist, who lived so many years just around the corner in the old Pariser Platz, would surely be unimpressed if he returned today.

Another area of less than happy compromise—between East and West—has been in the running of the city's railway system. From the moment of its inception, even before the days of empire and at least until 1939, it had been one of the city's main sources of pride and joy, as well as being a steady employer. The construction process of the several different railways, overground, overhead, underground, was virtually non-stop for decades on end. Since the division of the city, however, the demands made on what remained of the system have changed. Lines joining East to West have had to be closed, and some of the world's great railway termini have closed down, or have changed totally and been renamed. A few have become flea markets or Turkish bazaars.

A source of perpetual smiles over the post-war years was the fact that the East German transport authorities kept the name Deutsche Reichsbahn (German Imperial Railways) while they were managers. A source of discontent was the state of disrepair and neglect which pervaded so many of the stations, and the rolling stock, which they managed. Charlottenburg S-bahn station in the mid-1980s, for instance, from which the Friedrichstrasse station and crossing point were only a few stops away, was a strange and timeless place. Bomb and bullet marks could still be seen on unchanged sign and notice boards, the embankments remained uncultivated, and weeds intruded between some of the railway lines. The tired old carriages, predominantly a rusty red, provided some lingering fascination in themselves, but were at the same time relics only of a time that had been removed out of memory. In January 1984 the running of the city's railway system was handed to the West Berlin authorities.

★   ★   ★

Direct action came to West Berlin with a vengeance in the early 1970s. It was a period of 'anti-capitalist, anti-authoritarian' bombings and of State or city authority violence being met by violence. This would come from often armed representatives of groups who had rejected Marxism-Leninism as 'no longer progressive' and who were 'sustained solely by Utopia, the permanent motive for our actions'.

Various groups emerged, some very small and not all of them violent. They concentrated around communes that developed in delapidated houses in the racially mixed and apparently accepting distinct of Kreuzberg, and especially in the immediate vicinity of the old Bethany Hospital. The Red Army Fraction (RAF) was born in May 1970, when Andreas Baader, Ulrike Meinhof and others were 'sprung' from Tegel Prison, where they had been sent after the bombing of a Frankfurt department store two years before. The 2 June Movement was formed fourteen months later when a group escaped from the courtroom where they were being tried for beating up a *Quick* magazine journalist. This group offered a credo which said in part, in the words of one of them: 'Violence rules, from birth to the grave, and it is simply heightened if you fight against it—it becomes totally concrete.'

Berliners and others, not of their persuasion, slipped easily into the pre-digested designation of them as terrorists, thus alienating them even further. The response from the groups and their supporters was to play 'the authorities'—the 'bulls' was what they called the police—at their own game, a game which non-terrorist Berliners finally lived with equably enough, as preceding generations had lived with the violence of the attempted revolution, the *Freikorps*, the underworld and the various political and other scandals.

In December 1971, when members of the 2 June Movement engaged in a shootout with plain clothes policemen, and one of the Movement, Georg von Rauch, was killed, a Schöneberg citizen was able to give police a coherent eye-witness account of the whole incident as it happened. Several weeks later, the British occupation forces' Sailing Club at Kladow (across the Havel River from where Goebbels had watched the sun rise at Schwanenwerder) was a target. A bomb was planted and Irwin Beelitz, a sixty-six-year-old boat builder, was killed. Within a few months, the Movement's house (named after Georg von Rauch) at Mariannenplatz, facing the Bethany Hospital building, was raided and twenty-seven people were detained for questioning. Soon, some leaders of the Baader-Meinhof group were also arrested.

In June, Andreas Baader himself and several RAF members were held after a shootout in Frankfurt, and when, two and a half years later, one of the group died after a two-month hunger strike in prison, the President of the West Berlin High Court, Günter von Drenkmann, was shot and killed by the Movement's members in his own home. Further arrests and prison sentences followed and, in February 1975, Peter Lorenz, the CDU's law-and-order candidate for the mayoral elections in West Berlin, was kidnapped in Zehlendorf to be held as hostage pending the release of other Movement members. When these were flown to 'temporary sanctuary' in South Yemen, Lorenz was released unharmed the same night in a park in Wilmersdorf. Police raids on several 'dissident' homes in West Berlin came in the wake of his release.

The authorities of West Berlin once again showed themselves to be confronted by phenomena they did not adequately understand and by individuals whose language was not the same as theirs. Dialogue between the two Germanies, or, on occasion, the two Berlins, was manageable compared with the exchanges between themselves and the city's 'terrorists'. When Henry Kissinger, the US Secretary of State, came in the early summer of 1975 and renewed American 'guarantees'—a gesture directed at the Soviet Union—that too was easily assimilated. But the guerilla activities of their own children, metaphorically speaking, were virtually incomprehensible to Berliners, something with which they could not cope.

When four of these 'children' escaped from a women's prison in Lehrter Strasse in the summer of 1976, the Senator for Justice was forced to resign. Within a year, Klaus Schütz, who had also been intermittently at the centre of controversy, resigned as Governing Mayor. He was succeeded by the Senator for Federal Affairs, Dietrich Stobbe. None of these developments, however, hindered the leaders of the three Western guarantor powers— President Carter of the US, Prime Minister Callaghan of Britain, and France's President Giscard d'Estaing—from agreeing in London once again to reinforce the four-power agreement on Berlin as a gesture for détente and peace.

In the eight years from 1970 to 1978, it has been estimated that the RAF and other groups committed to violence, were responsible for the deaths of twenty-eight people, the wounding of more than ninety others and the taking of more than 160 hostages. The equivalent of nearly £2 million was the estimated yield from thirty-five bank robberies. In the course of 1977, however, Andreas Baader, Ulrike Meinhof and others of their group, were reported to have committed suicide in prison. Some of these suicides happened even as other Red Army members had hijacked a Lufthansa jet to Africa, where the passengers were held as hostages in return for the release of the group leaders. At the same time, Hans-Martin Schleyer, a director of Daimler-Benz, was kidnapped for the same purposes. In the end, the aircraft was stormed and re-taken by a German anti-terrorist unit, Schleyer was murdered, and the RAF was, in more senses than one, disarmed as well as leaderless.

The wave which followed the RAF and the 2 June Movement was different in character. Squatters and exponents of alternative ways of living have always inhabited odd corners of Berlin and are today to be found in both parts of the city. At the end of 1979, they became a 'movement' in their own right, even with a sort of grudging blessing from the authorities. One group, about sixty strong, took over the Universum film studios by the southern perimeter of Tempelhof airfield, where Marlene Dietrich had been filmed in *The Blue Angel* and where *Metropolis* had been made by Fritz Lang. The group, which speaks of itself as 'a sort of kibbutz but less organised', runs its own shops, educates its own children, and runs a circus troupe. Another, much larger group, occupies an old printing works at Mehringhof in Kreuzberg, bought in 1979. It is now the premises for about ninety co-coperatives, each employing half a dozen or more people in a variety of occupations—producing goods for sale, refreshments, music or, once again, education for the youngest inhabitants. It is seen, informally of course, as the headquarters for the alternative community. 'Where,' one inhabitant of Kreuzberg asked a journalist in 1986, 'can you meet so many nice, but crazy people?'

In 1979, too, some houses in Cuvrystrasse at the eastern end of Kreuzberg were taken over. They had been allowed to run down to a state where they were fit only for demolition, but the young people who now moved in, mostly in their early twenties, had other ideas—based also on peaceable living together, social services in the broadest sense, as well as their own pressing need for somewhere cheap to live.

In this case, the authorities had mixed feelings. By 1981, a total

170 buildings, mainly multi-occupancy tenement blocks, had been taken over. The police, unable to appreciate the finer points of latter-day flower power, moved in, and another cause was found for street demonstrations. The clashes increased in intensity after May, when the CDU won enough seats in the Senate elections to organise a coalition administration with the Free Democrats and to elect Richard von Weizsäcker as Governing Mayor. In June, 173 young people were arrested in a police raid on squats; more demonstrations followed, and in a clash the following September, and eighteen-year-old youth, Klaus-Jürgen Rattay, was run over and killed by a bus in the Potsdamerstrasse. Another movement had found another martyr, and a silent protest march wound its way through the city in sympathy.

Before and after Weizsäcker's appointment, the Western part of the city was rocked by a number of scandals on a scale that must have brought a wry smile to the faces of many of the older generation. One involved the financial affairs of a building company run by the architect, Dietrich Garski; another involved the mysteriously abrupt departure of the Senator for new buildings, Rastemborski, in the summer of 1983; a third involved the forgery, at a printing workshop in Siemensstadt, of millions of dollar bills.

The city's underworld, so graphically chronicled by Brecht and Döblin, remains vibrant to this day. Berlin would not be Berlin if it did not have strange creatures trading in the unexpected and the unlikely. In both parts of the city, entertainments readily associated with the era of Grosz or Isherwood are still plentiful; transvestites and homosexuals have in Berlin the sort of licence they enjoy nowhere else. Prostitutes and black marketeers are an irremovable part of the brash Kurfürstendamm landscape—and they also flourish within a stone's throw of the Friedrichstrasse.

By the mid-1980s, the dispossessed city was no longer the flash-point it once was. 'Competition' between the two constituent parts had modified in character as both matured into something resembling a coherent conurbation, each one a whole in its own right. The drive on each side to achieve dizzy growth and the compelling need to produce tangible evidence of 'progress'—often in the form of less than top-quality public buildings—slowed down. As the collapse of the cities of Beirut or Manila or Managua became momentary centres of global attention, Berliners paused to take breath, to reflect, and sought where they could, to consolidate.

According to Heinrich Albertz, the preacher who had briefly been Governing Mayor during the time of the student troubles of the later 1960s, a difficult era of normality had been reached. In an interview given in early 1986, he said it had been reached once the 'fraudulent' claim that West Berlin was 'a bulwark of freedom' had fallen apart and as soon as the Vietnam war had come to an end. The trouble in the late 1980s was that the era of normality was much harder to live with than what had gone before, he said, adding that, 'We are now a mediocre big city with special status and positive links with the other part of Germany.' If that was a depressing diagnosis, what of Rainer Ott, one-time student activist and in 1986 a leading member of the journalists' trade union? West Berlin, he told the same interviewer, had become 'a cultural Sahel zone'.

The mid-1980s also saw a clutch of anniversaries in which Berliners on both sides were invited, and sometimes obliged, to remember events in their common past. One of the anniversaries fell in 1985 when Germans of all shades debated the extent to which they had been 'liberated' in May forty years before. For the East German leadership there was little real debate. In a telegram to their Soviet counterparts, Erich Honecker and Willi Stoph declared that, led by the Party of Lenin (no mention here of Stalin), the Soviet people have saved 'mankind' from fascist barbarism. The Soviet people and their glorious Army, it was noted at the joint 'festive event' held in East Berlin, had borne the main burden of the struggle, had played the greatest role in eradicating the fascist plague. . . .

That, at least, was the public sentiment in East Berlin, reinforced without any ambiguity in military parades, watched by Soviet generals, along Unter den Linden, and by the participation of several thousand of East Germany's youngest citizens in ceremonies held at the Soviet memorial in Treptow Park. Wreaths were laid at the other Soviet memorial just inside West Berlin and a tour of inspection made by the Soviet visitors of the Berlin Wall. Marshal Semyon Kurkotkin paid tribute to the East German border guards and their work in 'protecting the achievements of socialism'.

In West Berlin, these ceremonies were noted with varying

measures of circumspection. The word 'liberation' sticks in the throats of older generation conservatives and their gratitude to the Red Army of 1945 is tempered by thoughts of East–West realities, and perhaps—it has to be said—memories of vandalism and rape in the days that were now being remembered. There being no special war memorials to Germany's military dead—in either part of the city—satisfaction had to be derived from weighty statements. There was a quiet smile or two in the West when Honecker ventured to make great play with words first attributed to Kurt Schumacher: 'Never again dictatorship in Germany, never again war emanating from German soil.'

In 1986, two anniversaries were celebrated by the East Germans coincidentally with the 11th Congress of the Socialist Unity Party. One marked the hundredth birthday of Ernst Thälmann, during which a statue of him was unveiled in East Berlin's Thälmann Park and he was described as one who tried to join forces with the SPD in the common struggle against incipient Nazism. In fact, he had had great reservations about the SPD. The second coincidence was the fortieth anniversary of the formation of the SED itself, through the merger pushed through at the Admiralspalast in Friedrichstrasse in April 1946. No one dwelt publicly on the fact that it was the SPD rather than the communists which had originally pushed for this merger, nor on the fact that as many as 20,000 SPD members were subjected in its immediate aftermath to 'discipline', deportation or even death.

In August 1986 came the twenty-fifth anniversary of the Wall. Shortly before that date, Helmut Kohl, CDU Chancellor, told the Bundestag that there could be no 'normal relations' between East and West Germany until the Wall, the barbed wire and the border guards' orders to fire were cancelled. He also announced that a foundation stone would be laid in West Berlin in 1987 for the building of a new Museum of German History. Hans Mommsen, an SPD member and a professor of modern history, dismissed this gesture as 'nothing but a futile attempt to reactivate the German nation-state tradition', which most Germans thought had been finally destroyed on the battlefields of the Second World War. This was a thought which, in turn, raised some eyebrows in East Berlin, where the old Armoury building in Unter den Linden houses a museum trading under precisely the same name.

The East German authorities brought together contingents from those units which had been responsible for the actual building work, much of it under the direction of Erich Honecker himself. He told a rally in East Berlin on 13 August that the building of the Wall 'saved peace for our people and for all other peoples of Europe', that it was 'an historic deed that preserved the liberty of our people'. It was a well-rehearsed argument but one which found little sympathy among several of East Germany's writers and artists. 'My first thought,' Helga Schubert had written, in a novel called *Das verbotene Zimmer* (The Forbidden Room), published in 1982, was: 'I'm the one who has been walled in. They have built a wall around me. . . .'

In a Federal Government statement issued to mark the actual anniversary, the Minister for Intra-German Affairs, Heinrich Windelen, was less shrill than his own Chancellor. 'In the course of the 1960s', he declared, 'German politics began to accept the Wall, as well as the entire inter-German frontier, as a basis of practical policy. This policy has now been pursued . . . the Berlin Wall had become more penetrable, at least for West Berliners as a result of the 1971 Four-Power Agreement. In this way, the danger of growing estrangement between the Germans of both states has been averted.'

In a second, accompanying statement, the information was of a different flavour. In the twenty-five years since the Wall went up, it said, at least 110 people have died attempting to 'flee' to the West, seventy-four of them on the East German side of the Wall itself. However, it went on, 'escape' attempts continued, with 160 succeeding in 1985. Hundreds of others got through by other means, such as forged documents or staying in the West on specified job assignments.

As if to counter this sort of information, the East Germans completed in 1986 the rebuilding of their most notorious crossing-point in the city, Checkpoint Charlie. New customs facilities and frontier barriers were erected to replace ramshackle wooden huts and less sightly barriers, the aim apparently being to make the act of crossing more efficient, even more attractive. Nothing was done, however, to limit the waiting, which can be considerable and tedious, while one's passport and/or visa papers are checked. On the Western side of the same checkpoint, soldiers from the US, Britain and France sit in a little wooden shed—almost informal in character—and wave people through without formal examination. They insist that Berlin is a united city.

A few yards away, the Museum at the Checkpoint, which has

graphic details and paraphernalia associated with every defection from East to West, is teeming with visitors. Across the road, the Checkpoint Restaurant and the Snack am Checkpoint coffee bar are open for business.

The year 1987 was designated by both sides to be the city's 750th anniversary. The celebrations were based on a date, found in the public records, which had been 'discovered' by Hitler when searching for a suitable grandiose event which could be marked fifty years before. Heads of State from the guarantor powers came to their respective charges, but did not cross, except through diplomatic representatives, to the other side. The division of the city, Chancellor Kohl said for this occasion, should not be seen as the last word. Berlin's history, said a committee sitting under Erich Honecker, was eloquent proof of the triumph of socialism on German soil.

The anniversary did lead to one significant meeting between East and West. For the first time since the division of the city, the Governing Mayor of West Berlin and the Mayor of East Berlin met in the communist area—but after a church service—to shake hands and exchange greetings.

For these celebrations, no expense seemed to be spared. Both sides invested enormous sums in the construction or refurbishment of areas which until recently had been either characterless of wilfully neglected. The West made the most of its International Building Exhibition, the latest in a periodic series, in which outside architects were invited to see through schemes, mainly in housing stock, which would somehow make amends for the now acknowledged errors of earlier planners and architects— some of whom had been carrying out commissioned work even since 1945. In East Berlin, pride of place in this respect was given to the restoration of the Nikolaiviertel, the area adjacent to the site of the Kaiser's palace surrounding the St Nicholas Church. This church, still a bombed-out shell of its earlier self as lately as 1982, is believed to be more than 800 years old, the oldest building in the entire city. Around this church a whole quarter, which included several medieval buildings and which was virtually flattened during the war, has been brought back to life again. Poles who had rebuilt Warsaw's old town so meticulously after the war were enlisted to assist in the project.

Dozens of exhibitions, seminars and other events—mostly cultural in character—filled the anniversary year on both sides. Old barrel organs were tarted up and new ones manufactured to give the city streets the sounds they last heard in pre-war 'golden' times. Everywhere there were cheery, exhortatory hoardings, flags and posters reminding Berliners—as if they needed reminding—that they indeed had a past. At the events themselves, what was offered was usually a selective and for the most part palatable resurrection of that past, with *sotto voce* reminders of the unacceptable.

Indistinct echoes of things disturbing were of course frequently heard, and words, music and images which had once been, at the very least, contentious, even banned, were deployed. But by 1987, such offerings had become merely remarkable. Berliners may have, like the rest of us, an intolerant side to their natures, but it can be difficult for them to display shock. I know some who suffer great anguish because they still do not know precisely what their own parents were doing during the Nazi period, and others who are saddened and perplexed because, however much talk goes on in the *Kneipen*, bars and private rooms, there is still a deliberate skating over the Hitler years. An experimental play I saw in late 1986 dealing with these years was only sparsely attended, and a dialogue which the main actor and author, Hermann von Harten, tried to initiate with his audience soon petered out. By the same token, people did not flock in anniversary year to see the Gestapo-SS exhibition in the old cellars of the former SS headquarters.

As indicated, this anniversary did wonders for the fabric of the city, facilitating and speeding up the removal of most of the remaining post-war ruins and the erection of many new buildings. In addition to the Nikolaiviertel, the East Berliners had the refined socialist realism of their Palace of the Republic at Marx-Engels-Platz, opened in 1976, where their legislators could meet in parliamentary session and where they themselves could go for a drink, visit the theatre, watch the cinema or make use of an indoor bowling alley. A world communist 'summit' of the same year, however, still had to be held in a Berlin hotel.

The East Berliners also had the Schauspielhaus, originally a Schinkel creation, now rebuilt, refitted, and refurnished in more or less the same glittering style. An evening spent listening in that hall even to the familiar music of Brahms and Beethoven can be exhilarating, and for the glimpse it gives of the very *bürgerlich* East Berliners, it can be revealing as well. Outside, meanwhile, the French cathedral nearby has also been refurbished and the

German cathedral (at this writing) is nearly done. The old Gendarmenmarkt, where once the cream—and the would-be cream—of Berlin society would promenade gently among the flower beds and the fountains, is being stage-managed back to a sort of life. The flower beds and the fountains have gone and the sweet atmosphere of the place then, a sort of annexe to Unter den Linden itself, will remain elusive: it is now called the Akademieplatz, and the clever photographer rather than the clever engraver will be turning it into a picture appropriate to the age.

In the spirit of this sort of rebuilding, imitating, however painstakingly, an irretrievable past, Berlin has become on both sides a centre for what might be called managed art. The uniqueness of its history and its position has drawn hundreds of creative artists and writers, all capable of being disturbed and stimulated at the same time to express the unease that it generates. A few have been genuinely, even outrageously, talented—the West Berlin painter and sculptor, Joseph Beuys, for instance, or the wayward East Berlin-based novelist, Stefan Heym. But the majority have been tortured—understandably perhaps—and too inward-looking for a wider audience.

There will always be odd gaps between the buildings in both Berlins and open spaces where they are least expected. The freeways for motor traffic, even though they sometimes run between formless blocks of concrete and glass, mean there is less congestion than in other cities and they are an asset. But the suddenly met, and not unwelcome, children's play area or car park, where once there was a great department store, tenement block or synagogue, are something else. Touring the city with an old Baedeker guidebook is an intriguing and depressing experience.

Talking to today's Berliners reveals other gaps: the old SPD and the KPD have gone from both sides and have been displaced by younger groupings with similar names but different clothes and different expectations. There is a Socialist Unity Party of Westberlin (sic), known as the SEW and heavily underwritten by the SED beyond the Wall—but it is a conservative grouping with policies that in recent years have appeared to be more hard-line than most ruling parties in Eastern Europe. In East Berlin, those who join the SED are not deeply versed in Marx or Engels or Lenin. The Marxism-Leninism Institute on Wilhelm Pieck Strasse is a cadaverously empty place.

In West Berlin, the CDU, in the mid-1980s, were firmly in

control, and the SPD, which once so dominated the city and its destiny, without effective leadership. The Governing Mayor of West Berlin was Eberhardt Diepgen, a thrusting and ambitious lawyer, born in the city and committed to the late twentieth century wish to see West Berlin blossom as a centre for technology and innovation as well as something approaching 'the cultural capital' of Germany. His counterpart in East Berlin was Erhard Krack, a former Food Industry Minister who was appointed in 1974.

Almost twenty years to the day after the shooting of Benno Ohnesorg and the outcry which followed it in 1967, there was rioting again in West Berlin—this time in anticipation of the anniversary visit to be made by President Ronald Reagan. In May and early June, the Kurfürstendamm was patrolled day and night by police in riot gear, while in Kreuzberg, burnt out buildings and wrecked motor vehicles—as well as urgently boarded up shops—were evidence of the violence and the panic. This time an anarchist group called the Autonomen were standard bearers for the radical Left. Sixty people were injured.

The violence, as (opposition) politicians later noted, came from over-zealous and heavy-handed police units as well as demonstrators and looters. Kreuzberg itself, the centre for a whole range of attractive life-styles, was still the place for the articulation of frustration about deprivation and poverty. Half the district's young people, in 1987, were unemployed; rents had recently been de-controlled and were rising, and amongst many, a 'no future' mentality seemed to be taking root. It was as if a wheel had come full circle.

Then, in another part of the city, there were further disturbances as a series of rock music concerts were held not far from the Wall, close to the old Reichstag building, as part of the anniversary celebrations. Thousands of young people gathered on the Eastern side of the Wall, not far from the Brandenburg Gate to hear, many climbing trees or on to rooftops to get a better view. Once again—as at a similar concert which had got out of control on the Alexanderplatz ten years before—the police moved in. They were unable to prevent dancing in the streets of the old city centre nor to stop a group of several hundred which broke through a cordon across Unter den Linden to gather outside the Soviet Embassy, chanting 'The Wall Must Go' and 'Gor-ba-chev' and singing the Internationale before some arrests were made and the whole group was finally dispersed by the police. Later the East

Berlin authorities denied that such a clash had taken place, while officials in Moscow expressed quiet pleasure that the name of their leader, a reformist, had been invoked in a state which had treated him until now with some scepticism.

Back in the Western part of the city, the evening before the Presidential visit, hundreds of black-clad anarchists, with possibly 20,000 others, marched noisily down the Kurfürstendamm, throwing stones and other missiles as they went. Once again, Bismarck's beloved avenue was being held to represent the wealth and the acquisitiveness which were rejected by the radical Left and readily associated by them with the US. The banners the demonstrators carried were anti-America in their message, and specifically against American missiles and American involvement in Nicaragua.

On Reagan's arrival, Kreuzberg was effectively sealed off from the rest of West Berlin, while elsewhere barbed wire was rolled out in such a way as to direct demonstrators and others as to where they could and could not go. The crowd which heard him when he spoke, just a few yards from the Wall and against the backcloth of the Brandenburg Gate, was mostly ticket-only, including many Americans bussed in from Frankfurt, and totalled about 35,000. Slogans painted on the Wall, urging him to 'go home' had been whitewashed over. His message, reminiscent of a few of the messages that had been delivered in the year of his death by President Kennedy, was that the Soviet leader should tear down the Wall. The thought was repeated by other West European leaders visiting Berlin in anniversary year, but was rejected as 'war-mongering' by the Soviets, while the East Germans suggested it would make the Wall 'even higher'.

East Berliners who gathered to hear the American president beyond that same Wall were not as numerous as they had been for the rock music recital the week before and were thwarted anyway because of defects in the loudspeaker system and a wind that blew the wrong way. The presidential suggestion that Berlin, both Berlins, should somehow host the Olympic Games between them as a gesture for peace, met with no response. The death of Rudolf Hess, the last Nazi war criminal in Spandau prison, in 1987, and the demolition of the prison to make way for a British Army leisure centre, ruffled few feathers in Berlin.

If the 1987 celebrations were intended to teach contemporary Berliners something more about their origins, they succeeded. If they were intended to raise consciousness and increase that sense of belonging which is essential if each entity is to work, they failed and they caused more problems than they solved. If the Reagan visit was intended to be a high-point of those celebrations, it too failed. However, the fact that Reagan himself and the younger generation of East Berliners had both addressed themselves to the Soviet leader, Mikhail Gorbachev, was something positive. When Günter Grass, the novelist, spoke in East Berlin (a week after the Reagan visit) for the first time in twenty-five years, it was somehow understandable that he should exhort the young people to back Gorbachev against the cold warriors. It was also understandable that the official East German press gave his talk only minimal coverage.

Berlin, the manic-depressive, dispossessed city, awaits a new initiative. But it waits, as secure as can be, with around 20,000 troops of the nationally occupying powers posted within easy reach on either side. How effective such numbers of troops would be in the event of a confrontation would of course depend on the nature of the confrontation. There are already about 20,000 Soviet dead buried in Berlin—most of them at Schönholzer Heide Park and Treptow. Soviet-led legions storming westwards to take the 'hostage', West Berlin, seems increasingly unlikely.

Everyone meanwhile continues to live on that extraordinarily rarified commodity, the air of Berlin, *Berliner Luft*. Berlin, they all agree, remains Berlin. Some, but not all, would like the Wall pulled down. Others, in the words of a respected West Berlin commentator, say the Wall represents a stabilisation of the impossible.

On paper at least, both sides remain ready for anything. Or rather they remain ready in a very Berlin fashion. Consider, for instance,the emergency stockpile of food that has been maintained in West Berlin for almost forty years as a precautionary measure against any repetition of the 1948–49 blockade. In mid-1987, it was found that millions of cans of food were probably inedible because they were too old, and that someone, possibly repre-senting one or more of the fourteen supplying companies, had been sticking new labels on them to make them appear fresh.

That discovery, like the discovery of other scandals that have periodically rocked the city in the last hundred years or so, has an oddly perverse *berlinisch* ring about it. Theodor Heuss, who became the first President of West Germany, said once that

Germany never properly conquered democracy for itself because democracy had come in the wake of defeat. A democratic Germany, he maintained, 'could not develop its own myth or acquire its own know-how'. Berlin may not have become totally democratic, but almost every street has its own 'myth' and few of its locally born inhabitants do not have their own very specific 'know-how.'

Finally, there will always remain the iconoclasm of Berliners. In the West it is apparent in the creations of the city's painters and other creative artists. In the more conformist East, it remains, for the time being, more restrained. It is on the Western side of the Wall that a graffiti artist has scribbled 'Dada lebt—in Ostberlin' ('Dada lives—in East Berlin'). But then, that scribble is a sort of Dadaist gesture as well. So, for that matter, is the Wall itself and the city that it divides.

Illustrations

Photographic sources

Landesbildstelle Berlin: Bismarck's statue, the Palace Bridge, Liebknecht in the Tiergarten, Gestapo headquarters, a 'rubble woman', Friedrichstrasse in 1946 and in 1898, Tauentzienstrasse in 1897, in 1946 and in 1985, Charlottenburg refugees, Clay and Kennedy, reinforcing the Wall, Kreuzberg in 1945 and in 1978.
Ullstein Bilderdienst: unemployment in Wedding, a meat queue in the Depression, the Romanische Café.
Bundesarchiv: the Jewish boycott.
Bildarchiv Preussischer Kulturbesitz: the armistice carriage at the Brandenburg Gate.
Bilderdienst Süddeutscher Verlag: gas masks on the Kurfürstendamm.

Bibliography

D'Abernon, Viscountess. *Red Cross and Berlin Embassy*. London, 1946.
Abrasimov, Pyotr. *West Berlin, Yesterday and Today*. Dresden, 1981.
Ardagh, John. *Germany and the Germans*. London, 1987.
Armytage, W. H. G. *A Social History of Engineering*. London, 1961.
Arnold-Forster, Mark. *The Siege of Berlin*. London, 1979.
Aronson, Theo, *The Kaisers*. London, 1971.

Baker, Leonard. *Days of Sorrow and Pain*. New York, 1978.
Bauer, Roland, and Hühns, Erik (Collective leaders). *Berlin—800 Jahre Geschichte in Wort und Bild*. Berlin, 1980.
Bielenberg, Christabel. *The Past is Myself*. London, 1968.
Biermann, Wolf. *Poems and Ballads*. London, 1977.
Boehm, Eric. *We Survived*. Santa Barbara/Oxford. 1985.
Botting, Douglas. *In the Ruins of the Reich*. London, 1985.
Brandt, Willy. *People and Politics*. London, 1978.
Bullock, Alan. *Hitler: A Study in Tyranny*. London, 1954.

Carr, William, *A History of Germany, 1815–1945*. London, 1979.
Carsten, F. L. *Britain and the Weimar Republic*. London, 1984.
Childs, David. *The GDR: Moscow's German Ally*. London, 1984.
Chuikov, Vassily. *The End of the Third Reich*. Moscow, 1978.
Cole, J. A. *Lord Haw-Haw: The Full Story of William Joyce*. London, 1984.
Coper, Rudolf. *Failure of a Revolution*. Cambridge, 1955.
Craig, Gordon A. *Germany 1866–1945*. Oxford, 1984.
Craig, Gordon A. *The Germans*. London, 1984.

Dawson, W. H. *The Evolution of Modern Germany*. London, 1908.
Documents on Germany, 1944–1985. US Department of State. Washington, 1986.

Eberle, Matthias. *World War I and the Weimar Artists*. Yale, 1985.
Esslin, Martin. *Brecht: A Choice of Evils*. London, 1980.
Everett, Susanne. *Lost Berlin*. London, 1979.
Evelyn, Princess Blücher. *An English Wife in Berlin*. London, 1920.
Ewen, Frederic. *Bertolt Brecht: His Life, His Art and His Times*. London, 1970.

Flannery, Harry. *Assignment to Berlin*. London, 1943.

Fowkes, Ben. *Communism in Germany under the Weimar Republic*. London, 1984.

Frecot, Janos, and Roters, Eberhard. *Berlin um 1900*. Berlin, 1984.

Friedrich, Otto. *Before the Deluge*. London, 1974.

von der Gablentz, O. M. *Documents on the Status of Berlin, 1944–1959*. Munich, 1959.

Gelb, Norman. *The Berlin Wall*. London, 1986.

Gisevius, Hans Bernd. *To the Bitter End*. London, 1948.

Grebing, Helga. *The History of the German Labour Movement*. London, 1969.

Grosz, George. *A Small Yes and a Big No*. London, 1982.

Grunberger, Richard. *A Social History of the Third Reich*. London, 1971.

Hamilton, Nigel. *The Brothers Mann*. London.

Harman, Chris. *The Lost Revolution*. London, 1982.

Harpprecht, Klaus. *Willy Brandt: Portrait and Self-Portrait*. London, 1972.

Hart-Davis, Duff. *Hitler's Games: The 1936 Olympics*. London, 1986.

Havemann, Robert. *An Alienated Man*. London, 1973.

Hayman, Ronald. *A Biography of Kafka*. London, 1981.

Heinicke, Hans Peter. *Berlins heimliche Sehenswürdigkeiten*. Berlin, 1986.

Heitzer, Heinz. *GDR: An Historical Outline*. Dresden, 1981.

Henderson, W. O. *The Rise of German Industrial Power*. London, 1975.

Henselmann, Hermann. *Drei Reisen nach Berlin*. Berlin, 1981.

Hitchcock, Henry-Russell. *Architecture: Nineteenth and Twentieth Centuries*. London, 1983.

Hitler, Adolf. *Mein Kampf—Introduced by D. C. Watt*. London, 1969.

Holmsten, Georg. *Die Berlin-Chronik*. Düsseldorf, 1984.

Isherwood, Christopher. *Mr Norris Changes Trains*. London, 1935.

Isherwood, Christopher. *Goodbye to Berlin*. London, 1939.

Jencks, Charles. *Le Corbusier—The Tragic View of Architecture*. London, 1975.

Keiderling, Gerhard, and Stulz, Percy. *Berlin 1945–1968*. Berlin, 1970.

Koch, Thilo. *Berlin ist Wunderbar*. Munich, 1986.

Kuby, Erich. *The Russians and Berlin, 1945*. London, 1965.

Lane, Barbara Miller. *Architecture and Politics in Germany, 1918–1945*. Harvard, 1985.

Lane, Peter. *Europe since 1945, an Introduction*. London, 1985.

Lange, Annemarie. *Berlin zur Zeit Bebels and Bismarcks*. Berlin, 1984.

Lange, Annemarie. *Dàs Wilhelminische Berlin*. Berlin, 1968.

Laqueur, Walter. *The Missing Years*. London, 1980.
Leber, Annedore. *Das Gewissen Steht Auf*. Mainz, 1984.
McAdams, A. James. *East Germany and Détente*. Cambridge, 1985.
Mann, Anthony. *Comeback: Germany 1945–1952*. London, 1980.
Mann, Golo. *The History of Germany since 1789*. London, 1968.
Manvell, Roger, and Fraenkel, Heinrich. *Doctor Goebbels*. London, 1960.
Manvell, Roger, and Fraenkel, Heinrich. *Göring*. London, 1962.
Masur, Gerhard. *Imperial Berlin*. London, 1971.

Nettl, J. P. *Rosa Luxemburg*. Oxford, 1966.
Nicholls, A. J. *Weimar and the Rise of Hitler*. London, 1968.
Noakes, Jeremy (editor). *Government, Party and People in Nazi Germany*. Exeter University, 1980.
Norden, Albert. *Thus are Wars Made*. Dresden, 1970.

Pascal, Roy. *The Growth of Modern Germany*. London, 1946.
Passant, E. J. *A Short History of Germany, 1815–1945*. Cambridge, 1962.
Peters, William. *In Germany Now*. London, 1946.
Pool, James and Suzanne. *Who Financed Hitler?* London, 1979.
Prittie, Terence. *The Velvet Chancellors*. London, 1979.

Quigley, Hugh, and Clark, R. T. *Republican Germany*. London, 1928.

Ramos Oliveira, A. *A People's History of Germany*. London, 1942.
Ratchford, B. U., and Ross, William. *Berlin Reparations Assignment*. North Carolina, 1947.
Reichhardt, Hans. *Berlin in der Weimarer Republik*. Berlin, 1979.
Reissner, Alexander. *Berlin, 1675–1945*. London, 1984.
Richter, Hans. *Dada—Art and Anti-Art*. London, 1965.
Röhl, John. (editor) *Kaiser Wilhelm, New Interpretations*. Cambridge, 1985.
Rürup, Reinhard. *Topographie des Terrors: Prinz-Albrecht-Gelände, Eine Dokumentation*. Berlin, 1987.
Ryan, Cornelius. *The Last Battle*. London, 1966.
Ryder, A. J. *The German Revolution*. London, 1959.

Schäfer, Hans Dieter. *Berlin im zweiten Weltkrieg*. Munich, 1985.
Schaffer, Gordon. *Russian Zone*. London, 1947.
Scheider, Richard. *Historische Stätten in Berlin*. Frankfurt/Berlin, 1987.
Shirer, William. *Berlin Diary*. London, 1941.
Shirer, William. *The Rise and Fall of the Third Reich*. London, 1960.
Shub, David. *Lenin*. London, 1966.
Smith, Howard. *Last Train from Berlin*. London, 1942.
Speer, Albert. *Inside the Third Reich*. London, 1970.
Spender, Stephen. *World within World*. London, 1951.
Stahl, Walter (editor). *The Politics of Postwar Germany*. New York, 1963.

Steele, Jonathan. *Socialism with a German Face*. London, 1977.

Sutcliffe, Anthony (editor). *Metropolis, 1890–1940*. London, 1984.

Taylor, A. J. P. *Bismarck*. London, 1955.

Taylor, A. J. P. *The Course of German History*. London, 1945.

Taylor, Fred (editor and translator). *The Goebbels Diaries, 1939–1945*. London, 1982.

Taylor, Simon. *Germany, 1918–1933*. London, 1983.

Trevor-Roper, Hugh. *The Goebbels Diaries: the Last Days*. London, 1979.

Trevor-Roper, Hugh. *The Last Days of Hitler*. London, 1947.

Trost, Heinrich. *Hauptstadt Berlin I*. Berlin, 1984.

Ulbricht, Walter. *Whither Germany?* Dresden, 1966.

Vassiltchikov, Marie. *The Berlin Diaries*. London, 1985.

Voss, Karl. *Reiseführer for Literaturfreunde, Berlin*. Frankfurt, 1980.

Welch, David (editor). *Nazi Propaganda*. London, 1983.

Willett, John. *The New Sobriety: Art and Politics in the Weimar Period*. London, 1978.

Wippermann, Wolfgang. *Steinerne Zeugen: Stätten der Judenverfolgung*. Berlin, 1982.

Wolff, Theodor. *Through Two Decades*. London, 1936.

To a list like this should be added some of the countless guidebooks and catalogues that the city has led to over the years. Baedeker's, without doubt, remains the best of the lot in spite of a certain arrogance of tone which creeps through occasionally. A special edition was produced for anniversary year in 1987. The same year yielded a number of worthwhile exhibitions in both parts of the city, usually accompanied by not inexpensive catalogues. In London, too, there have been displays, notably of selections of German art, that have been well worth visiting. The Institute of Contemporary Arts, the Royal Academy, the Oxford Museum of Modern Art, and the Goethe Institute, have all provided food for thought at one time or another.

Index

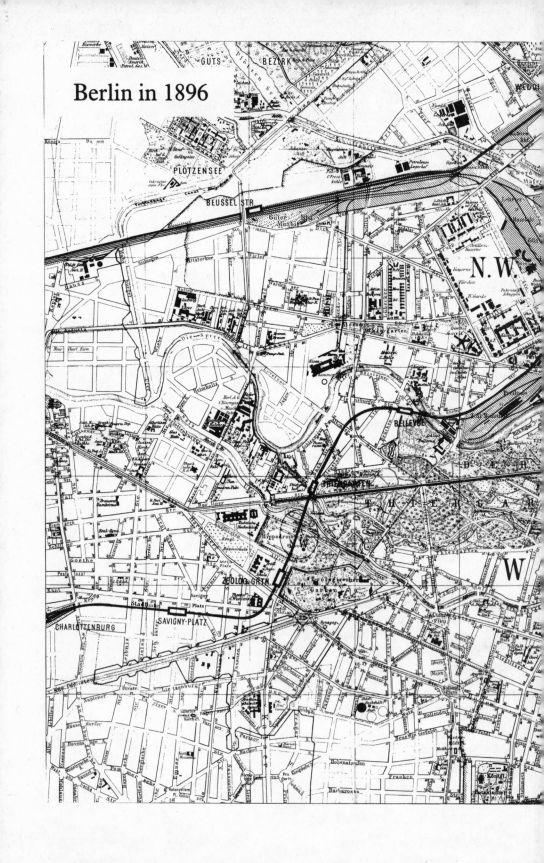

Berlin in 1896